# THE SECOND AMENDMENT

# THE SECOND AMENDMENT

*The Intent and Its
Interpretation by the States
and the Supreme Court*

Patrick J. Charles

McFarland & Company, Inc., Publishers
*Jefferson, North Carolina, and London*

Library of Congress Cataloguing-in-Publication Data

Charles, Patrick J.
    The Second Amendment : the intent and its interpretation
by the states and the Supreme Court / Patrick J. Charles.
        p.      cm.
    Includes bibliographical references and index.

    ISBN 978-0-7864-4270-6
    softcover : 50# alkaline paper

    1. Firearms — Law and legislation — United States.   2.  Gun
control — United States.   3.  United States. Constitution. 2nd
Admendment.   I.  Title.
    KF3941.C43  2009
    344.7305'33 — dc22                                            2008052737

British Library cataloguing data are available

Cover image: background ©2009 Shutterstock

Manufactured in the United States of America

*McFarland & Company, Inc., Publishers*
  *Box 611, Jefferson, North Carolina 28640*
  *www.mcfarlandpub.com*

# *Acknowledgments*

I would like to acknowledge the love and support of family, especially my mom (Constance Charles), Daniel & Sarah Charles, Katherine Charles, the rest of the Charles family, the Burkhart family, George & Marie Gusich, Jordan Gusich, the Metcalf family, Adam Morgan, and the Morgan family (Pinky especially). I would also like to thank the following friends for their support: Tom Burns, Elise Piatt, Grant Yochim, Canice Musiek, Greg Capoziello, Laura Delucia, Trista Chaney, Emily Chaney, Regina Fisher, Laura Kolat, Justin Fleming, Alex McCready, Carrie Lewine, Alex Reich, Gittle Chaiko, Allison Taller, Rick Ferrara, Fadi Boumitri, Milko Cecez, Klaus L., Kyle Lennen, Charlie Eisenstat, Marianne Lionell, Matthew Marshall, Shawn Romer, Randy Petrouske, Tanisha Bezue, Steve McIntosh, Matt Miller, Byron Moore, Hilary Michael, Bobby Nickodem, Alexis Osborn, Chris Pyanowski, Jim Templin, Shelia Downs, Danja Therecka, Michelle Todd, Amy Tumey, Rae Lynn Wargo, Dorothy Wolbert, Sarah Denney, Adam Fletcher, Jennifer Fogle-Weekley, Michael Gonzalez, Jeffery Jerome, Eric Long, Elias Hazkial, Samantha Lewis, Becky Sovol, Ross Ahern, Maura David, Brittany Parent, David Sires, Kevin Kovach, Courtney Tew, Jessica Groza, Shawna Slone, Elizabeth Bear, Emily Felker Beckmann, Nathan Repp, Lindsay Brown, Derek Newberry, Catherine Elyssa Brown, Michael Celone, Carrie Love, Jon Gagas, Andrew Hertel, Greg Kershaw, Loraine Martinez, Kara Webster, Dan Moss, Dana Rasmussen, Amy Stack, LeAnn Starlin, Monica Swintz, Tomar Thomas, and all his friends from George Washington University, Cleveland State-Cleveland Marshall School of Law, the Marines, and Pi Kappa Alpha Fraternity.

I would also like to thank my history mentors for their support: Adele Alexander, Nemata Blyden, Muriel Atkin, and James Horton. Lastly I would like to thank Mark Schamel for looking over the manuscript, Gary Klinga for editing the first draft, Professors Steven H. Steinglass and David F. Forte for their help and advice during my research, the Cleveland-Marshall School of Law library and staff for their help in obtaining all the necessary materials, and especially Mrs. Vera Brown and the Judge John Brown Excellence in Writing Foundation.

# Table of Contents

*The true barriers of our liberty in this country
are our State governments.*
— Thomas Jefferson to Destutt de Tracy,
January 26, 1811

*Let the American youth never forget, that they possess
a noble inheritance, bought by the toils, and sufferings,
and blood of their ancestors; and capable, if wisely improved,
and faithfully guarded, of transmitting to their latest posterity
all the substantial blessings of life, the peaceful enjoyment of
liberty, property, religion, and independence.*
— Justice Joseph Story's Commentaries

# Preface

For the past half-century, legal historians, analysts, judges, and commentators have all disagreed as to what the Second Amendment was meant to protect. Two main theories exist as to what the "right to keep and bear arms" was meant to afford. The first group of theorists have interpreted the Second Amendment as protecting an individual's right to own a firearm. Those who support this assertion are known as individual right theorists. To the second group, such a suggestion is preposterous; it does not make sense that the Framers of the Constitution were concerned with, nor ever intended that everyone would have, such a right. They interpret the Second Amendment as protecting the collective people's right to bear arms in relation to militia service. These individuals are known as collective right theorists. While both sides have found sources that support their position, neither has been able to adequately address the "right to keep and bear arms."

The individual right theorists draw out great points, such as the use of the word "people" to refer to an individual's right to "keep and bear arms." Meanwhile, the collective right theorists have definitively showed that there was a direct correlation between the "right to keep and bear arms" and some form of militia service. Unfortunately, though both sides have strong individual arguments, their reasoning and explanation lack continuity with their entire respective theories. Neither side has adequately researched the entire history behind the Second Amendment, the history of the militia, or fully incorporated their opponent's arguments.

The truth is that the evidence points to a right that Justice Antonin Scalia and the Supreme Court majority outright rejected, a right they described as "an absurdity that no commentator has ever endorsed." That right is the right of an individual to "keep and bear arms" in defense of his country, in a militia or military force, safeguarding against standing armies — foreign and domestic — and in defense of their liberties. That right, and that

1

right alone, is what the Second Amendment was meant to afford. It is a limited right that pre-existed the Constitution and was a right so essential to the founding of the nation that it "shall not be infringed." To interpret the Second Amendment in any other way is to take its wording out of context. In its recent ruling in *Heller*, the Supreme Court majority did just that. Not only did they take the "right to keep and bear arms" out of context, but they extended it as a right to own and use a gun for home self-defense purposes — an interpretation that is a far cry from the Framers' intentions.

Paul Helmke, the president of the Brady Campaign to Prevent Gun Violence, has conceded defeat on this issue, stating, "We've lost the battle on what the Second Amendment means." Helmke feels because "seventy-five percent of the public thinks it's an individual right," why argue theory anymore? There is no arguing that the majority of Americans believe the Second Amendment protects individual gun ownership. That does not mean that this is what the Founders intended. History, especially American history, often gets revised generation after generation. This is essentially what has happened with the Second Amendment. Helmke may believe the debate no longer centers on the Second Amendment anymore, but nothing could be further from the truth. For in reality, although a major battle was lost due to politics in America's highest court, the war over the Second Amendment and its meaning has just begun.

This book shows just why the decision in *Heller* is merely a battle in what will become an interpretative war. For although the Supreme Court has interpreted the "right to keep and bear arms" to extend to individual firearm ownership and use for self-defense in the home, state courts need not give the decision any weight in interpreting their respective "bear arms" provisions for two reasons. First, the Second Amendment is not a right that is incorporated under the due process clause of the Fourteenth Amendment. Second, each state court is allowed to interpret its constitutional provisions as it so chooses. This means that until the Supreme Court mandates the *Heller* decision be adhered to by the states, the research in this field will be paramount in interpreting each state's "bear arms" provisions.

Moreover, this means the Second Amendment issue will have to reach the Supreme Court once again for incorporation to occur. By then, research such as in this book will prove the Supreme Court erred in its interpretation, showing that the *Heller* decision should be overturned, was nothing more than politics spilling into the judiciary, and was a selective incorporation of all the evidence available to interpret the "right to keep and bear arms." This book not only proves the logic and research the Supreme Court used was historically and judicially inadequate, but also provides (1) exhaustive research into each state's gun, hunting, crime, and militia laws up to 1800, (2) an examination of the Second Amendment's placement in the Bill of Rights, (3) a textual analysis of the phrase "bear arms," (4) a textual analysis of the word "keep," (5) an historical analysis of the phrase "keep and bear arms," (6) a discussion of the intent of the Framers in drafting the Second Amendment, (7) a consideration of the legislative history and intent of the 1792 National Militia Act, (8) an examination of the history of the Founders confiscation of arms, (9) and a discussion of the Framers' intent of the word "state," and other historical and interpretative evidence.

Lastly, this book examines the state of Ohio's "bear arms" provision as a framework to show state courts how to understand and interpret similar provisions. It was Ohio's "bear arms" provision that aided the Supreme Court in interpreting that the Second Amendment protects an individual right. Unfortunately, the Supreme Court never researched this area. The statutory, textual, and legislative history of Ohio's "bear arms" provision shows the Second Amendment does not protect an individual right. To prove this, *The Second Amendment* will provide (1) a textual and statutory analysis of the phrase "bear arms" in Ohio's laws through 1859, when the first concealed weapon law was passed, (2) analysis and interpretation of Ohio's militia laws, (3) discussion of the history behind public arms and its effect on Ohio's national security policy, (4) differentiation of the "right to bear arms" provisions in the 1802 and 1851 constitutions, (5) a look into the legislative and secondary source material of the committee appointed to draft the 1851 Constitution's "right to bear arms" provision, and 6) analysis of Ohio's first concealed weapons law.

# Introduction:
# The Supreme Court and
# the Second Amendment

On June 26, 2008, the Supreme Court handed down its landmark gun rights decision in *District of Columbia v. Heller*. It was determined that the "District's ban on handgun possession in the home violates the Second Amendment, as does its prohibition against rendering any lawful firearm in the home operable for the purpose of immediate self-defense."[1] The Second Amendment reads, "A well regulated militia, being necessary to the security of a free State, the right of the people to keep and bear Arms, shall not be infringed."[2] The amendment has generally been read to have two parts or clauses — a prefatory clause and an operative clause; the prefatory is "A well regulated militia, being necessary to the security of a free State," and the operative is "the right of the people to keep and bear Arms, shall not be infringed." The distinction in the clauses is critical because the manner by which the courts have harmonized the two has resulted in ambiguity as to whether the possession of a firearm is an individual right or a collective right. The same held true in *Heller*.

The Supreme Court decision is significant for a number of reasons. First and foremost, it interpreted the amendment's prefatory and operative clauses in a manner that supports an individual right. Second, it overturned a ban on handguns in Washington, D.C., one the highest crime-rated cities in the United States. Of paramount importance, however, is that the Court's subjective analysis may have serious and far-reaching consequences on states' firearm regulations, as well as on interpreting the states' "right to bear arms" provisions.

*Heller* came before the Court as a result of the ruling in the District of

Columbia Appellate Court case *Parker v. District of Columbia.* In Heller, six residents challenged various District of Columbia codes that restricted the use and ownership of firearms.[3] Prior to that appeal the District of Columbia District Court had rejected the notion that the Second Amendment protects "an individual right to bear arms separate and apart from service in the Militia."[4] The plaintiffs appealed, and a review was granted, based on the claims by one of the plaintiffs, Dick Heller. Heller had been denied a registration certificate to own a handgun, thus bringing forth a valid Second Amendment claim.[5] The appellate court granted review because of the district court's failure to address the word "keep" in the Second Amendment.[6]

After review, the appellate court overturned the district court, holding that the Second Amendment protects an individual right and "the activities it protects are not limited to militia service, nor is an individual's enjoyment of the right contingent upon his or her continued enrollment in the militia."[7] The case would reach the Supreme Court when both the District of Columbia[8] and the original plaintiffs[9] petitioned for certiorari. The District of Columbia was only the third federal district to determine that the Second Amendment protected an individual right.[10] The remaining ten federal districts had adopted some form of the collective right model, and held that the Second Amendment was limited in its protective scope.[11] It was this lack of uniformity among the federal districts that ultimately led to the case reaching the Supreme Court.

One would have thought the Second Amendment, one of the original amendments within the Bill of Rights, was a legal issue that had been determined in the Supreme Court many times over. Unfortunately, this was not true. In fact, the Court had not directly addressed the amendment's protections since the late nineteenth century.[12] Outside of these limited holdings, the Supreme Court had been virtually silent[13] on matters related to the Second Amendment since the adoption of the Fourteenth Amendment,[14] except in the narrow ruling in *United States v. Miller.*[15] It was in *Miller* that the Court determined that the "possession or use of a shotgun having a barrel of less than eighteen inches in length" was not "any part of the ordinary military equipment" protected by the Second Amendment.[16] Although the Court only addressed whether a sawed-off shotgun was a type of arm protected, both collective right and individual right theorists interpreted the case to support their political agendas — another pivotal factor in the Supreme Court taking the case.

In the end, the *Heller* decision was nothing better. Just as both sides used subjective analysis to argue their stance on the Second Amendment, the justices split among similar lines. Led by Justice Scalia, the majority took a conservative stance, interpreting every facet of the Second Amendment to support the individual right theory. All evidence supporting the contrary was repressed, ignored, or referred to as erroneous. Meanwhile, the minority, with dissents by Justices Stevens and Breyer, supported the collective right theory. Their arguments often failed because they supported an incomplete, and often confusing, collective right model. This is not to say that the majority and the two dissenters did not have valid arguments. They certainly did. There was just no attempt to harmonize the two approaches. For if the Supreme Court had harmonized the two approaches by considering all the evidence and interpreting the true meaning behind the "right to keep and bear arms," the outcome would have been drastically different.

Scalia started off the majority opinion, citing *United States v. Sprague,* stating that "the Constitution was written to be understood by the voters; its words and phrases were used in their normal and ordinary as distinguished from technical meaning."[17] He initially argued that the collective right interpretation of the Second Amendment asserts a secret meaning that not everyone of the eighteenth century would have understood. Scalia provided no historical data to support this assertion, but he had a point. When the Constitution was drafted its words were incorporated in a manner the legislators in each state would readily understand. Or, in other words, the text in the Constitution had a natural legal meaning. This is supported by the *Heller* majority frequently turning to the legal documents of the founding era to come to its determination. While the majority believes this form analysis supports the individual right theory, it actually undercuts it. Through its dismissal, the majority was able to avoid the evidence that proves otherwise. A closer look into eighteenth-century practices paints a much different portrait, a portrait of a militia system that all citizens were required to know, familiarize themselves with, and practice.

The most important key to the majority coming to their individual right interpretation was not that they were interpreting the "right of the people to keep and bear arms" in an "ordinary" way; it was that they dissected every word of the operative clause, making two rights — the right to "keep arms" and the right to "bear arms." For if the Second Amendment was interpreted as it was meant to be read — as an entire phrase — the Court would have never come to their determination. It did not matter that the majority began by examining the operative clause before they addressed the prefatory clause. Indeed, Scalia was right that, no matter where one starts, one "would reach the same result,"[18] as the prefatory and operative clauses perfectly explain what right the Second Amendment was meant to protect. The debates and changes to the amendment during the Constitutional Convention testify to this protection. The Second Amendment was drafted in a manner that spoke directly to the people of the eighteenth century — that they had a right to "keep and bear arms" in defense of the ideals of the new republic.

The Second Amendment is unique in this regard. It is a right that "shall not be infringed." Those words are not to be taken lightly. No other amendment or provision in the Constitution uses such a phrase, meaning it was incorporated for a specific purpose. The individual right supporters and the majority interpret the phrase "shall not be infringed" as signifying a preexisting right. There is no disagreeing that the right to "keep and bear arms" was just this. This right existed prior to the creation of the Constitution through each state's militia system. All the same, what's more important is that the words "shall not be infringed" constitute a cogent language. To "keep and bear arms" was a right that was so important and so imbedded into eighteenth-century America that the Founders felt it should never be tampered with. It is not a right that can be "reasonably infringed" as the majority and minority opinions view it. It is something that can "never be infringed." When the word "shall" is incorporated into rules and laws, it indicates that something must happen or somebody is obliged to do something because of a rule or law. Thus the phrase "shall not" means the opposite — that something cannot happen or somebody may never do something because of a rule or law.

For those who have followed *Heller,* the outcome was not surprising. Even prior to oral arguments, it had been hinted by Justices Scalia, Thomas, Alito, and Chief Justice Roberts that the Second Amendment protected an individual right. It was just uncertain whether Justice Kennedy would join them. Oral arguments, including numerous proactive arguments by Justice Scalia in favor of the respondents, answered this question and, by doing so, solidified the outcome. While being critical of Walter Dellinger and the petitioners, Justice Scalia made sure to aid Alan Guru, who was arguing for the respondents. For example, when Justice Stevens was questioning whether the right in the Second Amendment was equal to or more expansive than the English Bill of Rights "bear arms" provision, the following transpired:

MR. GURU: It [Second Amendment] is quite clearly an expansion upon it [English Bill of Rights].

JUSTICE STEVENS: So that's not really your — you would not confine the right the way the English did then?

MR. GURU: I think the common law of English is a guide and it's always a useful guide because that's where the — where we — where we look to, to interpret.

JUSTICE SCALIA: It's useful for such purposes as what keep and bear arms means and things of that sort.

MR. GURU: It certainly is, Your Honor. And it's also useful to see how...

JUSTICE SCALIA: They certainly didn't want to preserve the kind of militia that America had, which was a militia separate from the State, separate from the government, which enabled a revolt against the British.

MR. GURU: That's correct, Your Honor.

Here Justice Scalia was saving Guru from Stevens' skepticism, making sure to chime in and answer the respondent's question. One can see, just prior to Justice Scalia stepping in, that Mr. Guru was about to be cornered with his answer. Scalia's judicial interference did not end there. When Justice Stevens was pointing out the inconsistencies with the individual right theory and the "shall not be infringed" wording, the following transpired:

JUSTICE STEVENS: Let me ask a question: are you, in effect, reading the amendment to say that the right shall not be unreasonably infringed instead of shall not be infringed?

MR. GURU: There is that inherent aspect to every right in the Constitution.

JUSTICE STEVENS: So we can — consistent with your view — we can simply read this: "It shall not be reasonably infringed"?

MR. GURU: Well, yes, your Honor, to some extent, except the word "unreasonable" is one that troubles us, because we don't know what this "unreasonable" standard looks like.

JUSTICE SCALIA: You wouldn't put it that way. You would just say it is not being infringed if reasonable limitations are being placed upon it.

MR. GURU: That's another way to look at it, Your Honor.

Here again, Scalia made sure to save the respondents. He wanted to make sure the individual right argument was well supported. Moreover, just as Scalia refused to be an objective judicial observer during the oral arguments, his opinion was not objective. In multiple instances he chastised the dissents of Justices Stevens and Breyer without adequately addressing their arguments.

When one looks at the full opinion, the holding is confusing. It does not examine any relevant legislative history immediately following the adoption of the Constitution, but rather uses commentary and cases drafted at least forty years later. It relies on state Constitutions' "right to bear arms" provisions after the adoption of the Second Amendment, without textually analyzing them or giving them a plurality meaning. Furthermore, the holding ignores the states' ratification of convention amendments that contradicted the individual right theory, but still erroneously inferred that these conventions all point to the individual right model. It added the word "because" to the beginning of the prefatory clause ("A well regulated militia, being necessary to the security of a free State"), changed the word "State" to "country," argued the word "against" would had to have been incorporated for the amendment to have some form of a collective right interpretation, and added a self-defense exception that never historically existed. In short, the opinion was a selective incorporation of the evidence to ensure the Second Amendment protected an individual right. The opinion clearly shows that politics had seeped into the United States' highest court.

The bad news is that this opinion may be used by federal and state courts to overturn many gun laws. Although the majority was clear not to apply the opinion as overturning gun prohibitions on "the possession of firearms by felons and the mentally ill, or laws forbidding the carrying of firearms in sensitive places such as schools and government buildings, or laws imposing conditions and qualifications on the commercial sale of arms,"[19] there is no telling how other courts will now interpret Second Amendment claims. The Supreme Court left that question unanswered. One can safely assume that the opinion was intentional. Scalia denied the need to identify any standard of review for such cases. He claimed such scrutiny will be defined as the circumstances present themselves. The truth is that, in all likelihood, the majority just could not agree on any form of scrutiny, nor could they agree on whether the Second Amendment was incorporated under the Fourteenth Amendment.

Without any direction from the Supreme Court in these regards, what is certain is that state courts do not need to give the *Heller* decision any weight. There is not one sentence that claims the Second Amendment restricts state governments from banning firearms. It is only applicable to the federal government, which has jurisdiction over the District of Columbia. The majority did state "banning from the home 'the most preferred firearm in the nation to keep and use for protection of one's home and family' would fail constitutional muster," but notice how any allusion to the states was omitted.[20] The decision only applies to the District of Columbia because it was the only place the respondents had standing to bring their claim. Moreover, there is no part of the opinion that claims the Second Amendment was anything more than a limitation on Congress. Unless a state's constitution protects individual firearm ownership or has been interpreted as protecting such, that state may impose any firearm legislation it deems proper.

This is not to say that a state or federal court's rejection of the application of the Second Amendment to a case would avoid a review before the Supreme Court. In fact, that is what Mr. Guru and individual right supporters hope will happen. It is just one of the many open-ended scenarios the Court left in question — especially as to whether the Second Amendment is incorporated under the Fourteenth Amendment. Section one of that amendment reads:

> All persons born or naturalized in the United States, and subject to the jurisdiction thereof, are citizens of the United States and of the State wherein they reside. No State shall make or enforce any law which shall abridge the privileges or immunities of citizens of the United States; nor shall any State deprive any person of life, liberty, or property, without due process of law; nor deny to any person within its jurisdiction the equal protection of the laws.[21]

It is argued by individual right theorists that the Fourteenth Amendment's reference to "No State" enforcing any law that abridges "the privileges or immunities of the citizens of the United States" makes clear that all States must abide by the Second Amendment — that is, all states must adhere to the Supreme Court's ruling on this matter, even without that Court incorporating the Second Amendment. There is no telling how state and federal courts will interpret this, for the Fourteenth Amendment is a larger debate in itself. Although the Supreme Court has answered this question in the *Slaughter House Cases*, there still exists much disagreement among legal analysts as to what rights constitute the amendment's "privileges and immunities." It is a hard sell to argue that having a firearm for self-defense in the home is an unenumerated right. Nevertheless, individual right proponents are making this argument. They believe the *Slaughter House Cases* should be overruled, but this is not all. They also pose the argument that no state may deprive individuals of their right to equal protection of the laws. This is the main argument Mr. Guru has already made in *McDonald v. City of Chicago*. He has challenged Chicago's handgun laws in that the restrictions prevent an individual from evoking his Second Amendment right to self-defense protection in the home. It is argued that since the states must give equal protection of the law to all citizens, Chicago must, under the Fourteenth Amendment, adhere to the Supreme Court's holding in *Heller*.[22]

The City of Chicago has responded by denying this claim for relief.[23] Their argument is simple: first, the Fourteenth Amendment does not apply in this case, and second, the Second Amendment is nothing more than a restriction on Congress. There is no precedent by which the states must incorporate that which does not apply to them. It is uncertain exactly how the district court will rule. What is for certain is that the outcome of the case will be crucial. The decision will give other court jurisdictions a basis to decide whether the Second Amendment is incorporated under the Fourteenth Amendment, but more important, though, the decision will surely be appealed to the Supreme Court. No matter which way the United States

Northern District Court of Illinois decides, the case is certain to spark the interest of four Supreme Court justices necessary to grant certiorari. It would not be surprising, therefore, that the Supreme Court would review such a case. Even the dissenting justices would want another opportunity to clear the muddy holding the majority created in *Heller*, or reverse it, for that matter.

The problem in examining the Second Amendment does not end with the Supreme Court. Just within the past year, individual right scholars have continually steeped further into revisionism in their attempt to shore up the individual right theory. Like the Supreme Court did in its decision in *Heller*, they too ignore where the evidence ultimately leads. It is as if they are determined to stretch the boundaries of the historical record by lawyering a right that many could argue has become outdated with the United States' creation of a permanent standing army.

For example, Stephen P. Halbrook's *The Founders' Second Amendment* makes three contentions about the Second Amendment, all of which assume the right to "keep and bear arms" was meant to protect an individual right. Halbrook's first assumption is that the militia laws that required every man be armed shows the Second Amendment protects an individual right.[24] Nothing could be further from the truth. For as will be shown in the subsequent chapters, the militia laws were the means by which the people defended themselves from dangers — foreign and domestic. These laws made it every man's duty to be armed; otherwise they were required to pay a fine or tax for their failure to comply. One can hardly say such laws are synonymous with the Founders' intent in drafting the Second Amendment.

Halbrook's second assumption is the British Ministry's policy of disarming the citizens of Boston, including those who were in open and avowed rebellion, was the influence behind the Second Amendment being drafted.[25] Here again, Halbrook is stretching the history behind the drafting of the Second Amendment. It is undoubtedly true that the British had employed a policy of disarming the colonists, but there is no substantiated evidence linking this fact with the drafting or the debates of the Second Amendment. As will be shown, not only did the patriots make similar efforts to disarm those who supported the crown, but at no time in the colonists' petitions to the crown did they cite such action as infringing upon their right to "bear arms."

Halbrook's last contention is one that many individual right theorists have assumed wrongly. It is that the states constitutions' right to "bear arms" provisions unequivocally support that one has a right to "bear arms" for defense their person.[26] Such a claim is been often made by individual right theorists without ever looking into the drafting and legislative history of each state's constitution. One can only come to a proper determination by doing so, not by assuming. Nevertheless, without doing the research, individual right theorists have continued to contend that State constitutional provisions, no matter how they are worded, support the belief that every individual has a right to own, carry, and operate a firearm.

Another piece of recent scholarship to examine the Second Amendment is David E. Young's *The Founders' View of the Right to Bear Arms*. Young, often cited in cases on the Second Amendment for his compilation of documents on arms in eighteenth-century America, here makes his first attempt to write on the subject. Young's approach is unique in that he argues that the colonists' familiarity with arms for hunting and everyday use is what made them an efficient militia fighting force. He particularly points to the colony of Pennsylvania to support his contention. Young argues although the Pennsylvania colony was different from other colonies in that it lacked a consistent militia system, its people were still well trained in the art of war. He contends this "military readiness" shows that even if we are to judicially interpret the Second Amendment in its militia context, using arms in the home and for everyday hunting served the purpose of a "well regulated militia."[27] Unfortunately, much like Halbrook, Young assumes too much. Young fails to address many facts, including that of Pennsylvania's policy of supplying its militia with the required arms. This fact not only disproves Halbrook's theory "that every man be armed" was linked to the Second Amendment, but also shows Young over stresses the fact that a Pennsylvanian's ownership and private use of a weapon was directly correlated to his service in the militia. This proves that Pennsylvania viewed arms ownership as a nonissue when serving in its "well regulated militia."

Because of these facts, it is of the utmost importance that the Supreme Court decision in *Heller* and the individual right theory be critically scrutinized under a legal and historical microscope. Critical analysis will not only show the faulty logic the majority used in coming to its individual right interpretation, but it will also provide the states with the necessary data to research, examine, and interpret their respective "right to bear arms" provisions. Some states' history and data will conclusively show that their constitution protects individual firearm ownership. Meanwhile, most others will not. Ohio, for instance, a state whose history the Supreme Court relied upon in reaching the individual right conclusion, actually does not support individual firearm ownership. A detailed historical analysis of Ohio's history and data supports the limited right the Second Amendment was meant to protect — the right of the people to maintain and use firearms to suppress standing armies, foreign and domestic, while defending their personal liberties.

This is the purpose of this book: to shed light on the Second Amendment and demonstrate that, although Congress and the states encouraged individual firearm ownership through the 1792 National Militia Act and other militia laws, it is a textual farce for the Supreme Court to imply that the Second Amendment protected individual gun ownership. Furthermore, the Court's refusal to properly address all the evidence was nothing better than revisionist history. One can easily come to a desired conclusion by revising history. All it takes is the omission of certain key historical facts and taking the history one chooses to adopt out of context. It is as if the Supreme Court majority looked at the historical record as rules of tainted evidence, and then decided to reject certain things it felt improper. For if the Court had reviewed everything more closely, they would have found that history definitively demonstrates that the "right to bear arms" provisions in both the Second Amendment and earlier state constitutions were synonymous in their limited protective scope. These provisions only protect one's right to use arms in the military (or militia context) in support of just government.

# CHAPTER ONE

# The Right of the People to Keep and Bear Arms Shall Not Be Infringed

Critics of the decision in *Heller* argue that it was the Supreme Court's focus on the operative clause which led to the textually perplexing decision. It is believed that because the majority ignored the prefatory language in textually examining the "right of the people to keep and bear arms," the individual right argument was therefore all but certain. This could be considered a valid criticism, but is not necessarily true. The Court could have just as easily come to a different interpretation by starting with the operative clause — the key being whether the Court viewed the operative clause in its entirety, rather than in piecemeal sections — for the phrase "keep and bear arms" speaks much differently than reading it as the right to "keep arms" and the right to "bear arms." Moreover, the operative clause includes that this right "shall not be infringed." This is strong language indicating just how limited the right is.

## *The Second Amendment's Placement within the Bill of Rights*

First, prior to examining the text of the Second Amendment, it is important to put it in its context within the Bill of Rights. This is an issue that the Supreme Court did not address, but shows just how awkwardly the Second Amendment was drafted. Firearms advocates have traditionally contended the Second Amendment's placement within the Bill of Rights shows that it was meant to bestow an individual right to "keep and bear Arms" to every citizen. Their argument, however, distorts both the historical and Congressional records. One cannot deny that Amendments III through IX of the Bill of Rights protect individual rights, with the Tenth Amendment reserving all other rights to the states. Whether the Second Amendment falls into this individual right category is debatable. This is because the First Amendment does not so much protect an individual right as it expressly restricts Congress.[1] The Virginia Senate even made a particular point of this during the ratification process.[2] While the Supreme Court has incorporated the First Amendment to protect an individual right to all of its citizens,[3] this was not the Framers' intention; the First Amendment reads "Congress shall make no law." Thus, the provision was initially intended to be a restriction on Congress, not an individual right.

Furthermore, the original Bill of Rights consisted of the Twelve Articles. If we take into account where the First and Second Amendments were placed within these articles, it can be fairly inferred that they were only meant to place restrictions on Congress. The First and Second Amendments were originally the Third and Fourth Articles. Articles One[4] and Two[5] were not adopted, thus making the Third and Fourth Articles the First and Second Amendments respectively. The First Article placed restrictions on how Congress would be represented, and the Second Article limited the manner members of Congress and the Senate could be compensated for their services.[6] While the Second Article was not even close to being ratified, the First Article almost made the Bill of Rights. It was one vote shy from being the First Amendment to the Constitution.[7] Thus, if we take into context how the Bill of Rights was originally to be structured by James Madison and the Bill of Rights Committee, the Second Amendment bordered the amendments restricting Congress and the amendments guaranteeing individual rights.

Nevertheless, there have been federal district court decisions, such as *Parker v. District of Columbia*, that have reasoned that the "setting" of the Second Amendment in the Bill of Rights "reinforces its individual nature."[8] It is believed by individual right supporters that, since the Bill of Rights "was almost entirely a declaration of individual rights," therefore the Second Amendment was intended to protect individual gun ownership.[9] To these supporters, to rule otherwise would be an "inexplicable aberration"[10] on the rest of the Bill of Rights. There is no doubt that the Second Amendment's setting is indisputably determinative of its intent. It does not, however, unequivocally support the individual right model. This is because the amendment was clearly meant to be a restriction on Congress, and in no way was meant to restrict the states or the rules surrounding the functioning of their respective militias. Thus, both individual right and collective right theorists have a legitimate argument that the amendment's placement in the Bill of Rights supports their stance.

## The Right of the People

What critically tips the scale between whether the Second Amendment protects an individual or collective right is the incorporation of the phrase "the right of the people." There is no doubt that the argument asserted by the individual right theorists and the Supreme Court majority regarding the meaning of the phrase is textually accurate, as the use of the word "people" is primarily incorporated in the Bill of Rights when referring to the individual. Collective right theorists disagree. They argue that because the militia was composed of a body of people, as the 1776 Virginia Declaration of Rights states, that the "right to keep and bear arms" can only be exercised by the collective people when in service of the militia. Herein, the argument is textually flawed. The word "people" in the Bill of Rights, coupled with its context in the recommendations by the state constitutional conventions, is used in a manner that is referential to the individual.

This is not to say that the entire individual right theory and Supreme Court decision is correct in interpreting what the "right to keep and bear arms" protects. It just means that it would be a textual farce to interpret "people" having one meaning in the First and Fourth Amendments and another in the Second Amendment. Moreover, the "right of the people" was incorporated in this manner in all the state constitutions as well. Therefore, to interpret "people" in any other light would essentially be throwing out the other guarantees in the Constitution.

## Bear Arms

If there is one phrase that stands out in the operative clause of the Second Amendment, it is "bear arms." The phrase was almost distinctly used to describe individuals performing military service. The Supreme Court majority claims the phrase was also used to denote other forms of arms use such as hunting, carrying of firearms, and self-defense. Nothing could be further from the truth. The Constitution was a legal instrument, drafted by America's greatest legislative and legal minds. Those that ratified the Constitution were familiar with how words and phrases were incorporated into their respective colony's statutes. When one looks at these statutes, there was only one common usage of the phrase "bear arms," it being that it was only incorporated in a manner that denoted military service.

## Gun Laws

During the eighteenth century, it was common practice for each of the colonial assemblies to pass laws governing the use of firearms. The purpose of the laws was no different than they are today: to protect the citizenry from the potential harms that firearms pose. In these laws there is not one instance of the use of the word "bear" or the phrase "bear arms." Instead, the word "carry" was usually used because the word "bear," in conjunction with "arms," always denoted using the latter in a military capacity.

For instance, a Georgia law to protect against potential domestic insurrections required that every man would bring with him "one good gun" or a "pair of pistols" to church at all times.[11] It was feared if all the white inhabitants were at church, the black slaves could incite an insurrection without the former being properly equipped to react. Therefore, in order to protect "this provinice against domestick insurrections, and other fatal consequences," it was required that "firearms be carried to all places of publick Worship."[12] In a Maryland law effectuating the trial of criminals, the improper use of firearms was one of the focuses. While addressing the fine for the commission of crimes within the colony, the law stipulated if any person shall "shoot, kill or hunt, or be seen to carry a gun upon any person's land," they were to forfeit "one thousand pounds of tobacco."[13]

Within laws governing the illegal discharging or firing of guns, the word "bear" was also never incorporated. In New York's law the phrase "shall fire or discharge" was used.[14] In Pennsylvania, the law used the words "discharge" and "throw or fire,"[15] while South Carolina's law used the phrase "shall fire or shoot off any gun or pistol."[16] Gun advocates will be quick to argue the laws governing the discharging of firearms did not address the carrying of firearms. Thus, they did not need to incorporate the word "bear" in such laws, but this reasoning is flawed. If the individuals in these acts were "bearing" arms in these instances, the acts would have easily identified them as such. This was not the case.

Furthermore, most colonies enacted some form of protection from riots, routs, and tumultuous assemblies. The primary concern of these laws was to prevent individuals from violently assembling and endangering the public. In 1786, the Massachusetts law described such individuals as "persons in arms," but did not incorporate the word "bear" throughout the act.[17] The laws included terms like "being armed," "in arms," and "appear armed." In 1797, for example, New Jersey worded its riot law in this manner, using the phrase "being armed."[18] Meanwhile, Pennsylvania chose to omit any reference to "arms" in its riot law. That law made it unlawful for people "of three or more" to "meet together with clubs, staves, or any other hurtful weapons."[19] These acts show that the word "bear" was intentionally left out because it was not an all-encompassing definition. If the word "bear" was applied to denote the act of "carrying," the use of the word would have been incorporated in such acts to define all forms of arms use.

### Slave Laws

The majority of the original thirteen colonies had adopted slave laws in some form or fashion prior to and after the adoption of the Constitution. These laws often incorporated provisions regarding slaves and indentured servants owning or carrying any arms whatsoever. Up to the adoption of the Constitution, none of these laws described a slave's ownership or possession of arms with the word "bear" or the phrase "bear arms." Instead, in every instance the word "carry" was incorporated.

New Jersey did not permit its slaves to "be seen to hunt, or carrying a Gun on the Lord's Day."[20] In 1721, a Pennsylvania law ordered any Negro slave to be whipped if they should "presume to carry guns."[21] In North Carolina, the master of a slave was required to give them a certificate to be allowed to "carry a gun."[22] Delaware made it unlawful for "any Negro or Mulatto slave" to "presume to carry any guns ... or other arms whatsoever."[23] In Georgia no slave was to "carry or make use of firearms."[24] Meanwhile, Virginia provided that no "negroe, mulatto, or Indian whatsoever" shall "keep, or carry any gun, powder, shot, club, or other weapon, whatsoever, offensive, or defensive, but all and every gun, weapon, and ammunition, found in custody or possession of any negroe, mulattoe, or Indian, may be seized by any person."[25]

These laws reinforce an intended distinction between the words "bear" and "carry." The words were vastly different in meaning when it came to the possession of firearms: "carry" denoted possession on one's body while "bear" was limited to and defined military service. Moreover, the distinction between the words "carry" and "bear" is further emphasized when referring to the incorporation of slaves into militia laws. Slaves were often exempt from such a duty as "bearing arms" because it was universally feared such a privilege should only be bestowed on its citizens, while the South also feared such incorporation would encourage slave insurrections.[26]

The Supreme Court majority in *Heller* did use a legal dictionary that seems to cite a slave law that used a form of "bear arms." Timothy Cunningham's 1773 legal dictionary states: "Servants and labourers shall use bows and arrows on Sundays, & c. and not bear other arms."[27] No one has found the specific source of this quote and it is uncertain whether such a law ever did exist. In fact, there exists no American law that used "bear arms" in this fashion. The majority tries to support Cunningham's dictionary with a 1797 Delaware slave law, but wisely did not include the text of that law because it does not use the phrase "bear arms" or any form of it. The law reads, "That if any Negro or Mulatto slave shall presume to carry any guns, swords, pistols ... or other arms and weapons whatsoever ... he shall be whipt."[28] Here again the Founders plainly differentiated between using "bear arms" and "carry arms." The distinction is significant because it clearly shows that they were aware of how using the phrase "bear arms" was to be used in its legal and natural context.

### Hunting Laws

Hunting laws were another common fixture of eighteenth century America. They were incorporated to prevent or restrict the use of firearms and duly protect property rights. Much like the gun and slave laws during that period, hunting laws differentiated between the use of the terms "bear" and "carry." There is not one instance of a hunting law that used the word "bear" to describe an individual's use of arms during hunting or the act of hunting in itself.[29] Nevertheless, it has been argued that the right to "keep and bear arms" was premised on activities such as hunting, and that the Second Amendment reflects and extends this.[30]

Supporters of the individual right theory, who contend that the word "bear" was meant to include "to carry" in hunting laws, cite a 1785 bill drafted by Thomas Jefferson, which James Madison proposed to the Virginia Legislature. The bill would have proposed penalties upon individuals who violated hunting laws if they "shall bear a gun out of his inclosed ground, unless whilst performing military duty."[31] The wording of the bill undoubtedly uses the word "bear" in a "to carry" definition, but the bill did not pass. The historical record does not provide us with the reason why Jefferson and Madison's hunting bill did not pass, but it probably had to do with Jefferson's use of the word "bear." There was not a single instance of any Virginia hunting law incorporating the word "bear," let alone to denote the term meant "to carry."[32]

Supporters of the individual right theory also cite the fact that a minority of the delegates to the Pennsylvania ratification convention proposed the following amendment to the Constitution:

> That the people have a right to bear arms for the defense of themselves and their own state, or the United States, or for the purpose of killing game; and no law shall be passed for disarming the people or any of them, unless for crimes committed, or real danger of public injury from individuals; and as standing armies in the time of peace are dangerous to liberty, they ought not to be kept up; and that the military shall be kept under strict subordination to and be governed by the civil powers.[33]

The amendment undoubtedly uses the term "bear" to denote "carry." However, what the supporters of the individual right theory fail to mention is the context of that document.[34] First, the document was drafted after Pennsylvania had ratified the Constitution, meaning the "bear arms" amendment may never have reached the floor debates during the Pennsylvania ratifying convention. Given there exists no record to show that it did reach the floor, this proposal should be given no consideration. Besides, only twenty-three of sixty-nine members of the ratification convention supported it. Thus the proposal was never even considered in Congress. Second, it is uncertain as to just how many of those twenty-three delegates firmly believed in the proposed "bear arms" amendment's provisions.[35] Out of the fourteen amendments proposed, all but two were elaborated on, in some form or fashion, within the remainder of the document. Those two amendments were (1) the "right to bear arms," and (2) that the "inhabitants of several states shall have liberty to fowl and hunt in seasonable times."[36] All the other amendments were supplemented with text that explained why they were deemed necessary. The same was not true for the "right to bear arms" and hunting amendments.

In sum, the Pennsylvania minority amendment, much like Jefferson's proposed hunting law, was nothing more than a textual anomaly. Neither proposal accurately used "bear arms" in its proper legal context. In fact, there is not a single instance of the Pennsylvania Assembly or any state, for that matter, incorporating the word "bear" in any hunting law. Like the other colonies, Pennsylvania used the word "carry" to denote possession in such legislation.[37] Hence, a textual analysis of the Pennsylvania minority's "bear arms" amendment does not support the individual right theory. For if we are to take anything from it, the amendment was never pushed forward or accepted because it did not accurately incorporate the proper meaning of the word "bear."

### Influential Philosophers and "Bear Arms"

When the Founding Fathers adopted the Constitution, much of their opinions and political ideals were based upon political philosophers such as

James Harrington, David Hume, Algernon Sidney, and Niccolo Machiavelli. For in every instance that the phrase "bear arms" was incorporated in the writings of these philosophers, the phrase was limited to mean the use of arms in a military capacity.

In *The Prince*, for instance, Machiavelli, in describing the different kinds of militia, stated one of the problems with the new Italian State was that the citizens were not "accustomed to bear arms," thus, causing them "to hire foreigners as soldiers."[38] Here Machiavelli clearly limits the phrase "accustomed to bear arms" to mean an individual's knowledge regarding the military use of weapons. Surely he was not referring to their ability to hunt, carry weapons, or use them for individual self-defense. Thus, to include these meanings in this instance would signify that the Italian populace could not hunt, carry weapons, or defend themselves. In addition, it is Machiavelli's phrase following "accustomed to bear arms" that supports its restricted military context. The reference of the need for Italy to seek foreign soldiers or mercenaries in "bearing arms" was not intended to help the Italians hunt or protect one's home or family in self-defense. It was purely referring to using arms for a military purpose.

Algernon Sidney's writing also shows the limited meaning of the phrase "bear arms." His *Discourses Concerning Government,* written in 1698, would receive much praise from the Founders. In his description of what constituted the Hebrew army, he uses the phrase "bear arms" in a military capacity. Sidney wrote that when Moses was dividing his forces into units, it was common practice to only count those "who were able to bear arms."[39] Another seventeenth-century philosopher, James Harrington, used "bear arms" in the same limited context. In his work *Oceana*, Harrington cites the phrase "bear arms" in multiple instances, none denoting anything that resembles the individual right theory.[40]

### Interpreting "Bear Arms"

Despite all the historical evidence available to support the contrary, the individual right courts have held there were just "too many instances" of the use of the phrase "bear arms" to conclude that the Founders intended to limit it in a military sense.[41] For example, the District of Columbia's Court of Appeals examined the use of "bear arms" in the *Oxford English Dictionary*[42] and *Webster's Dictionary*[43] to come to this determination.[44] It held that although the majority of sources "support the notion that 'bear arms' was sometimes used as an idiom signifying the use of weaponry in conjunction with military service," confirming "the idiomatic usage was not absolute."[45]

It was such a notion the Supreme Court majority supported using a dictionary from 1773.

Unfortunately such an interpretation does not coincide with "bear arms" use in adopted colonial statutes and legal documents. There is no arguing that "bear" by itself denotes what the Supreme Court states it to mean, namely, "to carry." Unfortunately we are not analyzing the word in a phrase such as "bearing a letter" or "bearing bad news." We are analyzing "bear arms," a phrase that was distinctly used to describe one performing military duty. What solidifies this implicit meaning is the reference to the "well regulated militia" in the prefatory language. Therefore, when we look at "bear arms" in this context and according to its statutory use in eighteenth-century laws, we come to a more accurate determination of how the phrase was meant to be legally defined within the Second Amendment.

It cannot be stressed enough that the United States Constitution was a legal document, a document binding the government to the people of the United States, and establishing rules and restrictions by which a nation was to operate. Furthermore, the words of the Constitution have a legal meaning and were drafted by the America's best legal and legislative minds of the eighteenth century. These men had drafted their own States' laws and statutes, and the use of these terms in those documents undoubtedly had the same or a similar meaning in the Constitution.

The use of the phrase "bear arms" was distinctively limited to use in each of the colonies' militia laws. The Supreme Court majority describes "bear arms" use in these laws as technical, but nothing could be further from the truth. For militia laws were constantly published and distributed; they were the means by which the militia knew when and how to muster, train, and arm. Usage of "bear arms" was natural to eighteenth century America, and nothing can be more clear and convincing. In Georgia, for example, it was required that "every male person from the age of sixteen to sixty years" be "liable to bear arms in the regiment, troop, or companies" in the province.[46] New Hampshire required that "all Male Persons from Sixteen Years of Age to Sixty ... shall bear Arms, and attend all Musters, and Military Exercises."[47] Meanwhile, New Jersey included "all able-bodied Men, not being Slaves ... between the Ages of sixteen and fifty Years" that were "capable of bearing arms" to be enrolled in the militia.[48]

Leading up to the adoption of the Constitution and the Bill of Rights, no law in any of the states, colonies, or territories had used the phrase "bear arms" in anything but a military sense.[49] This is because "bear arms" was only meant to apply to military service and the purpose of the Second Amendment plainly reflects that. For the Second Amendment was adopted to counter Article I, Section 8, of the Constitution,[50] which stated that Congress shall have the authority to "provide for organizing, arming, and disciplining the Militia."[51] Prior to the adoption of the Constitution, every state had control of these functions with their militia laws. These laws varied in content depending on the colony or state, each furnishing different provisions regarding the arming of its citizenry in times of insurrection or invasion. It was feared that giving Congress the discretion of arming their militias would not only prevent the states from being able to defend themselves from enemies, foreign and domestic, but more importantly would impede their ability to protect against an oppressive federal government.

This point was addressed during the Virginia Constitutional Ratifying Convention. There was concern that federal control over the militia would result in one state's militia subduing the people of another, but the larger concern was that some of the states' militias would be neglected.[52] Future Supreme Court Justice John Marshall helped subdue some of these fears when he addressed the convention, affirming "[i]f Congress neglect our militia, we can arm them ourselves."[53] Marshall knew that barring any restriction in the Constitution forbidding the states from arming, disciplining, and organizing their militias, the states "fully possessed" the right to govern their respective militias "as ever they had been."[54] This did not settle everyone's fears, though. Thus the Second Amendment was drafted to counter those fears. It guaranteed the federal government would never encroach upon the states' ability to govern the arming of its citizens in a militarily capacity.

The Supreme Court majority in *Heller* interpreted "bear arms" much differently. It primarily cited an article by Clayton Cramer and Joseph Olson entitled "What Did 'Bear Arms' Mean in the Second Amendment?"[55] The article argues that "bear arms" was not solely in reference to the military but also described everyday arms use. However, the article fails to cite any colonial law that was adopted prior to the adoption of the Constitution. The only documents the article does cite predating the Constitution were found in England. Furthermore, out of the insurmountable number of documents searched, the authors only found seven sources that used some form of "bear arms" that may have a meaning outside of a military context. Even these examples are not absolute, though.

The only American legal examples given by Cramer and Olson are those already addressed as erroneous: (1) the Madison and Jefferson hunting law that did not pass, and (2) the Pennsylvania minority amendment that did not reach either the floor of the Pennsylvania Ratifying Convention or the Constitutional Convention. The only other American example that needs further elaboration is a citation to John Adams' *A Defence of the Constitu-*

*tions of Government of the United States of America.* In it Adams writes: "In order the purge the city of its many popular disorders, they were obliged to forbid a great number of persons, under grievous penalties, to enter the palace: nor was it permitted them to go about the city, nor bear arms."[56]

Cramer and Olson claim "there is nothing in the context that would suggest this was a limitation on military service or duty, or that these disorderly persons were engaged in organized rebellion." Unfortunately for these authors, there is nothing that states that this refers to activities apart from military service. Admittedly, the wording of the sentence is awkward, but it does not support the individual right interpretation. What Cramer and Olson leave out is the sentence following their quote. It reads, "All this they were obliged to do to prevent collections of people in the streets."[57] This puts "bear arms" in its proper context and does insinuate Adams was describing military service, for the city of Bologna was preventing the people from bearing arms as a means to keep the streets clear. What Cramer and Olson are intentionally leaving out is that citizen militias existed throughout Italy during the period Adams is writing about —1269 A.D., meaning at that time, individuals were bearing arms when they were mustering for militia duty. It was a practice Bologna was trying to deter to "prevent collections of people in the streets."

It is interesting that the Supreme Court majority goes through great lengths to find documents that use "bear arms" in a context outside of military service, but in their search it only finds (1) laws or resolutions that did not pass, (2) a handful of documents drafted in England, and (3) an article that provides no adequate examples predating the Constitution. It shows just how much a role political stances and agendas play in determining the outcome of cases. Meanwhile, there exist countless examples of "bear arms" used in contexts that support its true military meaning, but they were dismissed as being too technical and were therefore considered not determinative of the Framers' intent.

Outside of the misguided Cramer and Olson article, the majority also cite states constitutions' "bear arms" provisions to support their understanding. They believed "bear arms" was so commonly used in everyday references to hunting and self-defense in these provisions that it could not be limited to a military connotation. Here again, the majority is misinformed. As will be addressed in detail in examining Ohio's "bear arms" provision, there is no substantiated evidence to suggest that state constitutional provisions were referring to anything outside of military service. For every one of the eighteen states that drafted constitutions by 1818, none ever used the phrase "bear arms" in any statute that was not referencing military service.

Thus, until such substantiating evidence can be brought forward they cannot be interpreted as such.

What is even more perplexing about the majority's interpretation of "bear arms" is its dismissal of an amicus brief submitted by the District of Columbia. The brief gave nearly a hundred examples of how "bear arms" was incorporated in the Founding era's documents — that being in reference to military service. Nevertheless, the majority believed these documents to show nothing more than an "idiomatic meaning that was significantly different from its natural meaning." They felt these examples were not clearly determinative because half included the preposition "against," a word causing the majority to believe the military "idiomatic" meaning could only be "unequivocally" borne when followed by "against." Such an interpretation is ludicrous. As has already been shown, the militia laws preceding and following the adoption of the Constitution unequivocally show that the majority's interpretation is a historical and textual farce. Likewise, irrefutable are the insurmountable references in Congress to "bear arms" in the military context.

The majority's response to the use of "bear arms" in these examples is that Congress and state legislators would not need to use the phrase in any other context outside of military service. In their opinion, neither Congress nor the state legislators "would have little occasion to use it *except* in discussions about the standing army and the militia." The majority further states that Congress and state legislators also often used the phrases "carry arms," "possess arms," and "have arms," arguing that these phrases were synonymous with "bear arms." To support this assertion, the majority cites the use of "bear" in Cunningham's 1773 legal dictionary which reads, "Servants and labourers shall use bows and arrows on *Sundays,* & c. and not bear other arms." This phrase is nonexistent in any of the states' statutes. Nevertheless, the majority insinuated that the Founders commonly used the phrase "bear arms" in everyday language.

This argument is spurious for the following reasons. First, the Court relies on a law that never existed, while ignoring all other germane legislative history that does not happen to support their stance, reasoning that "post-enactment legislative history ... betrays a fundamental misunderstanding of a court's interpretive task."[58] Meanwhile the Court had no trouble citing cases and post Civil War history to support its stance. Second, their example reads "not bear other arms." The majority is willing to take an example in which "other" separates "bear" from "arms," but it dismissed the District of Columbia's amicus brief because nearly half of the examples read "bear arms against." In their dismissal, the majority was clearly more than willing to take any textual examples as long as the words "bear" and "arms" were in the same sentence, but made sure to dismiss anything that impeded its individual right interpretation. Lastly, the majority implies the Founders used "bear arms" as common everyday language. If that is the case, then we should assume the following hypothetical conversation would take place:

GEORGE WASHINGTON: Good afternoon, Mr. Madison, how are you today?

JAMES MADISON: I am well, Mr. Washington, thank you for asking. When we last spoke you mentioned that you may go *bearing arms* to get some deer meat, how did that go?

GEORGE WASHINGTON: It was very successful. We *bore arms* near the woods in Alexandria. My slaves and I were fortunate to kill three deer on the expedition. We may go *bearing arms* against this weekend. Would you like to join?

JAMES MADISON: I would love to. I have not *bore arms* for some time. I could use the practice.

Given the majority's claims that one also would "bear arms" in self-defense or defense of property, we are to assume the following conversation could have also taken place:

GEORGE WASHINGTON: I was told of a robbery that took place in Arlington. Could you tell me what happened?

JAMES MADISON: Thomas Jefferson's Monticello was robbed, sir. The bandits attacked in the middle of the night. Fortunately, Mr. Jefferson was able to fend them off by bearing arms.

Both examples show just how erroneous the majority's claim is. No historian has ever found any personal letter, diary, or correspondence that described hunting or self-defense as "bearing arms." Yet the majority claims the natural language of "bear arms" denoted such meaning. Furthermore, of all the nineteenth-century cases the majority so heavily relies upon, none of the facts in those cases describe any of the party's actions with firearms as, to wit, "bearing arms." In fact, in not one case regarding self-defense, hunting, crimes, or the illegal carrying of weapons do the facts describe the actions as "bearing arms." The answer to these inconsistencies with the majority's interpretation of "bear arms" is simple. One did not "bear arms" when they were performing any of these actions; "bear arms" in its legal form clearly denoted the activity of one performing military service.

## Understanding "Keep"

The Supreme Court majority in *Heller* admits the phrase "keep arms" was "not prevalent in the written documents of the founding period," but nevertheless found the phrase to mean individual arms ownership. There is no disagreeing that "keep" had been used in many statutory provisions of the eighteenth century and, some cases, probably implied "to possess" or "to own." The Second Amendment regarded the rights of people as a militia; thus its words should only be understood in the context that was incorporated in militia and military statutes. If we examine the word "keep" in these statutory provisions, it becomes clear that the word no longer holds its broad definition. Instead it holds a more limited meaning — "to maintain" or "to service."

In 1782, Delaware's militia act required every militiaman to "keep the same [arms] by him at all Times, ready and fit for Service" or be required to pay a fine of twenty shillings.[59] In 1799, Maryland imposed restrictions on its militia's "keeping" of arms when it provided that if any "private or non-commissioned officer, to whom a musket is delivered ... shall use the same in hunting, gunning or fowling, or shall not keep his arms and accoutrements in neat and clean order, he shall forfeit" a fine.[60] Meanwhile, in Virginia's militia law, a foot soldier was required to "keep at his place or abode one pound of powder and four pounds of shot," and every horse soldier was required to "keep his horse, arms, and ammunition."[61] Furthermore, in 1784, Virginia also required its militia slave patrols to "constantly keep the aforesaid arms, accoutrements, and ammunition ready."[62]

Thus, "keep" in the context of militia law plainly equated to "maintain," not to "own" or "possess." If the state legislatures wanted to denote required possession or ownership in their respective militia laws, they generally used the terms "provide" or "furnish," not the word "keep."[63] There is no better example of this than a 1746 South Carolina act which was perpetuated by the Revival Act of 1783. It governed the regulation of militia slave patrols and required each militia man, who was delegated to do slave patrols, "shall provide himself and keep always in readiness ... one good gun or pistol."[64] The act shows that "provide" and "keep" were deemed as two dissimilar verbs within the context of militia laws. The militia man's requirement to "provide" denotes his duty to own, while his requirement to "keep" denotes his duty to maintain in service.[65]

Other examples showing that the word "provide" meant ownership existed in the overwhelming majority of militia laws. In 1782, Delaware required every militia man to "provide himself, and every Apprentice, or other Persons" with a "Musket or Firelock with a Bayonet."[66] In 1757, Georgia required each member of its militia slave patrols to "provide for himself one good gun or pistol."[67] In 1793, Maryland required "every citizen so enrolled" in the militia to "provide himself with a good musket or firelock."[68]

In Massachusetts, "every Officer and private Soldier of said Militia" was required to "be constantly provided with a good Fire-Arm."[69] Lastly, even the first National Militia Act adopted by the Continental Congress does not use the word "keep" to denote possession.[70] Like the other state and colonial militia laws of the eighteenth century, "provide" was used to denote ownership or possession.

Some militia laws used the word "furnish" to denote ownership or possession. In 1777, New Jersey required every militia man to "furnish himself with a good Musket."[71] In 1786, North Carolina ordered every "able bodied man" to "furnish himself with one good rifled or smooth bored gun fit for service."[72] In 1781, Rhode Island required each of its "non-commissioned Officers and Soldiers" to "furnish himself with a good Musket."[73] Meanwhile, in Virginia's 1757 militia law, it was required that "Every soldier shall be furnished with a firelock."[74]

The word "kept" was also sometimes incorporated within colonial and state militia laws. Much like the word "keep," the word "kept" denoted "to maintain" or "to service" one's arms and equipment. Massachusetts required a "Stock of Powder and Ammunition" in each town to be "constantly kept which shall be one Barrell of Good Gun-Powder ... three hundred Weight of Leaden Balls (of different sizes) and three Hundred flints for every Sixty Soldiers."[75] Pennsylvania required each company's captain in charge of the state's arms "to appoint a suitable person near the place where the company usually meets for training, in whose custody such arms shall be put; to be cleaned and kept in repair; for the use of such militia men as the officers of the company deem unable to procure their own arms."[76]

Lastly, Baron von Steuben's *Regulations for the Order and Discipline of the Troops of the United States* also provides great insight into how the word "keep" was incorporated in a military context and can be applied to understanding "keep" within the Second Amendment. Von Steuben's rules not only applied to the Continental Army during the American Revolution but also regulated the militia. In fact, his rules would remain the basis by which the United State Army was to be regulated, organized, and disciplined during much of the nineteenth century. Throughout the regulations, "keep" is used in multiple instances but never denotes ownership or possession. In the section regarding the preservation of arms and ammunition, "keep," or a form of the word, is used in two instances. The first instance reads, "It is highly essential to the service that the ammunition should be at all times kept complete."[77] In the second instance it reads, "The ammunition wagons shall contain twenty thousand cartridges; and in order to keep the same complete, the conductor shall ... apply to the field commissary ... for a supply."[78]

From the reading of both these examples it is clear that "keep" denoted the same meaning as has been shown within the states' militia statutes, i.e., to "keep" meant "to maintain" or "to service."

To further illustrate this definition of "keep," Von Steuben also used the word in his sections regarding the duties to be performed by different ranking officers.[79] Of particular note was one of the duties assigned to sergeants and corporals regarding "arms." His rules stipulated, "Each sergeant or corporal ... must pay particular attention to their conduct in every respect, that they keep themselves and their arms always clean."[80] Again, "keep" in this example also denotes "to maintain" or "to service." In fact, there is not one instance in Von Steuben's entire regulations where "keep" is used in a capacity that would imply ownership or possession. Hence, further weight is brought to bear on the argument that "keep" in the Second Amendment does not protect a right to own firearms.

Despite the availability of each state's eighteenth-century militia laws and Von Steuben's regulations, the Supreme Court refused to consider the word "keep" in this context. Instead, it interpreted the Second Amendment to encompass an individual right by taking the broad, all-encompassing meaning. The District of Columbia Appellate Court had construed the word "keep" as "a straightforward term that implies ownership or possession of a functioning weapon by an individual for private use."[81] The Supreme Court endorsed this interpretation, stating the phrase "keep arms" was simply a common way of referring to possessing arms — for militiamen "and everyone else." Such an interpretation is inadequate given all the language of militia statutes that disproves it.

It has long been established by the Supreme Court that every word in the Constitution "must have its due force and appropriate meaning," and that "no word was [to be] necessarily used or needlessly added."[82] Therefore, if it is absolutely necessary for the meaning of the word "keep" to have its "due force," it should have been placed in the context of the Second Amendment's prefatory language. That language reads, "A well regulated militia being necessary to the security of a free State," and thus signifies that the remaining words, "the right of the people to keep and bear arms, shall not be infringed," must be interpreted in that "well regulated militia" context. Given that the only "well regulated" militias were run or authorized by the state governments, the Supreme Court should have used the Second Amendment's prefatory text in this framework. For if this had been done, the majority would have undoubtedly found the meaning of "keep arms" to equate to "maintain" or "service" arms, not "possess" or "own" them.

## How Can One "Keep and Bear Arms" Without Individual Ownership?

If the Supreme Court had examined "keep and bear arms" in the military context, it would have been quick to question if "keep" only meant "to maintain" or "to service," for how were the militia to maintain such arms if they did not necessarily own them? The answer is that the states varied in their views as to whether individuals were required to own their arms or whether the government was to provide them. This issue has never been addressed, though, because the courts most commonly quoted the first National Militia Act of 1792, which compelled every militia man to procure his own arms for the national defense. It read, "That every citizen so enrolled and notified, shall, within six months thereafter, provide himself with a good musket or firelock, a sufficient bayonet," and so forth.[83] Although the act compelled every qualified citizen to "provide himself," which denoted self-ownership with the arms required, the states adopted their own varied practices on how to arm the national militia if ever called up.

Prior to the Constitution giving Congress the power to organize, arm, and discipline the militia,[84] each state retained respective control over such functions. Generally, the practice was that every man enrolled in the militia was compelled to provide for himself the required arms and equipments mentioned in each act. In 1782, Delaware required that "every Person between the Ages of eighteen and fifty ... shall at his own Expence, provide himself" with "a Musket or Firelock with a Bayonet, a Cartouch-Box to contain twenty-three Cartridges, a Priming-Wire, a Brush and six Flints, all in good Order."[85] In 1781, Massachusetts required "every Officer and private Soldier of said Militia" to "equip himself, and be constantly provided with a good Fire-Arm, with a Steel or Iron Ram-rod, and a Spring to retain the same, a Worm, Priming-Wire and Brush, and Bayonet fitted to his Gun, a Scabbard and Belt therefore, a Cartridge Box that will hold Fifteen Rounds of Cartridges at least, Six Flints, one Pound of Powder, Forty Leaden Balls fitted to his Gun, a Haversack and Blanket, a Canteen sufficient to hold one Quart."[86] Similarly, a 1786 New York law required that "every citizen so enrolled" shall "provide himself at his own expence with a good musket or firelock, each cartridge containing a proper quantity of powder and ball, two spare flints, a blanket, and knap sack; and shall appear so armed, accoutered and provided when called out to exercise or duty...."[87]

While many states required every enrolled individual to provide their own arms and equipment, the majority of the states' militia laws had provisions set in place to provide arms for apprentices, indentured servants, men between the ages of eighteen and twenty-one, and poor persons. These provisions compelled the state or masters to provide the required arms and equipment. In 1782 Delaware, it was enacted that "every Apprentice, or other Person, of the Age of eighteen and under twenty-one Years who had an Estate of the Value of Eighty Pounds, or whose Parent is rated as Eighteen Pounds towards public Taxes, shall, by his Parent or Guardian, respectively, be provided with a Musket or Firelock with a Bayonet...."[88] Massachusetts and New Hampshire adopted similar provisions, the former's law stating the "Selectmen of any Town" whom shall judge "any Person belonging to the Militia of their Town unable to equip and arm himself aforesaid, such Selectmen shall ... at the Expence of such Town, provide for, furnish, arm and equip such Person with Arms and Equipments; which Arms so provided by such Selectmen, shall be the Property of the Town at whose Expence they shall be provided."[89] Meanwhile, New Jersey exempted those individuals who were too poor and "unable to purchase the Arms, Accoutrements and Ammunition."[90] In 1757, New Jersey even financed the purchase of "Two Thousand Stand of Arms, Two Thousand Pounds Weight of Gunpowder, Eight Thousand Pounds Weight of Lead, Eight Thousand Flints, and Thirty Bullet Moulds" for such "poor Persons as are unable to purchase for themselves."[91]

There were also times where states chose to provide all the arms and equipment for their militia. Typically, this was often practiced during times of war, but in the cases of Maryland, Pennsylvania, and Virginia, it was also done to ensure the security of the state. In 1732, Maryland had adopted a system where its assembly was required to provide all the arms and ammunition necessary to arm the militia. The arms and equipment were distributed but not to be sold under penalty of law.[92] Maryland continued this practice up to and during the French and Indian War when it defrayed the expense of arms and ammunition to the colony.[93]

Pennsylvania had often supplied its public arms when it assembled, mustered or trained its militia up to and during the American Revolution. By 1777, it had adopted a system where it was to supply enough arms and equipment for "two classes" in each company. The class structure within the militia system was much like a draft. Different classes were called into service at different times, with these classes rotating during long conflicts. Since the arms and equipment were the property of the state, it was ordered that no person "shall sell, or knowingly buy, take in exchange, conceal, or otherwise receive ... any arms or accoutrements belonging to this State."[94] This practice continued through the 1780s, including the state providing firing cartridges for the militia to practice with.[95]

Virginia initially required every man enrolled in the militia to provide himself with the required arms and equipment,[96] but in 1757 began making exceptions to those who were "so poor as not to be able to purchase the arms" required.[97] For these poor individuals, the state was compelled to arm them out of the public treasury. Much like the other states, Virginia ordered that "if any person or persons so armed out of his majesty's stores shall detain or embezzle any arms or ammunition to him or them delivered for the public service, and shall not produce or re-deliver the same when ordered and required so to do, it shall be lawful ... to commit such offender to prison, there to remain until he shall make satisfaction for the arms or ammunition by him detained or embezzled."[98] By the time of the American Revolution, Virginia practiced arming its entire militia "at the expense of the publick,"[99] and even began procuring arms from individual owners to supply the war.[100] The practice of arming the militia at the expense of the state continued throughout the war.[101] In many instances, men that left their personal arms with the company after their term was up were paid a bonus.[102]

By 1784, Virginia had reverted back to requiring each individual be responsible for their own arms and equipment,[103] but this quickly changed with events such as Shays' Rebellion. In December 1787, the individual requirement was repealed, making it the duty of the state to provide the proper arms and equipment.[104] The governor was to use the Virginia Assembly's appropriated funds for the "purchase of arms, in procuring such artillery, small arms, accoutrements and ammunition, as may to him with such advice seem proper; and the small arms so procured shall be distributed to the different counties in proportion to the number of their militia."[105] Furthermore, "[e]very private receiving such arms and accoutrements shall hold the same subject to the like rules, penalties and forfeitures, as are prescribed for a poor private in and by the act of assembly."[106]

These examples clearly show that just because an individual did not own his arms, this did not prevent him from "keeping" them. A person could just as easily "keep" an arm belonging to the state as they could with one they were required to provide themselves. What's more, the state often required them to do so. In 1766 Virginia, even those individuals that had been exempted from bearing arms were not exempt from "keeping" arms. Some individuals, such as justices of the peace or physicians, were still required to "provide compleat sets of arms" for the use of the "county, city, or borough" where they resided.[107] The act further provided that such exempt persons "shall always keep in his house or place of abode, such arms, accruements and ammunition, as are by the said act required to be kept by the militia of this colony."[108] This act not only perfectly demonstrates that "keep" was statutorily defined as "to maintain" in good order, but that even those who were exempted could be required to "keep" arms to fulfill their duty to society.

## The Second Amendment Within the Bill of Rights, the Debates, and Its Meaning

Although a textual interpretation shows the Second Amendment does not afford an individual right to carry or own firearms, individual right advocates often point to the *Federalist Papers* from which they argue that there was a clear understanding that their definition of the "right to bear arms," i.e., that everyone has an affirmative right to own a gun, was meant to extend to all. It is believed that *Federalist* Nos. 8,[109] 28,[110] 46,[111] and 59[112] convey that the purpose of the Second Amendment was that an armed populace provided a political check on the abuses of federal government. Therefore, it is argued that the Second Amendment's purpose to ensure individual firearm ownership was constitutionally protected. To expand the meaning is to take the provisions of the *Federalist Papers* out of context. The purpose of the documents was to curb the fears of those who felt the federal government would raise a standing army to suppress the populace. The text within the *Federalist Papers* shows its authors were only suppressing this fear, and in no way addresses the individual right to own arms by any means. To infer that the *Federalist Papers* meant otherwise is neither historically nor legally supported.

In order to arrive at a more accurate understanding of the Second Amendment's meaning, it is necessary to examine the congressional debates on the issue. These debates show that the Framers had only one concern in mind when they were drafting the Second Amendment: There must be a provision to prevent the federal government from limiting the militia from being armed, thus, preventing the establishment of a standing army, foreign or domestic.[113]

On August 17, 1789, the Second Amendment debates began with the initial reading, "A well regulated militia, composed of the body of the people, being the best security of a free state; the right of the people to keep and bear arms shall not be infringed, but no person, religiously scrupulous, shall be compelled to bear arms."[114] Eldridge Gerry was concerned with the "religiously scrupulous" clause. He feared the inclusion of such a provision would allow the federal government to prevent certain individuals from bearing arms. The government could accomplish this end by excluding certain classes of people it deemed "religiously scrupulous," thus making the amendment useless.[115] After much debate as to whether the "religiously scrupulous" clause would impede the rights of the militia to bear arms, it was moved that the clause be struck. However, the motion did not pass, with 22 voting for it, and 24 against.[116]

Gerry also was not pleased with the amendment's reading a well regulated militia "being the best security of a free state."[117] He feared the section insinuated that while a militia was the "best security," it also admitted a standing army was a secondary choice. He moved it should read, a "well regulated militia, trained to arms," because this would make it the federal government's duty to ensure the militia was maintained.[118] Although the motion was not seconded, the language, reading "being the best security of a free state," would eventually be removed. The words "necessary to the" were put in place of "the best," thus making the amendment imply what Gerry wanted it to — that a well regulated militia was the only security of a free State.[119]

On August 20, the debate on the "religiously scrupulous" clause was once again initiated. Mr. Scott feared since religion was on the decline, such a clause would exempt those individuals from bearing arms.[120] Mr. Boudinot disagreed and preferred the clause remain. He felt removing the "religiously scrupulous" clause would not adequately protect those who "would rather die than use" arms in a military capacity.[121] To settle the debate it was moved that the words "in person" be added after the word "arms."[122] The proposed amendment now read, "A well regulated militia, composed of the body of the people, being the best security of a free state; the right of the people to keep and bear arms shall not be infringed, but no person, religiously scrupulous, shall be compelled to render military service in person."[123]

On August 25, the amendment was read to the Senate and, before it was returned to the House of Representatives, multiple changes were made. The words, "composed of the body of the people" and "but no one religiously scrupulous of bearing arms shall be compelled to render military service in person" were removed. In addition, the word "best" was removed in favor of "necessary to."[124] After all the changes, on September 9, the amendment now read, "A well regulated militia, being necessary to the security of a free state, the right of the people to keep and bear Arms, shall not be infringed."[125]

First, the debates multiple references to military service show this is what the "right to keep and bear arms" was in reference to. More importantly, though, the congressional debates' lack of anything resembling an individual right to "own" or "possess" arms shows that the amendment's purpose was not to protect such a right, but rather to maintain the militia system, while preventing the federal government from placing restrictions on arming people to accomplish that end. The colonies were fearful of the effects a standing army would impose. This was the sole purpose of the Second Amendment — to quell such fears. No other fact preceding the adoption of the Constitution better illustrates this point than the Militia Bill of 1775. The bill would have placed the New England militias under the control of Congress to provide a more efficient system to call up the militia in support of George Washington's army.[126]

During the American Revolution it must be remembered that American society, which balked at the idea of a standing army, had just created the Continental Army. For each colony or locality to assemble their militia in defense of their rights was viewed as philosophically viable, but creating a unified Continental Army was thought to be more dangerous than the British army already stationed among them. Moreover, the majority of revolutionaries felt the militia was the preferred manner to fight the British. John Adams preferred a militia-based society, since "it is always a wise institution" and, under "the present circumstances of our country" is "indispensable."[127]

Meanwhile, General Washington[128] felt the militia was a plague. It was undisciplined, improperly trained and equipped, and their enlistments lasted for only short periods.[129] Something had to be done to fix these problems. Thus, in an attempt to supersede each colony's control over their respective militias, and to aid Washington, Congress drafted the Militia Bill. John Adams felt the bill was "so necessary, at this critical moment, for the publick service."[130] Despite its necessity, there was much dissent surrounding the bill.

Samuel Adams queried, "Should we not be cautious of putting them under the direction of the generals ... at least until such a legislative shall be established over all America, as every colony should consent to?"[131] He hoped the militia would "always be prepared to aid the forces of the Continent in this righteous opposition to tyranny, but this ought to be done [through] an application to the Government of the Colony." Until a strong legislature could be formed, Samuel Adams thought it "dangerous to the liberties of the people to have an army stationed among them, over which they have no control."[132] Elbridge Gerry agreed. He feared whichever general was in control of the militia "might forget his station and conceive himself its master." Gerry suggested that for a "Continental General" to assume control over all militia, he must gain approval through each colony's legislature.[133]

Furthermore, the Militia Bill was not viewed favorably by the people. Militia privates of thirty companies in the surrounding Philadelphia area petitioned their grievances on the bill. They supported the principles of the revolution but disagreed on giving Congress control of the militia. In their estimation, the purpose of the militia was to ensure the safety of the colony, and to be called up only in the event of an emergency. In their view, the Militia Bill undermined this system, their individual rights, and the principles of which a militia was based.[134]

On November 4, Congress had initially granted Washington the authority to call upon any New England militia unit to support his army, but dissatisfaction with the Militia Bill caused its removal. A new resolution only allowed Washington to assume control of New England militias when he had "obtained the consent of those officers in whom the executive powers of Government in those Colonies may be vested."[135] Thus, even in the face of losing the revolutionary conflict, the politics of a standing army superseded the possible disintegration of the American Revolution as early as December 1775.

One can only imagine how history would have viewed the American revolutionaries if they had lost that conflict, especially when such a loss would have been due in part to the Founders' strong principles against standing armies. Had the colonies' uncompromising views about maintaining respective control of their militias held sway, the conflict's outcome would certainly have been different. It was only once rebellions such as the Whiskey Rebellion and Shays' Rebellion occurred that any further consideration was given by the states to grant even partial control over their militias to a higher governmental entity. This helps put the Second Amendment in its proper historical context. Although there was a need for the federal government to have control in organizing, arming, disciplining, and calling out the militia, it did not override the Framers' fears that such control could be potentially oppressive. For that reason, an amendment needed to be put in place to protect the people from such oppression.

Even following Shays' Rebellion, given the potential abuses the federal government could practice with control of the states' militias, there were some who believed such authority would never be supplanted to Congress. In June 1787, at the Philadelphia Constitutional Convention, Elbridge Gerry balked at such an idea. Regulating the militia was a matter on which the existence of a state depends, and Gerry felt giving that power to the national government "may enslave the states."[136] He honestly felt such an idea "would never be acceded to" since it has "never been suggested or conceived among the people."[137] Gerry's hypothesis was close to being correct. The states had never conceded such a right and to do so would be to give up much of their sovereignty.

In the 1788 Virginia Constitutional Convention, George Mason, the author of Virginia's Declaration of Rights upon which the Bill of Rights was modeled, conveyed his displeasure with the Constitution's proposed control over the militia. He feared the structure of the Constitution could potentially destroy the militia because Congress "may neglect to provide for arming and disciplining the militia."[138] Since Congress had "the exclusive right to arm them," Mason feared the states would be left without such power, rendering the militia "useless." Furthermore, Mason conveyed his feelings on the matter when he stated he would only agree to such a constitutional provision on one condition — if the federal government shall neglect to arm the militia, "there should be an express declaration that the state governments might arm and discipline them."[139]

James Madison could not have agreed more with his fellow Virginian George Mason.[140] He could not "conceive that this Constitution, by giving the general government the power of arming the militia, takes it away from the state governments."[141] Madison felt the power was "concurrent, and not exclusive."[142] Although many Federalists might have agreed with Madison's thoughts on Congress' concurrent power to arm the militia, this did not give a definitive textual protection against the federal government either failing or neglecting to arm the militia.

Patrick Henry shared these exact sentiments. He addressed his fellow Virginian delegates by showing why Madison's argument was flawed: that it did not afford a concurrent right upon the states and, if anything, would only infringe on the states' rights to appoint the militia's officers. Henry stated:

> As my worthy friend said, there is a positive partition of power between the two governments. To Congress is given the power of "arming, organizing, and disciplining the militia, and governing such part of them as may be employed in the service of the United States." To the state legislatures is given the power of "appointing the officers, and training the militia according to the discipline prescribed by Congress." I observed before, that, if the power be concurrent as to arming them, it is concurrent in other respects. If the states have the right of arming them, &c., concurrently, Congress, has a concurrent power of appointing the officers, and training the militia. If Congress have that power, it is absurd. To admit this mutual concurrence of powers will carry on into endless absurdity — that Congress has nothing exclusive on the one hand, nor the states on the other.[143]

This passage shows Henry knew that a constitutional protection would need to be put in place for the states to have any concurrent power in arming the militia. Otherwise the federal government could impede state constitutional provisions, and vice versa. In closing, Henry warned his fellow

Virginian delegates, "If you have given up your militia, and Congress shall refuse to arm them, you [will] have lost everything."[144] Therefore it was extremely pertinent that "if Congress do not arm the militia," the states "ought to provide for it ourselves."[145] It is this protection the Second Amendment was meant to afford when Madison drafted it.

## State Constitutional Ratifying Conventions

Individual right supporters not only contend the Congressional debates show that the Framers intended the Second Amendment to protect individual firearm ownership, but also that the states' ratifying conventions prove their point. As Mr. Guru explained it to the Supreme Court in oral arguments, it was the ratifying conventions that "demand[ed] a right to keep and bear arms," and which was to be "understood" as an individual right.

In its memorandum supporting an individual right, the Office of the Attorney General made a similar argument. It contended that the states conventions' proposed amendments were phrased as "individual rights ... even when accompanied by language concerning the militia and civilian control of the military."[146] Unfortunately, both Mr. Guru and the Office of the Attorney General are misinformed on this matter. Just as the Congressional debates provide no substantial evidence for the individual right theory, the same holds true for the states' ratifying conventions. In fact, if anything, the preponderance of the evidence hurts their argument more than it helps it.

The strongest and most frequently cited argument regarding the states' ratifying conventions and an individual right to firearm ownership rests with the Pennsylvania minority.[147] The Supreme Court majority described that minority as being "highly influential" in drafting the Second Amendment. An inaccurate assumption given its content was never proposed or debated on either the Pennsylvania or Congressional floor. As has already been addressed, this proposal was one of only two amendments[148] that were not further elaborated on. The remaining twelve amendments were all described in great detail by the Pennsylvania dissenters as to why they thought these amendments should be incorporated. So, it is exactly unclear as to why "for the purpose of killing game" was incorporated in its "bear arms" proposal. This inclusion is only more perplexing seeing that they included a proposal to "fowl and hunt in seasonable times" immediately after it.

If anything, the amendment was nothing more than a textual anomaly. Prior to the adoption of the Constitution, the Pennsylvania proposal and Jefferson's proposed hunting law[149] are the only two documents to use "bear arms" or some form of the phrase in a manner outside its military context. Neither of which passed; Virginia[150] and Pennsylvania[151] never incorporated "bear arms" in any law in a manner denoting "to carry." An exception was certainly not going to be made in the cases of these proposals. Meaning that these proposals were most likely struck down due to their inaccurate use of the word "bear" or the phrase "bear arms."

The Pennsylvania minority proposal also gives rise to other problems in supporting the individual right theory and may also explain why it was never adopted. It states, "[N]o law shall be passed for disarming the people or any of them, unless for crimes committed, or real danger of public injury from individuals." This language clearly was intended to mean that the federal government would not have been unable to confiscate an individual's arms unless one of two things occurred. Either (1) the individual was a criminal and deemed a liability to the safety of the community or (2) the government felt an individual's possession of arms posed a threat to the peace and security of the community at large. The former need not be elaborated on because even individual right supporters contend criminals may be prevented from owning or using firearms.

It is the latter section, in which the government may disarm people that pose a "real danger of public injury" that shows the Pennsylvania minority did not unequivocally support the individual right model. For this terminology gives the government great discretion as to whom it may disarm. "Public injury" is a broad term. Meaning if the government felt firearms in a certain locality or region were dangerous to those citizens, it could disarm the area. Thus, the individual right theorists have only selectively incorporated the terminology in the Pennsylvania minority's amendment. They undoubtedly support the bearing of arms "for the purpose of killing game." They just neglect the portion that restricts the right at the government's discretion for the public safety.

Another source cited about individual right supporters was the proceedings of the 1788 Massachusetts Convention. John Hancock had made a proposal banning standing armies. He believed standing armies should not be allowed "unless when necessary for the defence of the United States, or of some one or more of them."[152] It was here that Samuel Adams[153] proposed Congress should not be allowed to "prevent the people of the United States, who are peaceable citizens, from keeping their own arms." Adams' proposal, if it had been adopted, would give weight to the individual right argument. For if these words had been inserted it would clearly depict an individual's right to maintain a firearm in the home — no exceptions.

The amendment, like the Pennsylvania minority proposal and Jefferson's hunting law, did not pass. Individual right supporters will argue this is because gun ownership was naturally understood to exist, thus the Framers need not incorporate it. This argument has no legitimate basis. For its application in our understanding of the Constitution would be limitless. The Founders were clear to place affirmative rights and guarantees in the Constitution that they wanted to be protected. They were aware it served as a legal document that was to be interpreted literally. The words "own," "possess," "self-defense," "hunt" and so forth were common terminology and could have easily been inserted into the Second Amendment. Even so, none of these terms were included. In the meantime, individual right theorists still continue to argue that the right to own guns was understood to have existed in the Second Amendment. If the individual right theorists were to be correct in this regard, such an argument would be viable regarding any article in the Constitution.

For example, let's say one of the Framers proposed the First Amendment contain an exception allowing the government to restrict speech during times of war. The proposal is heard, but voted down. This leaves the question, "Because this proposal was submitted should we interpret the First Amendment to allow the government to restrict the First Amendment guarantees during time of war?" To argue against this example, one would state there was no legitimate historical basis by which such a proposal could be supported. The opposite is actually true because before, during, and after the American Revolution there exists a substantial amount of examples that show the Founders thought it was permissible to restrict individual speech and expression in times of emergency.

One needs to look no further than the American Revolution to prove this point. Loyalists, both before and during the American Revolution, were targeted and suppressed by Congress for their views on the conflict. Numerous pamphleteers, newspapers, and loyalist presses were forced out of business. John Mein, editor of the *Boston Chronicle*, was beaten up by a mob and forced out of Massachusetts for his criticism of non-importation.[154] James Rivington's *Gazetteer* was smashed by a Patriot group on November 25, 1775, and the type was carted off to Connecticut where it was forged into ammunition. The revolutionary intolerance of loyalist views was appalling when compared to the freedom of speech afforded in Britain. It was ironic to some loyalists that those in Great Britain who supported America's stance were not silenced and were free to express their dissenting views.[155]

In January 1776, Azor Betts was summoned to the New York Committee of Safety for "denouncing Congresses and Committees, both Continental and Provincial and for uttering that they were a set of damned rascals, and acted only to feather their own nests."[156] He was ordered to close confinement, but finally released in April upon penitence, paying a fine, and taking an oath of allegiance. Thomas Robinson of Delaware was ordered to stand trial for allegedly stating the Whig Committees "were a pack of fools for taking up arms against the King, that our charters were not annihilated, changed, or altered by the late acts of Parliament" and "the present Congress were an unconstitutional body of men, and also, that the great men were pushing on the common people between them and all danger."[157] Leonard Snowden, in 1775, had written letters to England that were abusive towards the Whig cause and, once they were found by the rebel authorities, he was consequently arrested.[158] A loyalist in Delaware, only described by the initial "C," was inspected for cursing Congress. Upon his trial, the audience called for the charge of treason, but the inspection committee called only for recantation.

Given these historical facts, let's now reconsider the question. Under the individual right theory of how to interpret the Second Amendment — that failed proposals should be given great weight in understanding the protections the "right to keep and bear arms" affords — should a failed proposal regarding the restriction of First Amendment rights during war allow us to include it in the First Amendment? The answer is "no." For while the individual right theorists are using such an argument to expand the meaning of the Second Amendment, one could just as easily use this argument to restrict protections within the Bill of Rights.

Nevertheless, the Supreme Court majority found no problem being hypocritical in this regard. It had no quandary in finding the Pennsylvania minority amendment's reference to hunting being persuasive in forming the right the Second Amendment was meant to afford. Meanwhile, in addressing the deleted conscientious objector clause, it found "it always perilous to derive the meaning of an adopted provision from another provision deleted in the drafting process." Thus, the majority believed it was okay to take the reference to hunting in a minority amendment that never reached the debate floor, but to dismiss how "bearing arms" was incorporated in an amendment that did reach the debate floor. The clause the majority ignored reads, "but no person, religiously scrupulous, shall be compelled to arms." Just like the states' ratifying conventions' use of "bear arms" in their proposals that did assuredly reach Madison and the Bill of Rights drafting committee, here again "bearing arms" is distinctly referring to military service. It is a textual mockery to say "bear arms" in the Second Amendment was not distinctly referring to what the conscientious objector clause was referring to.

The clause was not adopted because there was a fear that its inclusion might carve out exceptions. This would allow the federal government to prevent certain classes from taking up arms, thus potentially allowing a standing army to take hold. The Supreme Court majority dismissed this by arguing Quakers not only objected to military combat but to the use of arms in other contexts such as self-defense. So what the majority is essentially stating is the clause was removed partially because it was feared Congress might infringe on an individual's right to defend their home. There is nothing from the ratifying debates on the Second Amendment that even remotely insinuate this. Most importantly, the wording of the deleted section states no person shall be "compelled to arms." It is highly unlikely that the use of "compel" was meant to include hunting or self-defense. Congress could never "compel" someone to perform these actions. The use of "compel" is plain and clear — Congress would have been restricted from forcing individuals to go to war.

If the states' ratifying conventions tell us anything about the Second Amendment, they show that the amendment was only meant to protect one's right to repel standing armies, foreign and domestic. The Maryland Convention clearly supports this. Its majority made the following proposal: "That the militia shall not be subject to martial law, except in time of war, invasion, or rebellion."[159] In its reasoning for making this proposal, the majority's purpose was to "restrain the powers of Congress over the militia" because without such a check it would expose "all men, able to bear arms, to martial law at any moment."[160] Here the majority's use of the phrase "bear arms" is limited to its military context.

Even the Maryland minority used "bear arms" in the same limited context. They had recommended, "That no person conscientiously scrupulous of bearing arms, in any case, shall be compelled personally to serve as a soldier."[161] Seeming to foreshadow the removal of a similar clause in the Second Amendment's drafting debates, this too did not pass. Here again though, the phrase "bearing arms" in this proposal was purely referring to one's service in a military capacity, meaning it was universally understood that "bearing arms" was strictly associated with military service.

Another source the individual right theorists use to contend that the Framers intended the Second Amendment to protect individual firearm ownership is the New Hampshire Convention. In its twelfth amendment, the convention proposed "Congress shall never disarm any Citizen unless such as are or have been in Actual Rebellion."[162] First, the amendment does not address any word in the phrase of the "right to keep and bear arms," which means it has no textual comparison to the Second Amendment and therefore should have no weight in how we interpret its content. Second, the amendment did not pass and its terminology was not incorporated into the Bill of Rights. Lastly, the proposed amendment was not intending to address the "right to keep and bear arms." It was purely a response to the Massachusetts government's action following Shays' Rebellion. For in that instance the government not only confiscated the insurgents' arms, but also passed a law preventing the insurgents from owning or using arms for a period of three years.[163]

What further supports this last point is the convention's proposed third amendment. Following Shays' Rebellion the insurgents were also restricted from voting during that same three-year period.[164] The New Hampshire Convention addressed their dissent in its third amendment. It proposed:

> That Congress do not Exercise the Powers vested in them, by the fourth Section of the first Article,[165] but in Cases when a State shall neglect or refuse to make the Regulations therein mentioned, or shall make regulations Subversive of the rights of the People to a free and equal Representation in Congress. Nor shall Congress in any case make regulations contrary to a free and equal representation.[166]

It is clear that the amendment intended to limit Congressional authority to regulate elections. There is no debating this. It is the latter half of the amendment that asks Congress to step in when a state "shall make regulations Subversive of the rights of the people to a free and equal Representation of Congress," in which the convention was specifically referring to Shays' Rebellion. Thus, once we take in the totality of the circumstances in the drafting the New Hampshire Convention's twelfth amendment we see its true intent — that New Hampshire abhorred the actions taken by the Massachusetts government against the Shays' insurgents. It was in no way intended to touch upon what the "right to keep and bear arms" encompasses.

Another individual right argument worth addressing on using the states' conventions to interpret the Second Amendment is the Virginia Convention. The Office of the Attorney General memorandum claims that an amendment proposed by a Virginia Bill of Rights Drafting Committee, consisting of Patrick Henry, James Madison, George Mason, George Wythe, and John Marshall shows there exists an individual right.[167] The committee proposed the following:

> That the People have a Right to keep and bear Arms; that a well regulated Militia, composed of the Body of the People, trained to arms, is the proper, natural, and safe Defence of a free State; that Standing Armies in Time of Peace are dangerous to Liberty, and therefore ought to be avoided as far as the Circumstances and Protection of the Community will admit; and that in all Cases, the military should be under strict Subordination to, and governed by the Civil Power.

It is claimed the amendments prefatory use of the "People have a Right to keep and bear Arms" shows this right was distinct and separate from participation in a state militia. First, this is a contradiction in the individual right argument on the prefatory language in the Second Amendment. The individual right theorists claim the Second Amendment's prefatory language explains why the "right to keep and bear arms" exists. That this right is not limited to or restrained by the "well-regulated militia being necessary to the security of a free State." Now regarding the Virginia Drafting Committee proposal it can be seen that the "well regulated Militia" language appears after the "right to keep and bear Arms." So in this instance the individual right theorists claim that the subsequent language explains that right as well. In short, what the individual right theorists are saying is no matter where the "right to keep and bear arms" provision exists, this right is always separate to any of the other language regarding a militia. This defeats the whole purpose of interpreting statutory and textual construction. Such an argument and theory is especially dangerous in interpreting the Constitution; it would allow constitutional interpreters to take pieces of the Constitution, limit their context, and avoid prefatory and subsequent language.

Second, the individual right theory disposes of the fact that Virginia Declaration of Rights of 1776 included similar language.[168] The only significant difference is that it 1787 Virginia Bill of Rights Drafting Committee added the prefatory language, "That the People have a Right to keep and bear Arms." This fact further erodes the individual right argument that the "well regulated militia" language in the Second Amendment exists to explain why the "Right to keep and bear Arms" exists. For the Virginia Drafting Committee added the "right to keep and bear arms" to the existing Virginia constitutional right of a "well regulated Militia, composed of the Body of People, trained to arms, is the proper, natural, and safe Defence of a free State." Meaning that because the right of a "well regulated Militia" pre-existed the phrase "Right to keep and bear Arms," the Virginia Drafting Committee saw the "Right to keep and bear Arms" as specifically limited to a "well regulated Militia."

What's more, the individual right theorists and Supreme Court majority fail to mention the use of "bear arms" in Mason's nineteenth proposal. It reads, "That any Person religiously scrupulous of bearing Arms ought to be exempted upon payment of an Equivalent to employ another to bear Arms in his stead." The use of "bear arms" in this proposal is limited to its military context. It does not make sense that Mason would intend for "bear arms" to have the individual right expansive meaning in one amendment, while using it in a limiting context in another. What further supports this limited definition of "bear arms" is its placement within Mason's proposal. It is placed immediately preceding the proposals that "no Soldier ... ought to be quartered in any House" and that religiously scrupulous persons cannot be compelled to "bear arms." Proving that "bear arms" in legal documents such as this was in strict reference to military service. Lastly, one cannot ignore Madison's reference to paying an equivalent "to employ another to bear Arms in his stead." This clearly makes the Supreme Court majority's argument about what the removed conscientious objector clause in the Second Amendment meant to be nothing more than a shameful political explanation. It is doubtful that Quakers would pay an exemption or fee for not taking up arms in self-defense to deter an intruder.

The last convention the individual right theorists believe supports their argument is the New York Convention. It is contended because the New York proposal fell immediately after the right to religion that it stresses the individual nature of its "right to bear arms" proposal. That proposal reads: "That the People have a right to keep and bear Arms; that a well regulated Militia, including the body of the People *capable of bearing arms*, is the proper, natural, and safe defence of a free state."[169]

While it is accurately contended an individual's right to exercise religion precedes this clause, individual right theorists fail to mention that three military clauses immediately follow it: first, the right not to subjected to martial law except during times of war; second, the military should be in subordination to the civil authority; and third, the right that no soldier is to be quartered in any house without the consent of the owner all follow the "right to keep and bear arms" proposal. Thus, one could just as easily assert that the "right to keep and bear arms" was referring to military service in a militia as much as it is referring to an alleged individual right to own a firearm.

A closer examination of the wording shows that the proposed amendment specifically uses "bear arms" twice. It first uses it in conjunction with "keep" but also describes the militia as "including the body of the people *capable of bearing arms*." According to the individual right theory, similar to their understanding of Mason's drafting of the Bill of Rights, we are to take the first use of "bear arms" as meaning the right to hunt, self defense, etc. The second use of "bear" uses a limited meaning though. It is prescribing "bearing arms" as equating to military service. It is not logically viable that the Framers of this amendment meant for the first reference to "bear arms" to have a different meaning than in its reference to the latter's. The Framers were very conscious about the words they used, especially within constitutional provisions. Furthermore, there is no evidence that New York had ever incorporated the phrase "keep and bear arms" to mean anything but in the service of a militia or military. There is not one New York statute that the individual right theorists can point to in order to support such a claim.

In sum, the state conventions do not support an individual's right to own or carry a firearm. In fact, the individual right argument is actually undercut by the state statutes. Not only have the individual right theorists selectively incorporated portions of these "right to keep and bear arms" proposals, but they have even taken them out of context. These conventions do prove one individual right argument to be correct — that the right of the "people" was referring to individuals as well as to the collective militia body.

# CHAPTER TWO

# Revisionist Judicial Interpretation and Review

Given the Supreme Court majority's perplexing textual examination of the Second Amendment, it is not surprising that its members revised, inferred, and misinterpreted the majority of legal sources on the topic. When we are talking about ensuring a proper interpretation of the Constitution, one would think this would be done by taking everything into consideration: that the Supreme Court majority would do their research properly and not take sources out of context or revise them. At the very least, it would be more than sensible that the Court would examine legal and historical sources that have a firm rooting in the adoption of the Constitution. The Court failed to do so. Instead, the majority's best argument stems from a revisionist interpretation of legal commentators such as Justice Joseph Story, whose commentary was written nearly forty years after the adoption of the Constitution and which can hardly be considered as contemporaneous with that document.

Even if we were to view such commentary as contemporaneous with the Second Amendment, the sources do not support the individual right interpretation. The majority also relies on nineteenth-century case precedents: Cases the majority subjectively stripped apart and then pasted together, all to support its predetermined conclusion. Such reliance is a far cry from a proper historical interpretation. One certainly does not reference people's personal opinions from the twenty-first century to understand the Vietnam or Korean Wars, especially when those former individuals were not involved in either of those conflicts. This is essentially what the Supreme Court majority was in error of doing in *Heller*.

## Legal Commentators

One of the Supreme Court majority's strongest arguments derives from its use of post-ratification legal commentary. Selectively quoting the writings of St. George Tucker, William Rawle, and Joseph Story, the majority sought to illuminate an ideal that the Second Amendment was drafted to protect an individual's right to own a firearm. Just as was the case in their selective incorporation of historical sources in textually interpreting the Second Amendment, the same can be said regarding their use of legal commentary. In every instance the majority used a quoted passage of writing to support their argument, they likewise left out quotes and historical facts that countered their argument.

For example, in using St. George Tucker's *View of the Constitution of the United States*, Justice Scalia writes:

> Tucker elaborated on the Second Amendment: "This may be considered as the true palladium of liberty.... The right to self-defence is the first law of nature: in most governments it has been the study of rulers to confine the right within the narrowest limits possible. Wherever standing armies are kept up, and the right of the people to keep and bear arms is, under any colour or pretext whatsoever, prohibited, liberty, if not already annihilated, is on the brink of destruction." Tucker believed that the English game laws had abridged the right by prohibiting "keeping a gun or other engine for the destruction of game." He later grouped the right with some of the individual rights included in the First Amendment and said that if "a law be passed by congress, prohibiting" any of those rights, it would "be the province of the judiciary to pronounce whether any such act were constitutional, or not; and if not, to acquit the accused...." It is unlikely that Tucker was referring to a person's being "accused" of violating a law making it a crime to bear arms in a state militia.[1]

What Scalia fails to mention is that Tucker first brings up the Second Amendment in describing Congressional power to provide for "organizing, arming and disciplining the militia." In this section, Tucker reiterated the fact that the Virginia Constitutional Convention was deeply concerned about giving Congress power over the state's militias. The convention firmly believed that "a well regulated militia, composed of the body of the people trained to arms, is the proper, natural, and safe defense of a free state."[2] Therefore the convention made the following proposal: that "each state respectively should have the power to provide for organizing, arming, and disciplining its own militia, whenever congress should neglect to provide for the same." Tucker wrote, "all room for doubt, or uneasiness upon the subject, seem[ed] to be completely removed" with the inclusion of the Second Amendment.[3] Its incorporation added "that the power of arming the militia, not being prohibited to the states, respectively, by the constitution, is, consequently, reserved to them, concurrently with the federal government."[4]

This section of Tucker's *View of the Constitution of the United States* clearly denotes that the Second Amendment was meant to counter Article I, Section 8, of the Constitution. This is a fact that does not support the individual right model the Supreme Court majority adopted. Furthermore, Tucker goes on to discuss the importance of a well organized and disciplined militia. The Framers thought it essential there be uniformity in this regard because of the problems that the country faced during the American Revolution. Tucker describes the militia during that war as one of "uncertainty and variety." By giving the federal government the power to organize and discipline, the exact opposite would present itself. Now the country would present a militia that is "most safe, as well as [a] most natural defense of a free state."[5]

These facts put the Supreme Court majority's quotes of Tucker in their proper context. Without Tucker's early analysis on the connection between the militia powers and the Second Amendment, it is easy to see the majority's argument. Their quotes are obviously out of context. They ignore Tucker's earlier comments, and instead focus on his describing the Second Amendment as the "true palladium of liberty." Granted that the Second Amendment is just this, since the ability of the people to stand up against oppressive standing armies, foreign and domestic, ensures everybody has a hand in defending their liberty. This point is stressed when Tucker writes, "Wherever standing armies are kept up, and the right of the people to keep and bear arms is, under any color or pretext whatsoever, prohibited, liberty, if not already annihilated, on the brink of destruction." What he is stressing is that the people must have the ability to partake in defending their liberties. If they are left out of this process, it was feared they would have no redress. The people must fight to ensure the protection of their own liberties. Counting on others to protect them, or in the case of the Second Amendment, if they are ever restricted from the process, the people could essentially lose them.

This is why Tucker refers to hunting laws that confiscated English citizens' arms for non-compliance. It was suspected that the English government had used the gaming and hunting laws as a means to prevent the people from ever bearing arms. While an English hunting law might have stated its purpose was to preserve game and property rights, it was believed the hidden objective of these laws was to disarm the populace. This would prevent the people from having the capability of bearing arms in defense of their liberties.

These laws, however, did not conflict with the English Bill of Rights. For the 1689 Declaration of Rights only protected "subjects which are Protestants may have arms for their defence suitable to their conditions and as allowed by law." At no time were the English hunting and gaming laws making it illegal to own, procure, use, or bear arms. The laws either fined individuals for non-compliance, resulted in the confiscation of the arms that were used in breaking the hunting law, or resulted in the forfeiture of such arms to pay the fine. Thus, the hunting and gaming laws did not outright prevent an individual from bearing arms, but did have an effect on it indirectly. Tucker believed this is what the Framers were trying to prevent by drafting the Second Amendment. The strong language "shall not be infringed" was included to obstruct the passing of laws that prevented the people from being able to use arms in defense of their liberties. Tucker felt the wording of the English Bill of Rights left too much room for legislation that indirectly affected one's ability to bear arms.

William Rawle, another early nineteenth-century commentator whom the Supreme Court majority also inaccurately interprets, further illustrates this point. He points out that the English hunting and gaming laws were a disguise to prevent the people from inciting "popular insurrections and resistance to government."[6] To Rawle, it was unlawful to prevent the people from having the opportunity to defend their liberties. They must have access to and the ability to use arms in defense of their constitutionally protected rights. Parliament had prevented this by the maintaining of standing armies. No longer was the militia system in practice. Nor was it the means by which England protected or asserted itself.

Meanwhile the American states had a different system in place. Each had their own militia. Each was not relying on a standing army to protect its interests. Furthermore, each had different laws and means to provide its citizens with arms, i.e., to defend their liberties against an oppressive government — foreign or domestic. It was the people who made up the militia. They were the means by which each state defended itself. Thus, unlike England, the states had kept a system in place that allowed the people to "keep and bear arms," a system comprised of a well organized and disciplined militia.

The Supreme Court majority wrongfully interprets Rawle by focusing on his interpretation of the operative clause. Rawle writes:

> The corollary, from the first position is that the right of the people to keep and bear arms shall not be infringed. The prohibition is general. No clause in the Constitution could by any rule of construction [shall] be conceived to give to congress a power to disarm the people. Such a flagitious attempt could only be made under some general pretence by a state legislature. But if in any blind pursuit of inordinate power, either should attempt it, this amendment may be appealed to as a restraint on both.[7]

Much like the interpretation of Tucker's *View of the Constitution of the United States*, the majority leaves out an important part of the commentary in its understanding of the Second Amendment. The quote, as incorporated, insinuates that neither Congress nor the states may take away firearms from the people. This quote is out of context, however, without Rawle's interpretation of the prefatory language, i.e., that of a "well regulated militia is necessary to the security of a free state." He writes that this is "a proposition from which few will dissent," for the militia was the "palladium of the country." It must be "ready to repel invasion, to suppress insurrection, and preserve the good order and peace of government." What's most important is that Rawle described the "well regulated" portion as "judiciously added," as a "disorderly militia is disgraceful to itself, and dangerous not to the enemy, but to its own country." It was the duty of the "state government ... to adopt such regulations as will tend to make good soldiers with the least interruptions of the ordinary and useful occupations of civil life."[8]

This well regulated militia is what Rawle was referring to when he described the "right of the people to keep and bear arms." He even writes that the "well regulated" portion was "judiciously added."[9] It was, therefore, arbitrary for the people to just have arms without being trained, disciplined, and organized into a militia. The people using arms outside of this context is what Rawle was referring to when he wrote "the right ought not ... in any government ... be abused to the disturbance of the public peace,"[10] for an "assemblage of persons with arms, for an unlawful purpose, is an indictable offense, and even the carrying of arms abroad by a single individual, attended with circumstances giving just reason to fear that he purposes to make an unlawful use of them, would be sufficient cause to require him to give surety of the peace."[11]

The Supreme Court majority claims this last quote infers that the Second Amendment extends to other purposes, including self-defense. Scalia wrote the statement "makes no sense if the right does not extend to any individual purpose."[12] Yet, Scalia ignored Rawles' prefatory interpretation. When we do include Rawles' interpretation, a different and more accurate understanding of the statement becomes clear. The Second Amendment does not extend to anything but to the right of an individual to bear arms to defend one's liberties or repel standing armies through the militia.

Finally, the majority reaches the height of misinterpretation when it takes out of context the writing of Joseph Story, a notable nineteenth-century legal commentator. Justice Scalia wrote:

> Story explained that the English Bill of Rights had also included a "right to bear arms," a right that, as we have discussed, had nothing to do with militia service. He then equated the English right with the Second Amendment: "A

similar provision [to the Second Amendment] in favour of protestants (for to them it is confined) is to be found in the bill of rights of 1688, it being declared, 'that the subjects, which are protestants, may have arms for their defence suitable to their condition, and as allowed by law.' But under various pretences the effect of this provision has been greatly narrowed; and it is at present in England more nominal than real, as a defensive privilege." This comparison to the Declaration of Right would not make sense if the Second Amendment right was the right to use a gun in a militia, which was plainly not what the English right protected.[13]

Again, Scalia's interpretation could not be more wrong. First, Story writes that the English Bill of Rights provision is "similar," not synonymous or equal to the Second Amendment.[14] As has already been addressed by Tucker's commentary, England had passed hunting laws that had an indirect effect on the citizens' ability to bear arms. Yet, at no time did these laws directly interfere with that right. This is what Story was partially referring to when stating "the effect of this provision has been greatly narrowed." Furthermore, when Story states the English right as being "more nominal than real," he is referring to the fact that England had turned to standing armies.[15] It no longer looked to its militia as the means to defend the nation, an important historical fact the majority seemed to misplace. This was the whole purpose as to why the Second Amendment was adopted — to ensure that the federal government did not maintain oppressive standing armies.

In describing the Second Amendment, Story does not hint at the individual right as the *Heller* majority infers. If anything, Story's interpretation supports the understanding that the "right to keep and bear arms" is directly correlated to one's service in the militia. "The militia is the natural defence of a free country against foreign invasions, domestic insurrections, and domestic usurpations of power by rules," wrote Story.[16] The militia was important because standing armies "subvert the government, or trample on the rights of the people." This is why the "right of the people to keep and bear arms has been justly considered the palladium of the liberties of a republic." Story was simply elaborating on what Tucker and Rawle had tried to imply; in order for the people to ensure their liberties and freedoms, it must be the people that bear arms in defense of the country, not a standing army. Only by fighting for their liberties can the people truly covet these rights. Otherwise they are taken for granted.

What further illustrates the connection between the "right to keep and bear arms" and one's duty to serve in the militia is the following analysis by Story:

[T]he importance of a well regulated militia would seem so undeniable, it cannot be disguised that among the American people there is a growing indifference to any system of militia discipline, and a strong disposition, from a sense of its burthens, to be rid of all regulations. How it is practicable to keep the people duly armed without some organization, it is difficult to see. There is certainly no small danger that indifference may lead to disgust, and disgust to contempt; and thus gradually undermine all the protection intended by this clause of our national bill of rights.[17]

This quote clearly indicates that the "right to keep and bear arms" is directly connected to militia service, for Story could not see how the people could keep and bear arms without militia regulations. An unorganized, undisciplined, and unregulated militia was dangerous. As Story so eloquently put it, without a system of militia discipline, the people are "gradually undermin[ing] all the protection intended by this clause."[18]

There is another commentator the majority address in passing — Benjamin Oliver. The majority admits Oliver identifies the Second Amendment as only protecting a right through militia service. Other than wrongfully labeling him the "only" commentator to state so,[19] the majority chose not to refute his analysis — and for good reason. They did not have any argument to refute him. For Oliver was on point and stating what Tucker, Rawle, and Story were all also inferring. He saw the Second Amendment as applying to the militia service "and not to prevent congress or the legislature of the different states from enacting laws to prevent the citizens from always going armed."[20]

Oliver knew how courts and juries in certain parts of the country were expanding that right. They had begun to interpret a militia right as including an individual right to use or carry weapons for any purposes whatsoever; a construction of the "right to keep and bear arms" that Oliver felt was unsupported. He saw the prefatory language as "the reason assigned" and "sufficient to show its true construction." That reason being, "A well regulated militia is necessary to the security of a free State."[21]

## Case History

Just as the Supreme Court majority took the early American commentators out of context, so have they done with their interpretation of pre-twentieth century case history. The truth of the matter is that early case law on the Second Amendment is far from conclusive. First, the earliest case the majority points to was decided thirty-five years after the adoption of the Constitution — a period that cannot be deemed contemporaneous with adoption of the Second Amendment. Second, the majority infer facts from the cases that they do not know to be true. It is common judicial sense not to make assumptions without facts to support them. Nevertheless, the majority had no problem doing just that in these cases. Lastly, for every quote or case the majority cites supporting an individual right, there exists a different interpretation in another quote or case. Thus, just as twentieth-century courts had split in interpreting the language of the Second Amendment, the same held true from the 1820s and throughout the nineteenth century.

### Houston v. Moore

In 1820, the Supreme Court heard *Houston v. Moore*, which rightfully held the states have concurrent power over the militia, at least where not pre-empted by the Constitution. The majority in *Heller* reference this case, stating it shows the Second Amendment was not in relation to congressional power to "organize, discipline, and arm" the militia. They cite Justice Story's opinion where he states the Second Amendment "may not, perhaps, be thought to have any important bearing on this point. If it have, it confirms and illustrates, rather than impugns the reasoning already suggested."[22] This quote led the majority to believe that the Second Amendment does not have any important bearing in understanding the concurrent powers over the state militias. Yet again, Justice Scalia and the majority have taken Story out of context.

First, one need look no further than Story's commentaries to understand his feelings on the Second Amendment. In his writings, Story makes it clear that the "right to keep and bear arms" is directly correlated to militia service, including its well regulation and discipline.[23] Second, even in *Houston v. Moore*, Story's analysis supports this point. Story was making reference to whether the states or federal government had the authority to arm the militia. Regarding this power, Story states, "It does not seem repugnant in its nature to the grant of a like paramount authority to Congress; and if not it is retained by the States."[24] Story rightfully says the Second Amendment "may not, perhaps, be thought to have any important bearing on this point." This is because the Second Amendment was only meant to restrict Congress from disarming the state militias. It makes no reference to arming them. Story understood that the Second Amendment was not a concurrent power; it was a restriction. But if it was to have any impact on understanding concurrent power on the militia, Story was clear to state it "confirms and illustrates, rather than impugns the reasoning already suggested."[25]

The majority wrongfully states that Story's "confirm and illustrates" reference pertained to the "importance of the militia" in the Second Amend-

ment's preamble. There is no doubting that Story understood the importance of the militia in the Constitution. This is a moot point. However,
Story makes no reference to the preamble when he makes his "confirms and
illustrates" statement. Thus, the *Heller* majority is inferring something that
is not there and, as a result, has wrongfully interpreted *Houston v. Moore* in
this regard.

### *Johnson v. Tompkins*

The Supreme Court majority next cites *Johnson v. Tompkins*[26] as illus-
trating the point they wrongfully believed was demonstrated in *Houston v.
Moore,* namely that the Second Amendment is not connected to militia or
military service. In *Johnson,* the Honorable Henry Baldwin was riding cir-
cuit in Pennsylvania. The *Heller* majority quotes Baldwin, stating the Second Amendment and the Pennsylvania Constitution protect "a right to carry
arms in defence of his property or person, and to use them, if either were
assailed with such force, number or violence as made it necessary for the
protection or safety of either."[27]

The majority leaves out an important point. Baldwin makes no attempt
to examine the Second Amendment or Pennsylvania's "right to bear arms"
provision. Instead he groups seven state and federal constitutional protections:

> [T]he constitution of Pennsylvania declares, "that all men have the inherent
> and indefeasible right of enjoying and defending life and liberty, of acquiring,
> possessing and protecting property," "that no man can be deprived of his lib-
> erty or property but by the judgment of his peers, or the law of the land." Sec-
> tion 9. That the right of citizens to bear arms in defense of themselves and the
> state, shall not be questioned. Section 21. The second section of the fourth
> article of the constitution of the United States, declares, "the citizens of each
> state shall be entitled to all privileges and immunities of citizens in the several
> states." The tenth section of the first article prohibits any state from passing
> any law "which impairs the obligation of a contract." The second amendment
> provides, "that the right of the people to keep and bear arms shall not be
> infringed." The sixth, "that no man shall be deprived of liberty or property,
> without due process of law." In addition to these rights, Mr. Johnson had one
> other important one, to which we invite your special attention, and a compari-
> son of the right given and duty enjoined by the constitution of the United
> States with the eleventh section of the abolition act of 1780. "No person held
> to service or labour in one state, under the laws thereof, escaping into another,
> shall, in consequence of any law or regulation, be discharged from such service
> or labour, but shall be delivered up on claim of the party, to whom such
> labour or service shall be due." Const. U.S. art. 4, § 2, cl. 3. Pursuant to this
> provision of the constitution, the act of congress of the 12th February, 1793 [1

Stat. 32], was passed, not to restrain the rights of the master, but to give him the aid of a law to enforce them.[28]

When writing his opinion, Baldwin does not differentiate all these constitutional provisions. He combines them into one, when he wrote:

> We have stated to you the various provisions of the constitution of the United States and its amendments, as well as that of this state; you see their authority and obligation to be supreme over any laws or regulations which are repugnant to them, or which violate, infringe or impair any right thereby secured; the conclusions which result are too obvious to be more than stated. Jack was the property of the plaintiff, who had a right to possess and protect his slave or servant, whom he had a right to seize and take away to his residence in New Jersey by force, if force was necessary, he had a right to secure him from escape, or rescue by any means not cruel or wantonly severe, he had a right to carry arms in defence of his property or person, and to use them, if either were assailed with such force, numbers or violence as made it necessary for the protection or safety of either.[29]

Notice that Baldwin particularly combined the Pennsylvania Constitution's right to property with the "right of the citizens to bear arms, in defence of themselves and the state,"[30] without differentiating between the two or defining them individually. Little, if any, deference should be given to such a broad and overreaching interpretation of Pennsylvania's constitutional provisions; for at no point did Baldwin examine the Second Amendment, Article IX, Section 21, of the Pennsylvania Constitution, or what the "right to bear arms" encompasses.[31]

### Aldridge v. Commonwealth

The majority next cites an 1824 Virginia case that held the Constitution did not extend to free blacks. The court in *Aldridge* explained that "numerous restrictions imposed on [blacks] in our Statute Book, many of which are inconsistent with the letter and spirit of the Constitution, both of this State and of the United States as respects to free whites, demonstrate, that here, those instruments have not been considered to extend equally to both classes of our population."[32] The *Aldridge* court then stated it would only "instance upon the migration of free blacks into this State, and upon their right to bear arms."[33] The Supreme Court majority believe this last sentence "obviously" shows that the court was not referring to preventing blacks "from carrying arms in the militia." That notwithstanding, the majority cites no law or information to support their assumption.

If the majority had done their research on Virginia laws in this area they would have found their assumption was misguided. First, the *Aldridge* court stated it would only "instance upon" free blacks the "right to bear arms," but makes no further mention of it in the opinion. This meant the *Aldridge* court never actually elaborated on this point. It only made this one vague reference. Second, the Supreme Court majority will have us infer that the *Aldridge* court was referring to laws that restricted free blacks from carrying arms in Virginia, that these laws were infringing upon free blacks "right to bear arms." What the majority fails to mention is that the Virginia Constitution does not protect an individual's "right to bear arms." Section 13 of the Virginia Declaration of Rights only provided:

> That a well regulated militia, composed of the body of the people, trained to arms, is the proper, natural, and safe defense of a free state; that standing armies, in time of peace, should be avoided as dangerous to liberty; and that, in all cases, the military should be under strict subordination to, and be governed by, the civil power.[34]

Even if the majority were right in assuming that the Virginia Constitution protected a right to individually carry and use firearms, it must be remembered that by 1824, Virginia had not established any laws that infringed upon this alleged right. From 1776 onward there were no laws that explicitly banned free blacks from carrying or using firearms. There was a 1785 law that banned slaves from carrying arms. It stated, "No slave shall keep any arms whatsoever or pass unless with written orders from his master or employer, or in his company with arms, from one place to another."[35] It makes no reference of free blacks or mulattoes, though.

The only law in existence that had any resemblance to impeding the alleged right to carry a firearm was a 1811 act entitled *An act to amend an Act, entitled an Act for regulating the Navigation of James River above the Falls of the said River.* Section 2 read, "No free negro or mulatto shall be allowed to carry on board of his boat any gun, rifle, or other fire arms, under pain of forfeiting the same to the use of any white person, who may seize them ... nor shall any owner of any slave permit him to carry such arms, under the like forfeiture."[36] The law did not outright prevent free blacks or mulattoes from carrying firearms. It merely prevented them from carrying firearms while navigating rivers. This law may have been passed to prevent conflicts with neighboring states' laws, especially since such boats could travel into areas of interstate commerce. It is uncertain whether the *Aldridge* court was referencing this boating law, but it is highly unlikely. This is because that court did not provide any citation as to what laws it thought were preventing free blacks from bearing arms.

The *Aldridge* case had come to fruition to examine the constitutionality of an act entitled *An act farther to amend the penal laws of this common-wealth*. The court was particularly interested in Section 3, which read, "when any free negro or mulatto shall be convicted of an offence, not by law punishable by imprisonment in the jail and penitentiary house for more than two years, such persons, instead of the confinement now prescribed by law, shall be punished by stripes at the discretion of the jury."[37] This section makes no reference to arms, the carrying arms, or the use of arms. In fact, no part of the act regulated the use of arms in any facet.

Thus there is no certainty about why the *Aldridge* court made this reference to free blacks being restricted from bearing arms. If anything, the court was making reference to free blacks and mulattoes being prevented from performing militia duty. For the 1792 National Militia Act only allowed "every free able-bodied white male citizen of the respective states" to perform federal militia duty.[38] This meant free blacks and mulattoes were restricted from federal service. Now, Virginia did not have to include this restriction. When calling up its militia for state actions, it was free to include blacks and mulattoes if it so chose. In reality, this was not the case. For on December 22, 1792, Virginia adopted the National Militia Act as the basis for its own militia laws.[39] The act declared that free blacks and mulattoes were excluded from the Virginia militia, as well as the federal militia.

Given these facts, the Supreme Court majority's inference is wrong. To believe that the *Aldridge* court referred to free blacks and mulattoes being restricted from individually using arms is completely unfounded. After all, there existed no Virginia laws to support their assertion. The truth is the only laws that restricted free blacks and mulattoes from asserting a "right to bear arms" were those where one could exercise that right — state militia laws. For the majority of the states had excluded free blacks and mulattoes from serving in their respective militias. This occurred even though blacks and mulattoes, free and slave, were crucial to the success of the Revolutionary War.[40] The Founders just thought blacks and mulattoes serving in a republican army, in a society that allowed slavery to be a contradiction in practice.[41]

## Waters v. State of Maryland

Relying on its assumption about the *Aldridge* court's reference to free blacks and mulattoes bearing arms, the Supreme Court majority further cited *Waters v. State of Maryland*. In *Waters* the court stated "laws have been passed to prevent [free blacks from] migrat[ing] to this State; to make it unlawful for them to bear arms; to guard even their religious assemblages with peculiar watchfulness."[42] It was the *Waters* court's mention of "bear arms" without reference to a militia that the majority relied on. The majority believed the lack of any reference to a "militia," coupled with its reference to the laws, meant "bear arms" was referring to an individual carrying or owning arms. Here again, the majority has inferred something with no basis to support it.

It is uncertain what "laws" the *Waters* court was referencing. A clue rests with the fact that the case's purpose was to examine the constitutionality of an 1831 Maryland act. Section 6 of that act reads:

> That no free negro or mulatto shall be suffered to keep or carry a firelock of any kind, any military weapon, or any powder or lead, without first obtaining a license from the court of the county or corporation in which he resides; which license shall be annually renewed, and be at any time withdrawn by an order of said court, or any judge thereof; and any free negro or mulatto who shall disregard this provision, shall, on conviction thereof before a justice of the peace, for the first offence pay the cost of prosecution...[43]

At no point in the holding does the *Waters* court reference this section of the act. So it is uncertain whether this is what that court was referring to as "making it unlawful for [blacks] to bear arms." If it is, it does not make any sense for the act does not prevent blacks from owning, using, or carrying arms. It merely established a licensing system, one of the first of its kind. Thus, one really cannot classify this act as making the use or carrying of arms by free blacks as "unlawful."

What is for certain is, as was the case in Virginia, it was likewise unlawful in Maryland for free blacks to serve in the state's militia. The most recent militia act at the time *Waters* was decided was an 1834 act entitled *An act to Enroll, Equip, and Regulate the Militia of this State.* Section 1 of that act only permitted "all able bodied white male citizens between eighteen and forty-five years of age" to serve in the militia.[44] Thus, if anything, it makes more sense that the *Waters* court was referring to the following fact: that all free blacks were excluded from serving and participating in the militia system, even as volunteers.

### United States v. Sheldon

Like the other cases, the Supreme Court majority infers another court's reference to the "right to bear arms," without mentioning the militia, insinuates the individual right theory to be correct. In *United States v. Sheldon* the Michigan Supreme Court stated:

> The constitution of the United States grants to the citizen the right to keep

and bear arms. But the grant of this privilege cannot be construed into the right in him who keeps a gun to destroy his neighbor. No rights are intended to be granted by the constitution for an unlawful or unjustifiable purpose.[45]

Scalia believed it is impossible to read this quote as "discussing anything other than an individual right unconnected to militia service."[46] If the Second Amendment was related to militia service, Justice Scalia continued, "the limitation upon it would not be 'unlawful or unjustifiable purpose,' but any non-military purposes whatsoever."[47] Scalia is inferring too much from a quote that was being used to make a broader point. In *Sheldon*, Judge Chipman was trying to show that the protections offered in the Bill of Rights were not limitless, for the case presented in *Sheldon* was whether a newspaper could publish a misleading account of a case before a court. Because Michigan was merely a U.S. territory at the time of the case, the First Amendment applied and was the center of what was being analyzed.

The Michigan court addressed the issue by making clear the First Amendment is not an unlimited right. The court held that although Congress may not abridge the freedom of speech and of the press, the Framers "never ... dreamed that this inhibition can take away the common law action for slanderous words, any more than it can alter the law of libels for a printed slander."[48] It is during this First Amendment analysis that the *Sheldon* court references the Second Amendment in passing, the purpose of which was to make clear that no amendment within the Bill of Rights was absolute.

Furthermore, there is nothing in Justice Chipman's quote that insinuates an individual has a right to own a firearm for self-defense. What Chipman was stating is that the people should not construe the "right to keep and bear arms" as a right to use guns for any purpose whatsoever. He was simply dictating the Second Amendment is a limited right, nothing more, nothing less.

## Nunn v. State of Georgia

*Nunn v. State* is a case the Supreme Court majority actually quoted and articulated properly. There is no arguing that the Georgia Supreme Court interpreted the Second Amendment as protecting an individual right to own, carry, and use a firearm. It held the "right to keep and bear arms" as:

> The right of the whole people, old and young, men, women and boys, and not militia only, to keep and bear *arms* of every description, and not *such* merely as are used by the *militia*, shall not be *infringed*, curtailed, or broken in upon, in the smallest degree; and all this for the important end to be attained: the rearing up and qualifying a well-regulated militia, so vitally necessary to the security of a free State.[49]

The *Nunn* court may have been the first to make what would become one of the modern individual right arguments. This is a circular argument that articulates one cannot "bear arms" in defense of his country and liberties if they do not own and possess the arms to do so. It is believed an individual must be familiar with the use and exercise of arms to accomplish the Second Amendment's objective — to form a well regulated militia. The *Nunn* court flushed this out, querying:

> If a well-regulated militia is *necessary* to the *security* of the State of Georgia and of the United States, is it competent for the General Assembly to take away this security by disarming the people? What advantage would it be to tie up the hands of the national legislature, if it were in the power of the *States* to destroy this bulwark of defence? In solemnly affirming that a well-regulated militia is necessary to the *security* of a *free State*, and that, in order to train properly that militia, the unlimited right of the *people* to *keep* and *bear* arms shall not be impaired, are not the sovereign people of the State committed by this pledge to preserve this right inviolate? Would they not be recreant to themselves, to free government, and false to their own vow, thus voluntarily taken, to suffer this right to be questioned? If they hesitate or falter, is it not to concede (themselves being judges) that the safety of the States is a matter of indifference?[50]

First, the *Nunn* court errs in that it failed to conduct any research in analyzing the Second Amendment. It infers the meaning of the "right to keep and bear arms" without going into any of its history. This is particularly surprising given that the legal commentaries of Blackstone, Tucker, Rawle, and Story were all readily available at that time. One would think the court would have at least incorporated such significant legal writings. This was not the case, however. Instead the *Nunn* court focuses on its circular reasoning. It argued that any such statute "under the pretence of *regulating* amounts to a *destruction* of the right [to bear arms], or which requires arms to be so borne as to render them wholly useless for the purpose of defence, would be clearly unconstitutional."

Although the Georgia Supreme Court is definitively inferring that the Second Amendment protects an individual right, their analysis is inaccurate and incomplete. The Supreme Court majority believes otherwise, describing the *Nunn* opinion as "perfectly captur[ing] the way in which the operative clause of the Second Amendment furthers the purpose announced in the prefatory clause."[51] The majority herein relies on a court opinion that could not even correctly interpret the protective scope of the Bill of Rights. For the *Nunn* court incorrectly applied the Second Amendment to state law. It had been well settled prior to this case that the Bill of Rights only operated as a restriction on the federal government and, therefore, did not extend to the individual states.

Nevertheless, it was the *Nunn* court's view that the Second Amendment "does extend to all judicial tribunals, whether constituted by the Congress of the United States or the States individually."[52] It wrongfully determined that the "language of the Second Amendment is broad enough to embrace both Federal and State governments — neither is there anything in its terms which restricts its meaning."[53] The Supreme Court majority relies on this court's opinion to support their own stance, on a court that could not even correctly apply the Bill of Rights to state government. In fact, its opinion was ridiculed by the same judicial body after the Civil War. In *Hill v. State*, the Georgia Supreme Court overturned *Nunn*, stating "the amendments to the constitution of the United States ... are all restrictions, not upon the states, but upon the United States."[54]

The reason the *Nunn* court overstepped its judicial boundaries was due to the fact that there was no Georgia constitutional protection for the "right to bear arms." It would not be until 1868, twenty-two years after *Nunn*, that the Georgia Constitution would be ratified to incorporate such a provision.[55] Moreover, at the time the *Nunn* case was being heard, there was a growth of conceal carry laws. Just as politics spilled into contemporary federal district and state courts disagreeing as to the interpretation of the Second Amendment, so did politics affect conceal carry laws of the nineteenth century. The state courts were politically divided as to what their respective "bear arms" provisions protected. Thus, in order for the *Nunn* court to assert its opinion on conceal carry legislation, it had to turn to the Second Amendment. It could not turn to Georgia's Constitution, since no protection was offered. The *Nunn* court's Second Amendment application would be a stretch, but it shows that the court was looking for a way to overturn Georgia's conceal carry legislation.

Excluding these facts does not change the impact *Nunn* should have in interpreting the Second Amendment — that being none. Just as, prior to *Heller*, the federal district courts were split on the Second Amendment, the same held true in state court opinions during the nineteenth century. Those courts disagreed as to exactly what the Second Amendment and their respective "right to bear arms" provisions protected. The decisions are incomplete. They did not examine state constitutional ratifying conventions, drafting debates, or other pertinent history. These state court opinions also did not differentiate between the Second Amendment and their respective "right to bear arms" provisions, coupling the two. Also, the decisions were nothing more than the viewpoint of whatever justice happened to be sitting on the bench. All in all, it is easy and expedient to find select quotes or decisions that cut for and against any argument as to what the Second Amendment

protects. Yet, such sources can hardly be relied on as determinative or sup-
portive.

### United States v. Cruikshank

*United States v. Cruikshank*[56] was the first Supreme Court case to give
the Second Amendment any significant attention. The case presented was
whether an indictment for conspiracy of the 1870 Enforcement Act was present. The defendants were charged with conspiring to prevent the black citizens of the State of Louisiana from voting. They did this "well knowing the
said citizens to be well qualified and entitled to vote at any such election."[57]
The Second Amendment became an issue in this case not because the defendants had taken away black citizens' firearms or because they had been prevented from joining the Louisiana militia. It was argued by the United States
that in the defendants' conspiring to prevent black votes, they also intended
to "prevent and hinder" black citizens:

> [S]everal and respective free exercise and enjoyment of each, every, all and sin-
> gular the several rights and privileges granted or secured to the said L.N. and
> the said A.T. in common with other good citizens of the said United States by
> the Constitution and the laws of the United States of America, contrary to the
> form.[58]

Thus, the issue before the Supreme Court was if the defendants prevented black citizens from voting, whether, as of a result of said action, the
defendants had restricted black citizens from (1) peacefully assembling
together, (2) bearing arms, and (3) enjoying life and liberty.[59] It is the *Cruikshank* Court's analysis of the Second Amendment that the *Heller* majority
believed supported the individual right model. Justice Scalia wrote:

> The opinion explained that the right "is not a right granted by the Constitu-
> tion [or] in any manner dependent upon that instrument for its existence. The
> second amendment ... means no more than that it shall not be infringed by
> Congress." States, we said, were free to restrict or protect the right under their
> police powers. The limited discussion of the Second Amendment in *Cruik-
> shank* supports, if anything, the individual-rights interpretation. There was no
> claim in *Cruikshank* that the victims had been deprived of their right to carry
> arms in a militia; indeed, the Governor had disbanded the local militia unit
> the year before the mob's attack. We described the right protected by the Sec-
> ond Amendment as "bearing arms for a lawful purpose" and said that "the
> people [must] look for their protection against any violation by their fellow-
> citizens of the rights it recognizes" to the States' police power. That discussion
> makes little sense if it is only a right to bear arms in a state militia.[60]

Here again, the *Heller* majority wrongfully inferred what a prior Court was stipulating, the Supreme Court no less. It even does this given the avail-ability of the briefs of the defendant and plaintiff in that case. For if the *Heller* majority would have read these briefs, they would have found what the *Cruikshank* Court meant by the Second Amendment. That it "is not a right granted by the Constitution or any manner dependant upon that instrument for its existence."[61] First, at no point does the United States stipulate in its plaintiff's brief what the "right to keep and bear arms" was meant to encom-pass.[62] In fact, neither do they define what the right to peacefully assemble nor what enjoying life and liberty encompassed. These definitions were com-pletely left out.

It is only through the defendant's briefs do we come to find out what lawyers of the late nineteenth century felt the Second Amendment was meant to protect. What makes *Cruikshank* particularly advantageous in this regard is that there were four distinct defendant briefs. Three of the briefs have a different lawyer addressing what they thought the "right to keep and bear arms" protected. The fourth brief merely denied the Second Amendment as applying to the states. Out of the three briefs that did address the issue, only one gives a hint of arguing that the Second Amendment protects an indi-vidual right. Attorney David S. Byron wrote:

> The right to bear arms is not guaranteed by the Constitution of the United States. It has been said that "a man who carries his arms openly, and for his own protection, or for any other lawful purpose, has a clear right to do so, as to carry his own watch or wear his own hat." The right to bear arms, if it be a right, is a matter to be regulated and controlled by the State, as each State may deem best for itself; and the United States have nothing whatever to do with it; either to support the right or abridge it. The truth is, that the power to reg-ulate and control the bearing of arms on the part of the people, and their assembling together in great numbers, belongs to the police authority of the State, and it is a necessary power to be exercised by the State for the peace of society and the safety of life and property; and it is a power that the States have always exercised from a time before the General Government was formed until the present, without gainsaying or dispute.[63]

Interestingly enough, this quote goes both ways: It does not make any mention of the militia but hints at the "right to bear arms" as a "power that the States have always exercised from a time before General Government was formed." This could easily be referring to concurrent power over the mili-tia. Prior to the Constitution, the militia and all the laws governing it, was a police power of the state. This could just as easily be referring to gun laws, for that matter. It too was part of the states' exercising of their police pow-ers. Unfortunately, we are unable to know for certain.

Another argument could be made to Byron's reference to the right being something "the United States [has] nothing whatever to do with." This could be a reference to restricting Congress from infringing upon the Second Amendment, and essentially arguing that the United States can have nothing to do with regulating and controlling of how each state armed its respective militia. On the flipside, this could also be a reference to an individual's everyday use of firearms. Byron could be arguing that the "matter to be regulated and controlled by the State" was personal firearm use in areas such as hunting, self-defense, or protection of property.

Either way one looks at Byron's brief, an argument can be made by either side. Even so, a more plausible argument would be in reference to the militia. For Byron mentions the state regulating bearing arms in relation to the people "assembling together in great numbers." Only in service of the militia were people ever allowed to assemble with arms in great numbers. So it is likely that Byron was referring to militia musters and training. However, it is impossible to know with any certainty precisely what Byron was intending to mean by his "bearing of arms" language.

Thus, because Byron's brief leaves much room for interpretation, the remaining two defendant's briefs may explain what Byron was trying to infer. Both briefs unequivocally argue that the Second Amendment was in reference to service in the militia. One of the charges was that the defendants banded together "to hinder and prevent Nelson and Tillman in their right to keep and bear arms for a lawful purpose."[64] Attorney R.H. Marr argued in his brief that using arms "for a lawful purpose" outside of the militia was "not the right contemplated" by the Second Amendment.[65] Marr states:

> [T]he right which the people intended to have secured beyond the power of infringement of Congress, is the right to keep and bear arms for the purpose of maintaining, in the States, a well regulated militia, acknowledged in this article to be necessary for the security of a free State.[66]

Attorney John A. Campbell's brief included a similar statement. He had interpreted the United States government's argument stating the "right to bear arms" for "lawful purposes" as implying something improper. Campbell replied that the right to carry a gun "is not a right derived from or secured by the Constitution of the United States." The Second Amendment is a right that "relates to the organization and equipment of the militia."[67]

More importantly, though, it is from Campbell's brief that the *Cruikshank* Court gets its quote, stating the Second Amendment "is not a right granted by the Constitution [or] in any manner dependent upon that instrument for its existence." For Campbell had argued that the militia's "privilege of citizens to keep and bear arms ... is not a right or privilege which the United States granted, nor its government charged to guard and guarantee;

nor is [it] an interference with this right an offence against any law of the United States."[68] What Campbell was properly arguing was that, prior to the Constitution, individuals had the right to bear arms in defense of their state. Every state's militia, and its respective militia infrastructure, had guaranteed to every person the right to defend their liberties and the interests of the state. The Second Amendment was purely acting as a means to prevent the federal government from infringing upon that right. Thus, the *Heller* majority's argument is erroneous that the pre-existing right that the *Cruikshank* Court refers to is a right to have a firearm. The defendant's briefs make it clear where the *Cruikshank* Court derived its holding.

### Presser v. Illinois

Given the defendant's briefs in *Cruikshank* explain that the Court was referring to the Second Amendment in light of the militia, it helps place *Presser v. Illinois*[69] in its proper context. For the most part, the *Heller* majority dismissed the case. Although *Presser* concerned a state law that forbade men to "associate together as military organizations" unless authorized by militia laws, and concerned whether this conflicted with the Second Amendment, Justice Scalia wrote "this does not refute the individual-rights interpretation of the Amendment." He argued that "[N]o one supporting that interpretation has contended that States may not ban such groups." But Scalia and the *Heller* majority missed the larger point. For the Court in *Presser* first reiterated the holding in *Cruikshank*, writing:

> We think it clear that the sections under consideration, which only forbid bodies of men to associate together as military organizations, or to drill or parade with arms in cities and towns unless authorized by law, do not infringe the right of the people to keep and bear arms. But a conclusive answer to the contention that this amendment prohibits the legislation in question lies in the fact that the amendment is a limitation only upon the power of congress and the national government, and not upon that of the state. It was so held by this court in the case of *U.S. v. Cruikshank*, in which the chief justice, in delivering the judgment of the court, said that the right of the people to keep and bear arms is not a right granted by the constitution. Neither is it in any manner dependent upon that instrument for its existence. The second amendment declares that it shall not be infringed, but this, as has been seen, means no more than that it shall not be infringed by Congress. This is one of the amendments that has no other effect than to restrict the powers of the national government....[70]

Here the *Presser* Court was affirming that the "right to bear arms" in the states was a pre-existing practice throughout the militia system. This is especially true given Chief Justice Morrison Waite had delivered the opinion in *Cruikshank*, and the fact that he was still sitting on the Supreme Court at that time. What further illustrates that the *Presser* Court viewed that the Second Amendment was a militia right was the next paragraph of the holding. In it the Court held that "all citizens capable of bearing arms constitute the reserve militia of the United States as well as of the states." What is particularly significant is that the Court stated the Second Amendment protects against state laws that prevented "the people from keeping and bearing arms, so as to deprive the United States of their rightful resource for maintaining the public security." In other words, the states could not pass laws that eliminated the militia force that was necessary to handle federal emergencies. Any law short of this would be constitutionally permissible.

### United States v. Miller

In *United States v. Miller* the Supreme Court held the "possession or use of a shotgun having a barrel of less than eighteen inches in length" was not "any part of the ordinary military equipment" protected by the Second Amendment.[71] Despite this narrow ruling, both individual right and collective right supporters had claimed the decision supports their respective stance. The Supreme Court majority and dissenters were no different. At first the majority rightfully cast the opinion aside as not properly addressing the protective scope of the Second Amendment. This changed when examining what arms were protected. Justice Scalia wrote:

> We therefore read *Miller* to say only that the Second Amendment does not protect those weapons not typically possessed by law-abiding citizens for lawful purposes, such as short-barreled shotguns. That accords with the historical understanding of the scope.

Again Scalia infers something from a court opinion that is not there. At no time did the *Miller* Court make reference to "lawful purposes" or to the use of firearms for civilian purposes. The *Miller* opinion was short and brief; it only concluded whether a shotgun was the type of "arms" protected by the Second Amendment. Justice McReynolds, delivering the opinion of the court, stated, "[i]n the absence of any evidence to show that possession or use of a shotgun having a barrel less than eighteen inches in length at this time has some reasonable relationship to the preservation or efficiency of a well regulated militia, we cannot say that the Second Amendment guarantees the right to keep and bear such an instrument."[72] At the time of its decision, the *Miller* opinion was the most detailed opinion the Supreme Court had ever written on the subject. It was also the first instance in which that Court used a significant amount of congressional and state legislative history about the militia to come to a determination on the Second Amendment.

Outside of its narrow ruling, only one thing is for certain regarding the *Miller* decision: Its examination of eighteenth-century militia laws and history opened the door for the twentieth-century Second Amendment debate. The majority in *Heller*, like so many courts before it, incorrectly skewed the decision to support its stance, and in so doing, rendered a decision that couldn't be further from the truth. By improperly including *Miller,* the majority severely contrasts with what Supreme Court justices had previously stated regarding how they should interpret that decision. In 1997, Justice Clarence Thomas stated the *Miller* opinion "did not ... attempt to define, or otherwise construe, the substantive right protected by the Second Amendment."[73] Thomas further stated the Supreme Court "has not had the recent occasion to consider the nature" of that right.[74] Prior to hearing *Heller*, Chief Justice Roberts had also been on the record as stating the Miller decision had "side-stepped the issue" and had left "very open" the question of whether the Second Amendment protects an individual right as opposed to a collective right. Nevertheless, both Thomas and Roberts had no problem siding with an opinion that argued just the opposite.

## Revisionist Legal History

As has been shown, the Supreme Court majority in *Heller* went through great lengths to incorporate legal sources that supported its predetermined conclusion. Unfortunately, the sources it used did not actually support their contentions for the majority consistently made wrongful inferences of the facts, left out important commentary, or placed citations and quotes out of context. Such faulty judicial interpretation is scary, especially when interpreting the Bill of Rights. If the Supreme Court can go so far as to skew legal sources and history to support a political agenda, as was plainly evident in this case, there can be no telling what will be the consequences in future decisions.

Moreover, it is surprising that the Supreme Court uses these sources at all, especially cases decided at least thirty years after the adoption of the Second Amendment. For the decisions in these cases can hardly be considered contemporaneous with it. Most importantly, though, none of these cases examined with any particularity the protective scope the "right to keep and bear arms" actually affords. Thus, they cannot be used with any degree of certainty to support either stance. It would make much more legal and historical sense to turn to the history immediately following the adoption of the Second Amendment.

# CHAPTER THREE

# Placing the Second Amendment in Its Proper Historical Context

It makes much more judicial and historical sense to focus on the history immediately following the adoption of the Second Amendment to understand what the "right to keep and bear arms" was meant to afford. Moreover, given the Supreme Court majority makes a number of inferences and relies heavily on what it believed constitutes the eighteenth-century militia, it is important to examine its history. The majority was right to point out that Article I, Section 8, of the Constitution infers the militia was not something created by Congress, but that it was "already to be in existence." It is undeniably true that the militia was made up of the people and the people made up the militia. This does not mean the people — as a militia — were free from restrictions and regulations. The pre-existing colonial militia laws show that a citizen's duty to perform militia service was connected to the states' police powers. The history of the implementation of the 1792 National Militia Act that the majority so frequently cites shows this to be the case.

## The 1792 National Militia Act, the Constitution, and the Second Amendment

On March 4, 1789, the Constitution and Bill of Rights were implemented throughout the United States. Each state had different methods of arming, organizing, training, and disciplining their respective militias. Such diversity was not viewed favorably since the Framers had based the fledgling nation's security on the militia system. With the Constitution granting Congress the authority to "provide for organizing, arming, and disciplining, the militia, and for governing such part of them as may be employed in the service of the United States,"[1] Secretary of War Henry Knox and President George Washington began the push for a National Militia Act to better effectuate the nation's security.[2]

Washington felt such an act "to be of the highest importance to the welfare of our country," and, on January 21, 1790, asked Knox to lay a plan before Congress.[3] Knox and Washington actually hoped Congress would compose a plan for a select militia,[4] but this was exactly what the Anti-Federalists feared. Thus Congress adopted a plan that incorporated a larger contingent of the population. It took over two years for a plan to be drafted, and, on February 21, 1792, the National Militia Act was submitted for Congressional review.[5]

Upon reading the bill's first section, the conflict between federal and state militia authority became utterly apparent. There was much disagreement as to just how far Congressional power should reach in organizing, arming, and disciplining the militia. Jonathan Sturges believed the "States alone are to say of what description of persons the militia shall consist, and who shall be exempt," while Samuel Livermore thought it best to just leave the entire process of organizing the militia to the "respective States."[6] Although many delegates were concerned with just how far the National Militia Act would intrude into each state's sovereignty, Joshua Seney reminded them that negating this act "would be to render the power of Congress in organizing, arming, and disciplining the militia, entirely nugatory."[7] Congressman Sturges agreed with Seney's sentiments, but interpreted such constitutional power to be subordinate to the States' existing militia laws.[8] Sturges' constitutional interpretation was wrong and was quickly corrected. Congressman William Vans Murray informed him that the militia in the Constitution did not mean the existing militia system, but one "to be formed or created" by the federal government.[9] It meant that the power was concurrent.

As each section of the act was reviewed, the same debate lingered — how far could the federal government intrude on the states' right to govern their respective militias? The act's provision for arming the militia was debated no differently, and it gives great insight to understanding what the Framers interpreted the Second Amendment was meant to protect. Overall, the National Militia Act posed two major problems on "arming" the militia that are applicable to understanding the meaning behind the Second Amendment: (1) It did not provide an exemption for poor persons, and (2) it required every person enrolled to purchase a certain caliber rifle and bore.[10]

Unlike many of the states' militia laws, the National Militia Act did not exempt persons who were unable to provide arms for themselves.[11] The act specifically provided that "every citizen so enrolled and notified, shall, within six months thereafter, provide himself with a good musket or firelock, a sufficient bayonet or belt...," and they "shall appear, so armed ... when called out to exercise," with no exceptions.[12] This caused a major dilemma for those individuals who were unable to provide arms for themselves — how were they to meet the arms requirement of the National Militia Act if they did not possess the means to acquire them?

The requirement to provide arms was nothing more than a tax[13] to maintain the external security of the state. Given the great expense of procuring arms for the entire militia, the states often deferred the cost to the individual militia man who would bear the arms, but there were exceptions: (1) In times of war, rebellion, or insurrection the state usually supplied arms to those individuals who were called into service, (2) states such as Maryland, Pennsylvania, and Virginia had, at times, decided to provide the entire militia's arms at the expense of the government,[14] and (3) when a person was of too little property to provide such arms, the state procured and supplied such arms for him.[15] It is the legislation on this third exception that shows the National Militia Act's requirement to provide arms was nothing more than a tax, and if anything, shows the Second Amendment was not meant to bestow an individual right to "bear arms."

Following the adoption of the National Militia Act, many states revised their militia laws to conform and comply with its provisions. Kentucky,[16] Maryland,[17] New York,[18] South Carolina,[19] Tennessee,[20] and Virginia[21] all adopted militia laws that virtually mirrored the National Militia Act, especially the provision requiring each enrolled person provide himself with the required arms and equipment. The remaining states adopted most of the act's provisions verbatim, but had created arms exemptions for those who were too poor to provide them. Delaware,[22] Massachusetts,[23] New Hampshire,[24] New Jersey,[25] Pennsylvania,[26] and Vermont[27] all adopted these exemptions. Although the National Militia Act did not provide a clause authorizing the states to incorporate such exemptions, this was never questioned by the federal government or Congress. This is because the purpose of the National Militia Act was to organize the militia in a way that best effectuated the nation's security. The best way to accomplish this was to ensure that every able-bodied man had a set of firearms available, provided either by himself or the state.

The militia's access to arms was paramount to national security because the United States faced so many internal and external threats. The most dangerous internal threat was the institution of slavery. As early as the late seventeenth century, colonies such as Virginia established laws preventing slaves from carrying or owning guns,[28] but after slave uprisings like the Stono Rebellion,[29] the Southern colonies began requiring white masters to constantly have such weapons available in case of insurrection. Acts establishing patrols were the preferred method to prevent such events. These acts usually required the commanding officer of each company's militia to ensure slave patrols were carried out periodically. Like the militia acts, these laws stipulated that members of the patrol were usually required to provide their own arms for such duty.[30] The colonies of Georgia and South Carolina were so fearful of slave insurrections that they even required all males to bring guns to church on Sundays.[31] The theory was that if all the white inhabitants were at worship, it would give the slaves a perfect opportunity to assemble and revolt. Thus, it was required that "firearms be carried to all places of publick worship."[32] Failure to do so would result in a fine.

Furthermore, all the colonies had to deal with some form of an external security threat, whether from the Indians, French, or Spanish. Up to the commencement of the American Revolution, the British government had always provided security from these threats, but even under these circumstances the militia was often called up to assist. After the war the status quo changed. The newly formed United States no longer had professional armies defending its Western borders and, with a perpetual fear of a multitude of security threats, coupled with the enormous expense of maintaining a standing army, the best method of defending the frontier was to require every enrolled militia man to provide himself with arms. Such a policy not only protected the United States from external threats, but dually promoted the maintenance of the militia as an institution.

Initially, the National Militia Act seemed like the most effective method to protect the United States. Although the act firmly represented the nation's republican beliefs, it did not prevent it from being severely flawed. Within six months after its adoption, problems began to surface.[33] The act had been constructed as simple as possible to give the states the ability to organize the militia as they saw fit.[34] Nevertheless, the act lacked adequate enforcement because it did not establish a fine[35] for those individuals incapable of providing themselves with the required armaments.[36] Kentucky,[37] Maryland,[38] Massachusetts,[39] New Jersey,[40] North Carolina,[41] Pennsylvania,[42] South Carolina,[43] Tennessee,[44] and Vermont[45] resolved this problem by requiring their own fines for non-compliance. Meanwhile, the remaining states stayed true to the act's construction by not providing a fine, thus causing deficiencies in arming their respective militias.

Even if the Act had provided a fine for not properly arming, compliance with such a requirement was impossible for many of the states' militias.[46] William Vans Murray, delegate from Maryland, requested a repeal and revising of the arming clause because "it was oppressive in principle and impracticable in operation."[47] He argued that "wherever a tax was levied for the protection of society, its apportionment among individuals should be as exactly as possible correspondent with the property of each individual."[48] Murray disagreed with a "uniform expense on men of unequal property" not only because it was unjust, but also because "men of large fortune will thus contribute nothing towards this species of protection, while many of very small fortune will be obliged to furnish largely to it."[49] He did not understand how the "fundamental principles of property and taxation" had always proportioned according to an individual's economic standing — but in terms of the militia this did not apply.[50] His was a solution many of the states had already adopted — furnish arms at the public expense for those who are too poor.[51] Murray's argument for a repeal or revision of the act won over only six votes. Thus, the act was defeated. The overwhelming majority felt that they should give the act more time to take effect. [52]

The Congressional majority also did not support Murray's motion because he had argued that the federal and state governments should provide the arms at their expense. Given the enormous expense of performing such a function, it is not surprising that his idea was met with stern disapproval by the delegates. Jonathan Dayton was one of the delegates who was adamantly against giving either the state or federal government the power to provide such arms. He felt giving the governments such a right would also give them the right to dispossess the people of "their arms on any occasion."[53] He reasoned that whatever the government could grant, it could just as easily take away. This argument is noteworthy because Mr. Dayton did not mention the Second Amendment.

Throughout the debates on the National Militia Act, the Federalists often used the Constitution to support their arguments. Whenever an Anti-Federalist argued that the right to arm the militia should be deferred to the states, the Federalists were quick to cite the powers given to Congress under the Constitution. The use of constitutional text in House debates was common and, in fact, was the most effective manner any delegate, Federalist or Anti-Federalist, could support his argument.[54] Therefore, if the Second Amendment — or the National Militia Act, for that matter — was meant to protect and promote an individual right to own arms, why did Mr. Dayton not refer to it in his argument?[55] Why did not one delegate mention the Second Amendment in any of the eighteenth-century debates on the militia?

Why was there no mention of the Second Amendment in debates over the federal government interfering with the method by which the militia was to be armed? The simple reason such an occurrence never took place was because the Second Amendment was not intended to protect the individual right theory. The Second Amendment's only purpose was to prevent the federal government from infringing on a militia man's right to "keep and bear arms," not to possess them. As has already been addressed, an individual did not need to own the arms in order to "keep and bear" them. The government — state or federal — could easily decide to own such arms, but because it was often not economically feasible to do so, it was preferred the individual be taxed by being required to provide his own arms and accoutrements.

In sum, the federal or state governments' allocation of arms for the entire militia was too great of a cost to bear. In December 1796, Congress almost adopted such legislation,[56] which would have required the federal government to provide arms for the entire militia. This new militia bill would have also placed the security of the nation on a select corps of men from the ages of twenty to twenty-five. Thomas Henderson, delegate from New Jersey, was in favor of the bill. Henderson's argued that it was unfair that some paid a "very great expense" to comply with the National Militia Act while others did not. The current system caused "the defence of the nation" to fall "upon a few who were more rich, or more patriotic." Accordingly, there was placed too much of a burden on certain individuals, while giving many no responsibility whatsoever.[57] It followed, therefore, that taxing the people as a means to equip the militia at the national expense would require all men to be responsible for paying for it.[58] Subsequently, the bill failed to pass. Arming the militia at the expense of the United States, as Thomas Hartley stated it, was a "most considerable objection,"[59] but the issue would present itself again.[60]

By 1798, it was apparent that the idea and policy that each man could provide the required arms to comply with National Militia Act was completely impracticable. In December 1794, William Branch Giles, head of the committee to prepare a better plan for organizing, arming, and disciplining the militia, had reported to Congress the defects in the existing provisions for arming the militia.[61] Francis Preston of Virginia was "ready to submit to anything" that shall be proposed. Given the states had "neither money [n]or arms,"[62] he feared the militia system may already be at an end. But even if such an emergency may justify supplanting the militia for a military establishment, it ought to be viewed by a republican government with a "very jealous eye."[63]

Unfortunately, every attempt to reform the National Militia Act's deficiencies were unsuccessful.[64] Some states decided to take matters into their own hands. Delaware, which already had a provision in its militia law exempting poor persons, resolved the problem by being more diligent in providing the state's arms. In 1796, that state now required each county to "collect all the public arms" that had been given to persons "unable to equip themselves."[65] These arms were moved to a "convenient place where they may be safely kept; and shall cause every musket collected to be branded, on the butt of the stock" with the words "State of Delaware."[66] Delaware thought it more efficient that the arms, supplied by the state and given to poor persons, would be better kept and more readily available for defense if they were in its possession. In 1793, New Jersey had authorized the purchase of "two thousand Stand of Arms and Accoutrements complete" to make up for the National Militia Act's deficiency in providing arms.[67] Such arms were to be distributed throughout the colony to those persons "between the ages of eighteen and twenty-one, and others, as are or may be ... unable to procure Arms for themselves."[68] South Carolina had similarly appropriated funds for the purchase of 10,000 stands of arms but had been unsuccessful in acquiring them.[69] Lastly, by 1797, Pennsylvania took the most drastic step by reverting back to their pre–Constitution practice of providing arms for the entire militia.[70] The Pennsylvania government approved a law requiring the governor to procure "twenty thousand stand of arms" under the specification of the 1792 National Militia Act.[71] The arms were then to be divided among the respective companies and deposited until needed.[72]

In June 1798, Congress finally addressed the problem. The Arms for Militia Act, which provided arms for the militia throughout the United States, had reached the House and was under debate. Men like John Clopton of Virginia had been clamoring for such a bill, for he felt the militia was "undoubtedly the natural, proper and best defence."[73] It was important to "have this great resource of our real strength placed in a good state of regulation and an adequate supply of arms."[74] The act allowed the president to purchase 30,000 stands of arms to be distributed throughout the states and sold to members of the militia.[75] The great expense of procuring the arms was the issue of much debate but, once it was assured that the militia would be required to purchase the arms,[76] the bill was handily adopted.[77] Furthermore, any unsold arms were to be sold to the state governments for their general defense. Thus, the federal government would not lose any money on such an investment. Nonetheless, there were objections, to selling these arms to the states because, as Thomas Claiborne argued, the "arms should be put into the hands of the people."[78] William Edmond of Connecticut was concerned that, by allowing the States to purchase such arms to provide to their citizens, individuals will not be compelled to do so.[79] Regardless of these concerns, the Arms for Militia Act passed. This included the provision to sell the arms to the states. The purpose of the act was to supplement the National Militia Act which provided for the defense of the nation. The majority of Congress undoubtedly felt that the Arms for Militia Act accomplished this. As James Bayard from Delaware stated, the act's objective "would be accomplished, whether [arms] are sold to individuals, or to the State Governments."[80]

Immediately following the Arms for Militia Act, other states took steps to supplement their militia laws by authorizing their governments to provide arms for the militia. In 1799, Maryland revised its militia law by requiring the state to provide to each regiment's select militia "seventy-two muskets, seventy-two bayonets, and seventy-two cartridge boxes, in good order for service."[81] To those individuals that a musket was delivered, the state restricted its use by ordering if any "shall use the same in hunting, gunning or fowling, or shall not keep his arms and accoutrements clean and in neat order, he shall forfeit and pay not less than one, not more than ten dollars, at the discretion of the company court-martial."[82] Meanwhile, Georgia authorized its governor to purchase "one thousand muskets and bayonets, five hundred pair of horseman pistols, and five hundred swords" for its militia.[83] The arms were to be sold by the "keeper of the public arms or magazine to the militia of this state for self defence, at cost and charges."[84]

While individual right proponents continue to argue that the National Militia Act and state militia laws support the notion that Second Amendment was designed to bestow an individual right to firearm ownership, the evidence does not support such a conclusion. The Framers' desire to have every man armed does not reflect the meaning behind the Second Amendment but, in fact, was nothing more than the preferred eighteenth-century America national security policy. Individual right theorists and the Supreme Court majority need to remember to separate the constitutional protection the Second Amendment affords and eighteenth-century national security policy. The former is a constitutionally guaranteed restriction on the federal government, while the latter is a political question. This latter consideration is evidenced by the actions of the federal and state governments to establish policies that would best effectuate the providing of arms for all individuals, rich and poor. Sometimes such arms were owned and kept by the state. In some instances the individual was required to provide and keep his own arms, while yet in others the state provided and the individual kept the arms.

In short, both the federal and state governments wanted arms in the hands of their citizens to ensure the security of the nation — not because they wanted to comply with or support a notion the individual right theorists construed as the purpose of the Second Amendment. In all the debates regarding the National Militia and Arming the Militia Acts, not once was the Second Amendment brought up. This included debates regarding the federal government's confiscation of individuals' arms. Individual right proponents will probably argue this was because the Second Amendment was so universally understood as a natural right it need not be mentioned in the debates. This does make sense, though. In other congressional debates, delegates often turned to the Constitution to make their point. Needless to say, in all the debates, regarding a select militia or requiring the governments furnish arms for militia use, the Second Amendment was never brought up.

Lastly, the National Militia Act required that every man provide arms in accordance with it. It stipulated that "from and after five years from the passing of this act, all muskets for arming the militia as herein required shall be of bores sufficient for balls of the eighteenth-part of a pound."[85] As has already been addressed, complying with the National Militia Act proved to be difficult. It was hard enough for many individuals to afford any arms, let alone compel them to procure a new rifle that met Congressional requirements. Therefore, if the National Militia Act mirrored the individual right theorist's purpose of the Second Amendment, would it make sense to require everyone obtain the same bore of musket or rifle? For if the individual right theorists' point is to be supported, would it not make more sense that such an act allowed the militia to bring any serviceable rifle? Given the answer to these questions does not support the individual right theory, its proponents will attempt to show the Founders thought the taking away of an individual's possession of arms to be unconstitutional and a violation of a natural right. Unfortunately for individual right advocates, when addressing this issue, they will come to find individual firearm ownership was not an affirmed right. Like other property, firearms could be subjected to confiscation if an individual did not comply with state or federal authorities.

## The Founders and Confiscating Arms

Firearm ownership in the eighteenth century was a duty and a privilege. It was a duty because, throughout that century, the nation's security primarily rested on the militia system. That system often required individuals to provide their own arms and accoutrements, but not always. Firearms ownership was also a privilege because the government established laws restricting their use. These restrictions covered safety, hunting rights, and even one's loyalty to the government. In most circumstances, they placed a fine[86] upon those individuals who violated the laws, but in some circumstances arms were liable to be confiscated and even sold.

In a 1783 Boston act regarding the town's gunpowder, it was required that all gunpowder be turned over to the "Firewards" for safe keeping and storage.[87] The act further stipulated any "Fire-Arms" found in any "Dwelling House, Outhouse, Stable, Barn, Store, Warehouse, Shop, or other Building, charged with or having in them gunpowder" were liable to be seized by the "Firewards."[88] Furthermore, a jury would decide whether the firearms seized "shall be adjudged forfeit, and be sold at public Auction."[89] In a 1771 New Jersey deer preservation law that outlawed the hunting or carrying of "any Gun on any Lands not his own," it was enacted that "Non-residents" who offended this law were not only required to pay "Five Pounds," but were also compelled to "forfeit his or their Gun or Guns."[90] Meanwhile, in another deer preservation law passed in 1745 North Carolina, it was resolved that any person that did not have a certificate to hunt on public lands "shall forfeit his gun, and five pounds proclamation money, for every such offense."[91]

While these firearm confiscation laws prove that firearm ownership may be restricted by the government, individual right theorists will be quick to argue that such laws did not prevent an individual from purchasing a new firearm to replace the one confiscated. Since these laws did not interfere with an individual's natural and constitutional right to firearm ownership, it will be argued such laws should have no bearing on how the Supreme Court should interpret the Second Amendment. Furthermore, individual right theorists will be quick to state that firearm ownership was a natural and constitutional right to check the power of government ever since the Glorious Revolution of 1688. Therefore, although the government could seize firearms for violations of public safety and hunting rights, it would have been unconstitutional for the government to infringe on an individual's right to purchase or own firearms because it kept the government from usurping the rights of the people. In short, firearm ownership was considered to be the people's only way to keep the government, state or federal, honest.

Certainly the American Revolution, or its inspirational precursor — the Glorious Revolution — would have never occurred had the Lockean principle been philosophically incorporated, i.e., the people have a right to overthrow tyrannical and oppressive governments. It was the essential argument behind the Declaration of Independence,[92] but said argument and philosophy did not guarantee a right to firearm ownership. It is true that the people were compelled to take up arms "in defence of the freedom that is our birthright,"[93] but their taking up of arms, as cited in the *Declaration of Causes and Necessity for Taking Up Arms,* was never described as a "constitutional" or "natural" right. It was something they were "compelled by our enemies to assume."[94]

Besides, the *Declaration of the Causes and Necessity for Taking Up Arms* never described any of the crown's confiscation of colonial arms as "unconstitutional" or as an infringement of a "natural" right.[95] The document even cites Thomas Gage's order that all Boston inhabitants deposit their arms with a magistrate. It described Gage's actions as an "open violation of honour, in defiance of the obligation of treaties, which even savage nations esteemed sacred," but did not state such an act was in violation of their "natural" or "constitutional" rights. In fact, Thomas Gage was not the only crown official to order or partake in the confiscation of the colonies' arms. As early as October 19, 1774, Lord Dartmouth had ordered the royal governors to take the "most effectual measures for arresting, detaining, and securing any Gunpowder, or any sort of Arms or Ammunition which may be attempted to be imported into the Province under your Government."[96] Governors Lord Dunmore of Virginia[97] and Josiah Martin of North Carolina[98] complied with the order by confiscating public stores and sabotaging arms. These events paled in comparison to the most infamous British attempt at confiscating colonial arms — the Battle of Lexington and Concord.

The event has been called "the shot heard around the world" because it is often cited as what sparked the outbreak of hostilities in the Revolutionary War. At least it, coupled with the Battle of Bunker Hill, is what Jefferson penned to be the beginning of hostilities in his *Declaration of the Causes and Necessity to Take Up Arms.*[99] It began on April 19, 1775, when Thomas Gage ventured to Concord in order to retake stolen munitions. These munitions were being stored at the British garrison Fort William & Mary in Newcastle, New Hampshire, prior to being raided by patriot General John Sullivan.[100] The fort was only defended by a corporal's guard and, since the fort contained large quantities of ammunition, arms, and supplies, it was deemed an easy target by the patriots. Thus, what is often lost in American history is that the events at Lexington and Concord were actually nothing more than a British attempt to recapture arms and ammunition that had been forcefully taken by the rebels. Nevertheless, one would think if the right to own and possess arms was a "natural" and "constitutional" right passed down to our country's Founders since the Glorious Revolution, that these British efforts and attempts to seize the colonists' arms would have been stated as such. They were not, though. In fact, the crown's confiscation of colonial arms was never described as "unconstitutional" or as a violation of a "natural right" in any of the colonies petitions to the crown. This includes the nation's most sacred and inclusive document of grievances — the Declaration of Independence.

The final draft of the Declaration of Independence lists twenty-seven grievances, not including the two that were deleted, none of which even mention the crown's confiscation of arms. Given that Jefferson had drafted the document, it is surprising that he did not even mention Virginia Governor Lord Dunmore's multiple attempts at seizing the colonists' arms. Certainly, Jefferson had mentioned Dunmore in his initial draft of the Declaration, but the grievance was not accepted by the Continental Congress to be included in the final draft.[101] Nevertheless, even if the deleted grievance had been included, the confiscation of arms still would not have been addressed. This leads one to ask the following question: If the Founders felt it important that the Declaration of Independence cites as a grievance that "he has called together legislative bodies at places unusual, uncomfortable, & distant from the depository of their public records, for the sole purpose of fatiguing them into compliance with his measures," and left out the British confiscation of arms, which would impede on what individual right theorists claim is a constitutional right passed down from the Glorious Revolution's Petition of Right, how is one's ownership of arms a constitutional or natural right of this country, let alone important, if the Declaration of Independence was the most inclusive list of colonial grievances?

The answer is that it was neither a constitutional nor a natural right. In fact, the revolutionaries confiscated arms themselves. Outside the incident of Fort William & Mary, four months prior to proclaiming independence, the Continental Congress passed a law ordering the confiscation of all loyalist arms. It read:

> That it be recommended to the several Assemblies, Conventions, and Committees or Councils of Safety of the United Colonies, immediately to cause all the persons to be disarmed in their respective Colonies who are notoriously disaffected to the cause of America, or who have not associated, and shall refuse to associate, to defend, by arms, these United Colonies against the hostile attempts of the British Fleets and Armies; and to apply the Arms taken from such persons in each respective Colony, in the first place to the arming the Continental Troops raised in said Colony.[102]

Confiscation of arms was actually a common punishment administered on those who did not support the revolutionary cause. "Bearing arms" was thus a conditional right in support of just government. When in Connecticut, Benjamin Butler was arrested for defaming the Continental Congress, he was deprived of bearing or wearing arms, and forbidden to hold public office.[103] Meanwhile, loyalist Josiah Chauncey, upon being examined, was forced to surrender his firearms and forced to burn all the royal commissions he had ever received.[104] In sum, firearm ownership, excluding those arms (depending on the state or colony), that were required to be provided for militia duty, was not anymore constitutionally guaranteed than any other personal property. No event serves as a better example of this than Shays' Rebellion.

In August 1786, three years after the end of the Revolutionary War, Captain Daniel Shays, a war veteran from Massachusetts, led a group of dissolute farmers against creditor merchants and lawyers of seaboard towns. The farmers were having their land confiscated for failure to pay their debts. Years prior to the outbreak of hostilities at Lexington and Concord, revolutionaries had shut down all the Massachusetts courts to prevent the crown from seizing their lands due to their failure to pay taxes. It took nearly 15 years for the Massachusetts courts to reopen. When they did reopen, there were many outstanding debts that created many insolvent farmers. Shays and others took action by taking up arms to prevent any of the courts from sitting. The event is significant because the members of Shays' Rebellion had taken up arms under the same philosophical principle of the American Revolution — to suppress governmental injustice.

Shays' Rebellion is often referenced as a significant event that led to the calling of the creation of the Constitution, for it had shown just how weak the federal government was in suppressing insurrections and rebellions. Although many sympathized with the plight of the rebellious farmers that made up Daniel Shays' force, it was predominantly believed the situation needed to be handled swiftly. The longer the rebellion went on, the more concerned the federal and state governments became. Something had to be done to ensure that the political experiment known as the United States of America succeeded.

The solution to dismantling Shays' forces was initiated by a private entrepreneur, Benjamin Lincoln, a Revolutionary War veteran who raised a private army made out of the Massachusetts militia. By January 1787 the rebellion had been put in check.[105] Regarding the rebels' punishment, Lincoln wrote to Washington that it "must be such, and be so far extended as thereby others shall be deterred from repeating such acts of outrage in [the] future."[106] On the other hand, the government could not be too stern. Lincoln felt that, in the "hour of success," the government should "hold out such terms of mercy."[107] Such an act of forgiveness would "apply to the feelings of the delinquents, beget them such sentiments of gratitude and love by which they will be led to embrace with the highest cordiality that Government which they shave attempted to trample under foot."[108]

Unfortunately for the rebels, the Massachusetts legislature and Governor James Bowdoin did not propose such favorable terms. On February 16, it was enacted that the governor may pardon anyone who participated in the rebellion, but on the following terms:

> That they shall keep the peace for the term of three years ... and that during that term of time, they shall not serve as Jurors, be eligible to any town office, or any other office under the Government of this Commonwealth, and shall be disqualified from ... giving their votes for the same term of time, for any officer, civil or military, within this Commonwealth, unless such persons, or any of them, shall after the first day of May, seventeen hundred and eighty eight, exhibit plenary evidence of their having returned to their allegiance... That it shall be the duty of the Justice before whom any offender or offenders aforesaid may deliver up their arms, and take and subscribe the oath aforesaid ... and it shall be the duty of the Justice to require such as shall take and subscribe the oath of allegiance, to subjoin their names, their places of abode, and their additions, and if required, to give to each offender who shall deliver up his arms ... a certificate of the same under his seal ... and it shall be the duty of such Major General or commanding officer, to give such directions as he may think necessary, for the safe keeping of such arms, in order that they may be returned to the person or persons who delivered the same, at the expiration of said term of three years, in case such person or persons shall have complied with the conditions above-mentioned, and shall obtain an order for the re-delivery of such arms, from the Governour.[109]

Furthermore, any offenders who attempted to vote during the three-year period lost their protection of such pardon and were to be treated as "rebels and open enemies."[110] The act is particularly significant to understanding the protections the Second Amendment affords because the State of Massachusetts had confiscated the arms of all those who had participated in the rebellion. The rebellious farmers considered their actions justified under the same principle that led to the success of the American and Glorious Revolution — that the people have a right to usurp oppressive government by force. It is interesting to note that the 1780 Massachusetts Constitution even had a provision in its Declaration of Rights that mirrored what would eventually become the Second Amendment. It secured the right of the people to "keep and bear arms for the common defence."[111] If we are to understand the individual right theorists' understanding of the Second Amendment, then were not the rebels of Shays' Rebellion doing just that? Was it not essential that the people have arms to keep the government in check and act with force to protect their natural rights when that government interfered with them? Though a general individual rights interpretation of the Massachusetts "keep and bear arms" provision would appear to encompass such a right, this was not, in reality, the case.

Fortunately, an act passed a week later gives great insight into just what the "keep and bear arms" provision in the Massachusetts Constitution was meant to protect. In *An Act for the more speedy and effectual suppression of tumults and insurrections in the commonwealth*, the Massachusetts legislature resolved:

> Whereas in free government, where the people have a right to keep and bear arms for the common defence, and the military power is held in subordination to the civil authority, it is necessary for the safety of the state that the virtuous citizens thereof should hold themselves in readiness, and when called upon, should exert their efforts to support the civil government and oppose attempts of factitious and wicked men who may wish to subvert the laws and constitution of their country.[112]

The act implies that the Massachusetts right to "keep and bear arms" was limited in scope. Specifically, the right may be extended only in a militia capacity, and under the direction of the government to support the people, government, and constitution. This meant it was for the governor and legislature to decide what the "common defence" encompassed, making the issue a political question depending on the individuals elected to government. This eighteenth-century interpretation is a far cry from that of the Supreme Court majority in *Heller*. Here the majority actually used the Massachusetts 1780 "bear arms" provision to support their individual right interpretation of the Second Amendment. It is not to say the majority ignored any consideration to the limited scope that "for the common defence" encompasses. They did, for that matter, state that "common defence" could be thought to "limit the right to the bearing of arms in a State organized force." They did not adopt this stance, though. Instead of referring to eighteenth-century statutes and history, Scalia quotes an 1825 libel case, *Commonwealth v. Blanding*. In it, Chief Justice Parker wrote:

> The liberty of the press was to be unrestrained, but he who used it was to be responsible in cases of its abuse; like the right to keep firearms, which does not protect him who uses them for annoyance or destruction.[113]

First, the case in no way was addressing an individual's "right to bear arms" or its synonymous provision in the Massachusetts Constitution. It was a libel case addressing whether a newspaper in another state could be sued in Massachusetts. Second, the quote the majority uses nowhere cites that an individual has a right to use a firearm outside of military service. It only details instances when a firearm may not be used. Lastly, it is an analogy showing that a right, no matter how expansive, is not unlimited in its protective scope.

Notice that the quote of the "right to keep firearms" does not cite the Massachusetts Constitution. The reference by Justice Parker is merely being used in a way to prove the court's point. When one reads the quote and considers how it is placed in the entire paragraph, his intention becomes clear. At the beginning of the paragraph, Justice Parker cites Articles XI and XVI of the Massachusetts Constitution to describe what the liberty of the press was meant to protect. When he gets to the "right to keep arms" reference, he does not cite the Constitution.[114] This is because he was only making an analogy. In no way was his quote intended to supersede what the Massachusetts Congress stated the "right to bear arms for the common defence" encompasses when it was dealing with the Shays' insurgents. The Massachusetts Constitution's right to bear arms provision meant the people have a right to serve and protect the state.

Certainly, many of the nation's eighteenth-century leaders were not happy with the steps the Massachusetts government had taken. Even Benjamin Lincoln, who was in charge of subduing the rebellion, stated "the conduct of the Legislature will make a rich page in History."[115] He hoped the insurgents would have been "at liberty to exercise all the rights of good Citizens; for I believe it to be the only way which can be adopted to make them good Members of Society."[116] It was an opinion Washington was "perfectly coincident" with.[117] Washington also felt "that measures more generally lenient might have produced equally as good an effect without entirely alienating the affections of the people from government."[118]

Neither Washington nor Lincoln were even remotely upset that the insurgents' arms were confiscated. The issue that upset them both greatly was the fact that those men would not be allowed to participate in government, as either voters or representatives, for three years. They could not see "how, upon republican principles, can we justly exclude them from the right of Governing."[119] Even James Madison, the man considered to be the main architect of the United States Constitution, did not question the constitutionality of disarming the insurgents. He surely believed such punishment could bring on a "new crisis,"[120] especially since it "disfranchised a considerable proportion of the disaffected voters," but did not question the constitutionality of confiscating the insurgents' arms.[121] When Madison conveyed his sentiments to Washington on the matter, he stated Massachusetts' actions "betray a great distrust," not because the insurgents were disarmed, but because they were disqualified from voting and was to have a standing army stationed among them to enforce their pardon.[122] Washington concurred.

He thought the "State of Massachusetts have exceeded the bounds of good policy in its disenfranchisement — punishment is certainly due to the disturbances of a government, but the operations of this act is too extensive."[123]

Surprisingly, the Massachusetts act would be overturned in less than a year after its passing. Although the insurgents had been prohibited from voting, most of them would participate in the 1787 spring election. Through the political process, they were able to remove those officials whom had voted for their disenfranchisement and restructure a legislature that was more sympathetic to their cause.[124] It was through the political process that the insurgents regained their arms and rights to participate in government. At no time did anyone claim the Massachusetts government's actions to be unconstitutional or in violation of their natural rights. This was the case even though the Massachusetts' Constitution expressly protected the "people have a right to keep and bear arms for the common defence."[125] Thus, as the Founders showed us through the crisis of Shays' Rebellion, it is through the political process that we should understand the right to own arms, not through the Constitution. The Constitution only protects the right to maintain and bear arms through the militia system. That is what the wording of the "right of the people to keep and bear arms" so expressly represents.

If the drafters wanted to protect every citizen's right to own guns, the Second Amendment would have been drafted much differently. As has already been addressed, New Hampshire Ratifying Convention's disarming proposal clearly puts this into context. It had proposed a constitutional amendment that stated, "Congress shall never disarm any Citizen unless such as are or have been in Actual Rebellion."[126] It must be remembered that New Hampshire was very sympathetic to the plight of the Shays' insurgents. In fact, it had harbored many of its participants, refusing to give them up to the Massachusetts authorities. This is why New Hampshire proposed and worded the amendment as it did.

With this history now available to them, individual right theorists will now argue that the taking away of the insurgents' arms was exactly what the Second Amendment was drafted to prevent. Furthermore, they would argue, Madison and the Bill of Rights Committee had kept the event in mind when drafting it. Nothing can be further from the truth. First, the New Hampshire proposal omits the important Second Amendment language that individual right proponents claim supports individual firearm ownership — the phrase "keep and bear arms." Thus, the textual construction of the New Hampshire proposal alone does not equate to the protection the Second Amendment affords.

Second, it is clear from the wording of the 1784 New Hampshire Constitution that "bearing arms" was a distinct reference to military service. That constitution did not afford a provision similar to the Second Amendment, but its wording of Article I, Section XIII shows the state was well aware of what "bearing arms" encompassed. It provided, "No person who is conscientiously scrupulous about the lawfulness of bearing arms, shall be compelled thereto, provided he will pay an equivalent." Just like the other conscientiously scrupulous provisions in other state constitutions, this provision is clear about the limited scope of "bearing arms." For no one would have been forced to pay an equivalent for refusing to perform self-defense or hunt.

Third, there does not exist any New Hampshire hunting, crime, or gun law that uses "bear arms" in anything denoting what individual right theorists suggest. It is thus clear that the New Hampshire Ratifying Convention was well aware of what right "bear arms" actually protected. The only laws that do use "bear arms" were those regarding the militia. For example, in the 1718 New Hampshire militia act it was required that "all Males persons from Sixteen Years of Age to Sixty ... shall bear Arms, and duly attend all Musters, and Military Exercises."[127] Nearly the exact same wording was used in the 1759 act,[128] proving "bear arms" was meant to infer its military meaning.

Lastly, Madison's lack of any negative reaction to the disarming of Shays' insurgents shows he did not believe their right to "keep and bear arms" was infringed. While the Second Amendment may not have existed at that time, the Massachusetts Constitution did protect the "right to keep and bear arms for the common defence." As was addressed by the Massachusetts legislature at that time in *An Act for the more speedy and effectual suppression of tumults and insurrections in the commonwealth*, this only protected one's right to perform military service. Moreover, one cannot forget there still existed the individual right coveted 1689 Declaration of Rights provision. That provision stated, "subjects which are Protestants may have arms for their defence suitable to their conditions and as allowed by law." It was a provision the Supreme Court majority endorsed as not only being a precursor to the Second Amendment but that it gave Protestants the right to own arms. If Madison and the Founders truly believed this English Bill of Rights provision protected individual gun ownership, why was it not cited by contemporaries following the disarming of the Shays' insurgents? The answer is that neither English Bill of Rights nor the Second Amendment offer such individual ownership protection. While the English Bill of Rights conditioned arms on "as allowed by law," the Second Amendment conditioned this right in service of the militia.

## The Protection the Second Amendment Affords

An original and textual construction of the Second Amendment does not support the Supreme Court majority's determination in *Heller*. While the opinion certainly provides us with a colorful historical and theoretical argument that the "right to keep and bear arms" provision protects every individual's right to own firearms for personal protection, self-defense, and hunting, such an interpretation is not part of the Second Amendment's protective scope. Comparing the words within the Second Amendment to how they were incorporated within every state's militia laws shows the phrase "keep and bear arms" was not meant to reference civilian possession, ownership, or use of firearms. This is supported by the fact that (1) there was not one instance of the word "bear" being adopted within any of the states' eighteenth-century hunting, slave, or gun laws denoting the term meant the anything outside using arms in a military capacity, and (2) the word "keep" within the textual construction of eighteenth-century militia laws equated to "maintain" or "service." Therefore the phrase "keep and bear arms" was only meant to be accurately construed as a protection to maintain and carry arms in a military capacity.

If the Framers truly wanted to protect individual firearm ownership within the Second Amendment, they would have used the words "provide," "furnish," "own," or "possess" to denote such a right. All these words were commonly used at the time the Constitution was drafted. Even the 1792 National Militia Act used "provide" to denote a militia man's duty to own the required firearms. individual right supporters are correct in pointing out that the federal and State governments promoted firearms ownership through their respective militia laws — so much so that such firearms were protected from judicial liens and forfeitures.[129] This statutory protection was often incorporated to legally shield the arms from property liens. This is because even though such arms were often purchased by the individuals, they were also quasi-government property that acted like a tax on all males that met the age qualification.

The requirement that one provided the mandatory arms in these militia laws is not a reflection of how we should interpret the Second Amendment, but instead a political issue. In 1790, Mr. Jackson, speaking before Congress, said it best when he described "carrying arms" as a "privilege."[130] While he was of the opinion that the "people of America would never consent to being deprived" of that privilege, he didn't refer to it as a right, let alone a constitutional right. Neither did Jackson say Congress was incapable of taking that privilege. He just preferred Congress not remove the privilege because in a "Republic every man ought to be a soldier and be prepared to resist tyranny and usurpation."[131] Most importantly, just like all the other debates on arms, no one in Congress disagreed with Jackson or referenced the Second Amendment as preventing Congress from regulating the "carrying" of arms.

The ownership of firearms was a political issue because in many instances militia men were not required to provide their own arms. The state often provided the militia with the arms if its legislature thought it prudent to do so. In fact, even Congress had debated the issue. They decided against enacting such legislation, not because it interfered with the spirit of the Second Amendment, but because it would not effectuate a good national security policy. Moreover, Shays' Rebellion supports arms ownership, and the manner one was able to use them was a political issue. Shays' insurgents lost their firearms for a period of three years. At no time did the Framers question the constitutionality of Massachusetts confiscating these arms. This was the case even though the Massachusetts Constitution protected the "right to keep and bear arms." Only through the political process did the insurgents regain their arms.

Furthermore, one cannot ignore the prefatory language in understanding the Second Amendment. The majority believes it to be explanatory, inserting the word "because" in front of it. Up to this awkward interpretation, federal and state courts had held varied opinions on exactly what a "well regulated Militia" encompassed, with some of the courts turning to the language of the 1792 National Militia Act and the current congressional definition of the "Militia" to come to their respective holdings.[132] The 1792 National Militia Act required that the federal militia system include every "able-bodied white male citizen of the respective states" who is "eighteen years, and under the age of forty-five years."[133] Compare it with the current congressional definition which includes "all able-bodied males at least 17 years of age ... and under 45 years of age, who are, or who have made a declaration of intention to become, citizens of the United States and of female citizens of the United States who are members of the National Guard."[134] Both sources are close in definition to understanding what a "militia" is, but neither definition gives any insight as to what "well regulated" was meant to encompass.

For example, in what would become the *Heller* case, the District of Columbia had argued to the appellate court that "well regulated" meant a collective body acting in concert, and one person could never constitute a militia. Therefore, the District of Columbia believed the Second Amendment only protects a group of individuals acting in a militia capacity, and does not protect individuals within that militia.[135] The appellate court was not convinced by this argument. It believed such an interpretation turned the "popular militia" embodied in the 1792 National Militia Act into a "select militia." Instead, that court determined that since the act required every person was obligated to arm themselves, "regardless of the organization provided by the states, and the states were obligated to organize the militia, regardless of whether individuals had armed themselves in accordance with the statute," it followed that the "authors of the Second Amendment contemplated" a "well regulated Militia" distinct from the organization of the states' militias.[136] Therefore, according to the appellate court, a "well regulated Militia" equated to include the entire population. This notion was what the Supreme Court majority essentially supported. It held that "well regulated" implied nothing more "than the imposition of proper training and discipline," inferring that people only need to have arms to meet this standard.

Unfortunately, both the District of Columbia Appellate and Supreme Court are misinformed on the history of the 1792 National Militia Act, and failed to take any steps to incorporate pertinent legislative or statutory history. An examination of the act's debates shows its requirement that every individual shall "provide himself with a good musket or firelock"[137] was not a supplementary provision to understanding the Second Amendment.[138] The arms requirement was a political consideration. On multiple occasions Congress had debated whether they should supply the national militia with federal arms, but given the national security needs of the new nation, coupled with the great expense it would entail, it was believed such action would undermine the effectiveness of the militia.[139]

In its search for a more accurate definition of what a "well regulated Militia" encompassed, one would think that the majority needed to look no further than the Virginia Constitution of 1776. Given that the Court relies heavily on Madison's opinions, since he is considered to be the chief architect of the Constitution and one of the main contributors to the Federalist Papers, would it not make sense to refer to Madison's definition of a "well regulated Militia" in the Virginia Constitution of 1776 of which he was also one of the main architects? Although the Supreme Court majority cites the Virginia Constitution, they do not give it proper consideration. Therein the provision clearly states a "well regulated Militia" is "composed of the body of the people trained to arms," and it "is the proper, natural, and safe defence of a free State."[140] Noteworthy is that nowhere does the provision state that a "well regulated Militia" is composed of a people "who own arms" or through "individuals trained to arms." It affirmatively states it is "composed of the body of the people trained to arms."[141] Given the facts that (1) the states defined whether the individual was required to provide his own arms, (2) that Virginia and other states chose whether to provide those arms through the state, and (3) eighteenth-century militias were only mustered and trained by the direction of the state, it is conclusively clear that a "well regulated Militia" was a militia organized and regulated by the state.

This point is further supported by examining the construction of the word "State" within the Bill of Rights and a statutory analysis of those states that adopted a "right to bear arms" provision within their respective constitutions. Although the Second Amendment's placement within the Bill of Rights has left scholars disagreeing whether its intent was to guarantee an individual right or was purely a restriction on Congress, the use of the word "State" gives great insight into understanding the protective scope it was meant to encompass. In the original Bill of Rights to the Constitution, the word "State" is incorporated three times, the first being within the Second Amendment, with the Sixth[142] and Tenth Amendments[143] also incorporating the word. In the Sixth and Tenth Amendments, the use of the word "State" shows the word was referring to the respective states within the newly created United States. Therefore, the Second Amendment's phrase that a "well regulated Militia being necessary to the security of a free State" was in reference to a "well regulated Militia" in the context of service to the "State," not in the context of the federal government.[144]

Moreover, out of the eight states that adopted a "right to bear arms" provision up to 1818, none incorporated any part of the phrase "[a] well regulated Militia being necessary to the security of a free state."[145] Such language was not incorporated in the states' "right to bear arms" provisions because it would serve no purpose other than to explain that right. These provisions contrast the Second Amendment in this regard. For the Second Amendment needed to incorporate this language to secure that right. It was through state governments that the people formed a militia, with each state's militia laws dictating how its respective militia was meant to "keep and bear arms." The variance in how each state performed this function serves as evidence to illustrate this point.

The Supreme Court majority and District of Columbia's Appellate Court's interpretation of this evidence is a constitutional anomaly. First, the appellate court argued since Madison's first draft stated a "well regulated Militia was necessary to the security of a free country,"[146] and the House committee changed "country" to "State," the court believes the final draft should be interpreted as Madison initially drafted it.[147] Thus, according to the court, the word "State" is not supposed to maintain the same meaning as it is incorporated within the Sixth and Tenth Amendments. Instead, the appellate court claimed we must interpret the Second Amendment's use of "State" differently and to equate it with "country."

Since the Supreme Court majority had already dismissed language deleted in the drafting debates as "perilous," it had to take another approach to come to the same determination. Instead it equated "State" to "country," using Joseph Story's treatise on the Constitution. In it Story writes, "the word 'state' is used in various senses [and in] its most enlarged sense, it means the people composing a particular nation or community."[148] It is clear that Madison and the Bill of Rights Committee had initially drafted "country," but this was intentionally changed by the ratifying convention. Consequently, the Supreme Court majority has decided to alter and amend the Constitution as it sees fit.

Most importantly, this contradicts the Court's earlier determination on what the phrase "the people" means in the Second Amendment. The Supreme court made a textual interpretation when it used the manner the phrase "the people" is incorporated within the First, Fourth, Ninth, and Tenth Amendments to determine what the Framers intended the phrase to equate to. But in regards to the word "State," it chose to accept a meaning different than is indicated within the Bill of Rights.[149] This unequivocally shows the majority's opinion is a contradiction of textual interpretation. It is not judicially viable to interpret one part of the Second Amendment textually, and another based on a personal opinion. What this also shows is that the Supreme Court majority was doing everything in its power to affirm the District of Columbia Appellate Court's holding. What undermines the latter's holding is what the court admitted when making its determination on this matter: "[w]e have no record on the House committee's proceedings." Nevertheless, it felt "it is not credible to conclude a profound shift was intended in the change from 'country' to 'State,' particularly as there was no subsequent comment on the change."[150]

In sum, it is a constitutional farce to fall short in one's duty to understand the "right to keep and bear arms" without putting it in its proper context — "A well regulated Militia necessary to the security of a free State." This prefatory language indicates one's right to "keep and bear arms" cannot exist without a "well regulated Militia" composed by a state. The Supreme Court majority's belief that "State" equates to "country" is a textual farce. There was no legislative historical evidence to support such a conclusion. Nevertheless, individual right advocates would like us to believe, by virtue of their reasoning, that any word or phrase of Madison's initial draft of the Second Amendment that was substituted for another did not change in meaning.

Thus, according to their argument, we should instead interpret the Second Amendment as it was first proposed. Such an argument is erroneous and ignores the political process by which our Constitution and Bill of Rights was adopted. It is frightening that the Supreme Court allowed such a determination to stand. For such reasoning could be applied to any part of the Constitution, and in doing so, irrevocably undermine our affirmative rights and protections.

It must be remembered that the Second Amendment was adopted to check Article I, Section 8, of the Constitution, which states Congress shall have the authority to "provide for organizing, arming, and disciplining, the Militia." This means the Second Amendment was a provision governing the "Militia." It is a point the Philadelphia *Independent Gazetteer* addressed in its September 9, 1789, issue. The gazette described what would become the Second Amendment as a provision that did not "abridge" the "absolute command vested by [the Constitution's] other sections in Congress over the militia."[151] The provision was described as such because the Second Amendment did not prevent the militia from being "subjected to martial law" or from being "marched from state to state."[152] It only prevented the federal government from impeding on the states' ability to arm its militia.

# CHAPTER FOUR

# The Conditional Right to Keep and Bear Arms

Courts that have analyzed the meaning of the Second Amendment have often done so without mentioning the three conditions upon which the right is based. The conditions are that the individual must be (1) in support of just government, (2) willing to "keep and bear" arms during times of emergency, rebellion, or invasion, and (3) willing to be subjected to martial law. It is important the individual be willing and able to meet all three conditions to have a claim in exercising their "right to keep and bear arms." For these conditions were put in place as a means to check unjust, unruly, undisciplined, and vigilante behavior.

Excluding the ruling in *Heller,* and prior to that decision, both the individual right and collective right courts had addressed the first condition — that the individual must be in support of just government. It is logically and historically viable that an individual does not have the right to perform military service against the very country that gives him that right. Such action is not exercising one's right to "keep and bear arms." It is treason. While some may argue that the Second Amendment reiterates Locke's theory that the people may employ arms to usurp unjust government, the historical evidence of the Framers does not support such an assertion. There were numerous laws against the practice of groups assembling with arms outside of militia duty.

Moreover, the Constitution set up the means by which the people may alter and abolish unjust government. The people's ability to participate in elections, local and national, allows them to change the government frequently. There exists only one exception that would allow the people to exercise their "right to keep and bear arms." This would occur if the national government used its standing armies to suppress the people's constitutional

95

rights. The Founders were not only fearful of what foreign standing armies might impose, but of the consequences an unchecked domestic standing army could bring with it as well. It is in this limited instance that the people's exercising of the Second Amendment would be constitutionally permissible.

The second condition — that the individual must be willing to serve their country in times of emergency — has never been mentioned. Service in the militia, both state and federal, was not an option. It was a duty. Outside of the exemptions provided by the governments, individuals were required to register with their local company, attend musters, often but not always required to purchase and maintain their own arms and accoutrements subject to fine, and perform patrols. The only way an individual was excused from these requirements was if he were religiously scrupulous to bearing arms, paying a fee, or finding a substitute. One's militia service was, therefore, not something to be taken lightly. One never knew when the next conflict would arise. At any moment an Indian conflict or slave insurrection may require the calling out of the militia. In a sense, the militia was a perpetual military draft. Individuals were often put into militia classes. One's class decided when, where, and for how long they were to be deployed.

The courts have also never addressed the third condition — that the individual must be willing to be subjected to martial law. This phrase is somewhat confusing because what we know today as "martial law" has a very limited meaning. The eighteenth-century definition differed in that it had two applications. Its first application involved what we associate with martial law today. This is where there is a suspension of the legal structure, replacing it with law at the discretion of the executive. The second application is not, in truth, associated with this contemporary definition. It involved laws governing the exercise of the military, or in other words, what we today call military law. While the two forms of martial law seem ostensibly different, the Framers found both applications to operate on the same foundation — the fear of standing armies.

Only through standing armies could martial law be used to subdue the populous. It was also only through the maintenance of standing armies that martial law was made necessary. For without martial law, it was universally feared an army could never be tried under the common law. This was because a standing army's purpose was to either protect the populous against an invading threat or to invade another country, making their actions deemed to be above the law. Thus, some other form of law had to be instilled outside of the common law as a means to check an army from carrying out lawless actions. Even though its application was necessary, the theory behind it was the issue of much debate and reform from its Roman inception up to the adoption of the United States Constitution. For many saw how its unfettered exercise might undermine the democratic underbelly of a Republic.

This third condition has never been mentioned for good reason. This is because when the Founding Fathers drafted the Constitution in 1787, they did so without alluding to martial law. This is particularly surprising given their disdain for its exercise during the eighteenth century. It is not to say that the Constitution does not offer any protection against the use of martial law. Article I, Section 9, does guarantee that the writ of habeas corpus will not be suspended.[1] In spite of this, the article offers little insight into the Founding Fathers' opinions on the use and exercise of martial law. For example, in what circumstances it can be applied, for martial law imposed a stricter form of justice that in many instances could subvert individual guarantees. The potential impact on individual rights was essentially unchecked. Nevertheless, the Founding Fathers saw its second application — military law — essential to the formation of the new country. Without it, it was feared the military would subvert the civilian authority and deem the populous a distinct class.

## Martial Law and American Independence

First, a brief history of the exercise of martial law, in reference to the military taking over the normal administration of justice, is necessary to understand its military application. It was in 1775, that the colonial governors' declarations of martial law would have a significant impact not only on the American colonists taking up arms, but also in their push for independence. Following the Proclamation of 1763, English administrators in multiple instances had considered declaring martial law in the colonies. It would not be until the colonists thought it was necessary to take up arms that martial law was ever declared, though. In every instance before this the civil law was never subverted in favor of martial law.

For example, revolutionary fervor heightened in October 1768 when Massachusetts Governor Francis Bernard requested the aid of two regiments to maintain order in Boston. The action only provoked further resistance from the colonists. The event was marked by a frantic preparation of arms. While the colonists were reacting in fear of a standing army and portraying a picture of an "iron-fisted military dictatorship, its inhabitants cowering in terror, [and] its legal constitution abandoned," nothing was further from the truth.[2] By January 1769 things had gotten much worse. Lieutenant Governor Thomas Hutchinson had been informed that Samuel Adams had remarked, "Let us take up arms immediately and be free, [by] seiz[ing] all the King's officers," and "we will destroy every soldier that dare put his foot on shore; His Majesty has no right to send troops here to invade the country, I look up on them as foreign enemies."[3] Even in the face of these threats of rebellion and insurrection, Hutchinson and Bernard maintained the civil system.

Tensions continued to escalate when a loyalist printer, John Mein, refused to adhere to the non-importation agreement. In broad daylight, patriots assaulted his person. In self-defense, Mein drew a pistol and fired into the mob. In the heat of the scuffle Mein was somehow able to escape to the town's main guard, begging Hutchinson for protection.[4] Hutchinson was now alone. Bernard had sailed for London that same month to discuss Massachusetts' state of affairs with the king.[5] In the meantime the lieutenant governor had to make a decision regarding the incident and the troops in Boston. While Mein would be given no redress, and forced to sail to England disgraced,[6] Hutchinson would again give way to the rebels by ordering one of the regiments removed from the town.[7]

It was actually not until June 12, 1775, that martial law was ever declared by Thomas Gage.[8] Just months prior, Gage had been advised by Lord Dartmouth that he had the power to proclaim martial law under the Massachusetts Royal Charter "in time of War, Invasion, or Rebellion."[9] Even though Gage was aware of this power, like Hutchinson, he chose against such action. In fact, Gage recommended to his superiors that all attempts of peaceful discourse be exhausted before such a proclamation should ever be made. Instead he proposed that a proclamation pardoning all treasons be issued, only prescribing to offer a reward for the capture of the members of Congress.[10] It wasn't until nearly 30,000 rebels surrounded Gage that he would finally issue his proclamation of martial law. It was an act of desperation and one of the minimum options available to him for on the same date, he would also conceive of plans to incite the slaves and recruit the Indians to his cause[11] — anything in order to ensure his men's safety as well as maintain the crown's prerogative.

On November 7, 1775, Virginia Governor Lord Dunmore would issue the most infamous declaration of the martial law. He offered freedom to all rebel slaves and indentured servants that would join the British standard.[12] Like Gage, Dunmore's declaration came as a result of many frustrating events. It was only once Dunmore felt he was unable to restore order in Virginia and forced to preside as governor aboard the ship HMS *Fowey,* that he resorted to declaring martial law. Although the actual physical contribution of Dunmore's declaration was miniscule, with only three to six hundred slaves flocking to his standard, the psychological impact was immense.[13] The fear of slave insurrections had perpetually existed in the Southern colonies throughout the eighteenth century since the Stono Rebellion.[14] Now, for the first time, slaves would not have to flee Virginia for their freedom. They would merely have to escape to the closest British garrison. The only condition of their freedom being they had to support the war effort against their former masters.

The overall impact of Gage and Dunmore's declarations of martial law was indeed telling on American independence and the formation of state constitutions. Even before independence was declared, Congress had addressed Gage's declaring of martial law as one of the five reasons why the colonies had taken up arms.[15] It was the "General, further emulating his ministerial Masters" proceeding to "supersede the course of the Common Law, and instead thereof to publish and order the use and exercise of the Law Martial" that aided Congress in proclaiming "Our cause is just."[16] The impact of the governors declaring martial law could also be seen in the Declaration of Independence. Out of the twenty-seven grievances comprised in it, two can be implied to refer to Gage and Dunmore's declaring of martial law, including (1) "he has affected to render the military independent of, & superior to, the civil power," and (2) "he has abdicated government here by declaring us out of his protection and waging war against us."[17]

Through the authority of the Continental Congress allowing each state to form its own government, each state made sure to address the issue of martial law. Virginia's Declaration of Rights of 1776 stipulated "all power of suspending laws, or the execution of laws, by any authority, without the consent of the Representatives of the people, is injurious to their rights, and ought not to be exercised."[18] The 1780 Massachusetts Constitution would guarantee the "power of suspending the laws, or the execution of the laws, ought never to be exercised but by the legislature, or by authority derived from it, to be exercised in such particular cases only as the legislature shall expressly provide for."[19] Meanwhile, in 1776, North Carolina's Declaration of Rights would read "that all powers of suspending laws, or the execution of laws, by any authority, without consent of the Representatives of the people, is injurious to their rights, and ought not to be exercised."[20]

It is clear that the Founding Fathers abhorred the idea of exercising martial law because they believed such an imposition subverted the rights of the citizens. Furthermore, it was believed this subversion of rights undermined the democratic principles of the Republic. Although this explains the principle reflecting strong objections to martial law, it also must be remembered one could not exercise martial law without a sufficient military force to enforce it. Thus, this is how the other form of martial law — military law — developed and even became a prominent staple of justice in order for the Founding Fathers to create their own republic.

## Martial Law's Beginnings in the Roman Republic

The first Western treatise to examine the need for martial law governing the military would appear in *De re Militari*. It was written by Flavius Vegetius Renatus between the late fourth and early fifth centuries as a discourse of Roman warfare and military principles. Flavius' work shows the late Roman Empire was well aware of the problems that arise from the maintaining of a standing army. It was observed that the army, when gathered together but not engaged in battle, "occasionally raises riot, and when in fact it is unwilling to fight, it pretends to be angry at not being led out to battle."[21] It was because of these potential riots that soldiers "should be held to every article of discipline by the strictest severity of tribunes, 'vicars' and officers, and observe nothing but loyalty and obedience."[22]

As a means to accomplish such control, it was believed that, when the soldiers were not in combat, they should be in constant training in the "review of arms," "shooting of arrows," or "throwing [of] javelins." This would give the soldiers no opportunity to take a leave of absence and cause mischief.[23] If they were well-trained and disciplined as a means to be in a constant state of readiness, not only would they be a competent and efficient fighting force, but they would also not undertake dangerous mutinous actions that could endanger the Republic.[24]

In regards to punishment, Flavius disciplined soldiers that behaved in a "disorderly or mutinous" manner by segregating them from camp as a means to: (1) maintain order, and most importantly, (2) maintain the army's moral. He knew if these individuals that behaved mutinously were harshly dealt with, it might lead to a large mutinous retaliation.[25] This did not mean that unruly or mutinous soldiers ever eluded punishment. In some instances, "extreme necessity" would require the "medicine of the sword." If this had to be done, it was preferred that the "ancestral custom" was followed by punishing only the "ringleaders" of the crimes, so that "fear extends to all, but punishment to a few."[26]

What is interesting about military law during the late Roman Empire period is that it was not very expansive and was not much different from the civil law. When Emperor Justinian codified all the Roman laws in the *Cor-*

*pus Juris Civilis of Justinian* only a handful of the thousands of pages cover the military.[27] It is uncertain why the military was not subjected to the more stringent legal structure that we know today. It can be inferred that the severe punishments in Roman criminal law, in addition to the expansiveness of the civil code, caused little need for the military class to be treated much differently from the civilian population. The section of Roman law that did affect the military mainly referenced issues that only affected the army. The majority of these laws referenced crimes such as desertion, who may serve, when a soldier may purchase land, and rules regarding military arms. Most punishments, especially regarding the different forms of desertion, were by penalty of death, but even a soldier that "lost his arms in time of war, or has sold them, [was] punished with death."[28]

Although most of the military punishments were of a capital nature, soldiers did not appear before a magistrate for crimes committed. In fact, it would not be until Emperor Constantine that a judicial reform would be made allowing soldiers to be tried by the civil authority.[29] Until that time it was standard practice that the commanding officer administered justice in all cases affecting soldiers.[30] The theory behind this was circular. It was believed that due to the necessity that the soldiers follow the orders of the commanding officer, and because the commanding officer was the enforcer of discipline, it should be the commanding officer that administered the justice because there could be no law besides his orders.[31]

The reigns of Julius and Augustus Caesar led to a change. It had been Roman custom during times of peace that the military disband. This practice ceased. No longer could the soldiers be discharged in the same manner as republican armies. This meant that for the next two centuries a dangerous military *esprit de corps* flourished throughout Rome.[32]

Only after many abuses by this new militaristic and imperial power were the military structure, organization, and discipline reorganized by Constantine. This included separating the civil and military jurisdiction in the provinces. Now the commanding officers were restricted to the military jurisdiction of their territories, while civil governors were given jurisdiction over the civil population in the same area.[33] Although this change did not prevent commanders from hearing civil cases involving soldiers, it dually opened the door for the civil authority to try soldiers in certain cases. No longer were the soldiers to be strictly adjudicated by their commanding officers.

This did not mean the new judicial system was free of problems. For example, during the reign of Emperor Anastasius, the soldiers stationed in the eastern portion of the empire were being tried by civil magistrates for both civil and criminal violations. Anastasius would write to the general of that sector "both civil and criminal cases which affect the soldiers aforesaid shall not be brought for hearing before the magistrate of highest authority in the East, but shall be determined by the tribunal of your Highness."[34] This was not intended to prevent the civil authority from assisting the military in coming to a just determination in all cases arising. Such practice was actually encouraged. The emperor simply hoped both the civil and military authorities would "aid one another, so that the examination of public and private causes, and even executions, shall not take place in their absence."[35] The civil authorities were not to try the soldiers unless the commanding general chose to abstain from hearing the case. The commanding general could always exercise the option of turning over the case to the civil magistrate. The emperor just wanted to be sure both the civil and military authorities were not trying the soldiers. Anastasius stipulated:

> But as We have ascertained that certain persons have been so rash and unjust as to bring some of the soldiers above mentioned not only before the tribunal of Your Highness, but also before that of eminent magistrate who presides in the East, for the purpose of accusing them at the same time before both tribunals, and obtaining different judgments against the same persons for the same causes, in order that, hereafter, such snares may not be laid for Our soldiers, and to prevent confusion from arising in complaints brought against them, no one shall be permitted to accuse any soldier, or soldiers, before the tribunal of your Highness, and prosecute him, or them, either civilly or criminally, even though he may have obtained an order of the judges, or of the commanders, when the former have any matter before you which has not yet been decided.[36]

Furthermore, because of the perpetual fear that the military would subvert the civil authority, the Romans deemed it important to keep the military class separate from the civil for other reasons. For instance, it was law that any man employed in the army was forbidden to perform civil duties. Any attempt by a soldier to work outside of his employment in the army would cause him to be "immediately dismissed," and "deprived of all privileges."[37] The practice would also be adopted by the Founding Fathers. They too saw the importance of keeping the military separate from civil affairs. An unchecked collaboration of the two classes could lead to a military dictatorship, the enactment of martial law, or a subversion of the civil authority, thus undermining the principles of the Republic.

## Martial Law in England

Given the Roman Republic's heavy influence on Western culture even today, it is not surprising that England adopted much of the same structure.

For the demise of the Roman Republic had been well studied as a means to ensure the success of English democracy, serving as an example of what to and what not to do. One of the principal "not to do's" was the maintaining of a standing army. To ensure this, England had subscribed to a quasi-militia system. By the seventeenth century this would change. Standing armies were becoming a common practice by the Stuart monarchy, and the issue of martial law in times of peace would present itself.

For example, in 1624, England was facing many internal threats from the maintenance of its standing army. It was no fault of the army itself. King James I and his government simply had not established any system of supplying, feeding, clothing, and handling the creation of a large force of men within the small British island. As a result, much lawlessness occurred. Theft of cattle, food, and other essential articles were rampant, some of which led to the deaths of soldiers. It was the lack of a sufficient system to properly maintain an army that led many exasperated townspeople to resort to self-defense as a means of protecting their property.[38]

The problem rested with the lack of a sufficient judicial enforcement to try soldiers for crimes committed. The civilians were unable to obtain any form of justice due to the soldiers being exempt from the courts' jurisdiction. As a remedy, appointments for commissioners of martial law courts were given to town magistrates to try soldiers for violations under military law. Initially there existed overlapping jurisdiction between the common, civil, and military legal systems. It was at the commissioner's discretion as what type of law he wished to apply.[39] In 1628 this would change. There began to be too much confusion as to when the military could, if ever, be subjected to the jurisdiction of the civil authority.

The problem specifically arose when King Charles I's army, stationed in Banbury, had threatened to set fire to the town. A multitude of other outrages were committed, leading the town's constable, George Phillipes, to ask for redress.[40] There was no debating that the army was stationed there to thwart off a potential invasion by the French or Spanish, but these enemy forces had not arrived. Thus, the town was left in the hands of the military, a standing army on English soil, in a time of peace. This left Parliament to debate whether martial law or common law should apply to soldiers during times of peace.

Apparently the surrounding legal authorities had been told that "no justice was to commit any soldier but for treason or felony," leaving many soldiers unpunished for crimes committed.[41] The secretary of state, Viscount Conway, supported the notion of coexisting jurisdictions. There should be cooperation between the civil and military, with the officers having primary responsibility over exercising what discipline was to be enforced. Conway was for such a proposal because he thought it was too burdensome for the soldiers to know the law of the land. Henry Montagu, a former chief justice, disagreed. He thought it was wrong for soldiers to believe their officers shall only govern them without being held liable to the civil authority. He reminded his fellow members of Parliament of the importance in distinguishing common law from martial law. Martial law could not be above the common law because of the need for cooperation between the civil and military authorities. If the military were superior to the civil in the administering of justice, then the military would also be superior to the civil in authority and governance.[42]

Meanwhile, John Williams proposed a medium between Conway and Montagu's approach to the issue without addressing the relationship between martial and common law. Williams thought the soldiers should not only submit themselves to discipline of the military law but, in addition, be subjected to the laws of the land, with neither form of law being superior to the other.

The issue was not immediately resolved. What did not make sense to Sir Edward Coke was how martial law should apply at all in this instance. He felt that martial law should be contained by the common law because it was illegal to exercise in times of peace. "When the Chancery is open, this law sleeps," he argued.[43] Coke's comments did not create a consensus, and the debate was moved to a later date. Parliament was left to consider the following: "first, to consider the extent of martial law; 2ly, to know what validity it is in time of peace, and whether the common law may add or diminish strength to it, then the continuance of it."[44]

On April 15, when the debate reconvened, Coke's resubmitted his argument — that only in times of war when the king's courts are closed could martial law be executed. It was further pointed out by Robert Mason, that even treasonous and rebellious subjects received trials when such courts were open. Thus to Mason, he did not see the validity of martial law in this instance.[45] He felt that the common law clearly placed a restriction on the use or exercise of martial law in such circumstances. Humphrey May disagreed on the grounds that the common law did not cover the disciplining of soldiers. May argued, "It is impossible an army should be governed without martial law ... [because] if a soldier draw a weapon against an officer, the common law will not give any remedy for it."[46]

May's point was valid. For if the military was only subjected to the jurisdiction of the common law in times of peace, how were treasonous or mutinous activities to be tried? How was an officer to discipline his soldiers without the punishments afforded by martial law? Unfortunately for May, there was no legal precedent to support this argument, only his logical conclusion. John Selden reminded the members that the Romans also had their *de re militari* to show there had existed a system where the martial law worked in conjunction with the civil law. This argument failed, though, because even Roman martial law was limited to operating during times of war. The Roman laws had never been intended for martial law to apply outside this context, because their armies were forbidden from being stationed among the citizens.

It was well known by Parliament that the king could execute writs of martial law to areas that had been invaded or stricken by war, foreign or domestic. Thus, as Francis Ashley stated, it would seem that martial law was meant to serve "for a supply in defect of the common law when ordinary proceedings cannot be had."[47] The potential abuses that may result from martial law were why it was so limited. But if "martial law is merely for the necessity for things that the common law cannot take notice of," as Henry Rolle asserted, was it not necessary that there always be some form of martial law whenever armies are raised? What remained unanswered was: Where were the limits to its exercise?[48] For armies may be raised in peace when preparing for war and vice versa, or as Selden so eloquently stated it, "war is peace because it is a preparation to peace, and peace to war."[49]

Sir Henry Marten was willing to concede the point that the military should always be subjected to martial law whenever raised. He just preferred that the common law take precedent whenever it may be executed with "convenience." Otherwise the martial law should take precedent in trying soldiers for crimes committed.[50] What was to be considered convenient, though? Selden reminded Marten that "convenience does not make law," and certainly it should not in such a dangerous case as martial law. Selden, and other advocates of the common law being superior to the martial law, would have to make a fundamental concession. Somehow the common law and martial law had to work together to quell the dangerous nature of armies.

It is with this regard that Coke felt the common law would have to give way to the exercise of martial law in some form. For when there is preparation for an offensive or defensive war, the people must give way to martial law becoming a precedent in the justice system. It was not only necessary to protect the people from unruly armies, but to aid in the discipline of the soldiery when it came time for war. Certainly the people, especially the soldiers serving, would have to sacrifice some of their natural and civil rights for the benefit of the whole. As Marten had advocated, marital law was a necessity because it was very difficult to control soldiers unless they were "governed under known, preferably published regulations."[51] This was true even if its exercise superseded a man's rights such as trial by jury of his peers.

In the end, the debates settled nothing except to create a few theories as to how and when martial law may be applied to the soldiery. The only thing that was certain, and which did become an issue of contention, was that martial law, in its military law form, should never apply to the citizenry in times of peace. Even the 1628 Petition of Right would not settle the matter. That document only addressed the impropriety of quartering of soldiers, stating:

> Whereas of late, great companies of soldiers and mariners have been dispersed into divers counties of the realm, and the inhabitants, against their wills have been compelled to receive them into their houses, and there to suffer them to sojourn, against the laws and customs of this realm, and to the great grievance and vexation of the people... And that your majesty would be pleased to remove said soldiers and mariners; and that your people may not be so burdened in time to come.[52]

Throughout the seventeenth century, the issue remained unsettled. Standing armies became a staple of the times, especially with the creation of the Cromwellian Protectorate. Thus, when the Stuart monarchy was restored to power in 1661 there was a large anti-standing army sentiment.[53]

The issue would resurface again in 1688. James II raised a force of 50,000 men in response to a rebellious attempt to overthrow him as king. Moreover, he also decided to give military commissions to Catholics, causing great fear that Catholicism would usurp the Protestant religion. These events, coupled with a multitude of other grievances, led to the Glorious Revolution of 1689, which ultimately led to the Declaration of Rights of 1689. Article 6 of that Declaration ensured the "raising or keeping a standing army within the kingdom in time of peace, unless it be with the consent of Parliament, is against the law."[54] Technically, the Declaration of Rights did not immediately take effect due to the presence of William of Orange's standing army. Once a full transition in authority occurred, though, Article 6 was supposed to take effect.

The transition never occurred. England's empire began to flourish in the start of the eighteenth century, causing the need for a permanent standing army to exist. The Machiavellian principle that a militia was "necessary to a free State" remained entrenched in English Whig ideology. Nevertheless, an army would have to be maintained in order to prevent James II and the Stuart line from reclaiming the crown. Besides, William and Mary were currently embroiled in an unending conflict with Holland and France. Consequently, an army would be required until those wars ceased. Lastly, a militia-based military was no longer thought to be an adequate fighting force against the trained professional armies of the European continent. William Blackstone even logged, in his commentaries:

> But, as the fashion of keeping standing armies ... has of late years universally prevailed over Europe ... it has also for many years past been actually judged necessary by our legislature for the safety of the kingdom, the defense of the possessions of the crown of Great Britain, and the preservation of the balance of power in Europe, to maintain even in time of peace a standing body of troops, under the command of the crown; who are, however *ipso facto* disband at the expiration of every year unless contained by parliament.[55]

Even with a standing army deemed as a necessity by the majority of Parliament, fundamental opposition to the idea persisted. Philosopher Algernon Sidney was one of these critics, borrowing from the radical Whig ideals of the militia and from Machiavelli and James Harrington. Sidney argued against the maintenance of a standing army, not only because it infringed upon the civil liberties of the people, but also because it perpetuated dependent relationships in society.[56] It was up to the people to respond against any efforts to maintain a standing army and to demand the reestablishment of the militia. For he further argued that if the citizenry failed to do so, then they — the people — must be corrupt. It was up to the people to claim their "birthright to bear arms." Furthermore, Sidney believed citizen armies had greater military potential than and were far superior to any hired mercenary army. He attributed this to the "quality of commanders and the courage of rank and file" a citizen army had over any standing or mercenary army. While standing and mercenary armies were fighting for specie and plunder, a citizen army was fighting for much more — their national pride and property.[57]

Other prominent philosophical opponents of a standing army would publish their sentiments regarding the subject. Robert Viscount Molesworth used, for purposes of exemplification, the history of Denmark (in his *Account of Denmark as It Was in the Year 1692*) to show the effects of what happens when a freely-based militia system is overridden by an absolute monarch's standing army. Molesworth attributed Denmark's decline as a free nation to the moment when the citizenry failed to accept their civil responsibility in maintaining the militia. It was Denmark's inability to defend their liberties that led to the rise of that country's absolute monarchy.[58] John Trenchard, John Toland, Walter Moyle, and Andrew Fletcher also published popular tracts regarding the impropriety of a standing army. Like the writers before them, these radical Whigs pushed the idea that professional soldiers were an immediate threat to the constitutional balance of Britain.[59]

These philosophers still did not answer the question as to when and under what circumstances martial law was justified. Neither were the issues addressed of under what particular circumstances the common and civil law applied to soldiers, nor whether martial law superseded the authority of other forms of law in times of peace. The philosophers of the era were so adamant on the impropriety of having and maintaining a standing army that the issue was somehow never addressed. In their view, standing armies were illegal to the principles of the republic. The applicability of martial law in times of peace was, therefore, a moot point. Because if standing armies did not exist in times of peace, then there would be no need for the exercise of martial law in times of peace.

In the beginning of the eighteenth century, Parliament would devise a temporary solution to the problem — the passing of annual Mutiny Acts. Given its authority to raise standing armies in times of peace, Parliament would also need to pass laws for the governing of those troops. The political and international climate of the time deemed it a necessity that troops be kept in a constant state of readiness. Although Parliament only authorized the existence of a standing army for a year at a time, the authorizing of these troop levies coincided with the passage of the Mutiny Acts as a means to keep the soldiery trained and disciplined. The acts provided a happy medium between the exercise of martial and common law. Now, any crime in which military personnel could be punished under the common law was to be tried by the civil magistrate, including the crime of blasphemy or of speaking "against any known Article of the Christian Faith."[60] Only when the civil authority made no application within eight days of the offense could the accused be tried by court-martial by the Articles of War.[61]

What also derived out of the Mutiny Acts was something that had never been considered before — the trial of civilians under martial law in times of peace. Prior to 1689, civilians had never been tried under martial law in times of peace, unless the civilian was charged with the crime of treason, but even this type of circumstance had long been dealt with in Roman and English common law. Now, civilians who were camp followers could be held liable to some of the regulations of the Articles of War, thus, subjecting themselves under the jurisdiction of martial law courts.[62]

The first major English commentator to remark on the function of martial law within the judicial structure of English society was Blackstone. Just as the many interpreters preceding him, Blackstone could find no well-established precedent regarding its exercise. For he observed that martial law "is built upon no settled principles, but is entirely arbitrary in its decisions."[63] He only viewed its function being the "necessity of order and discipline" within the army, and therefore "ought not to be permitted in time of peace."[64]

Despite this, Blackstone supported the function and purpose of martial law and the Mutiny Acts governing it. He only differed in the opinion of punishments. He did not see how the same punishments should be inflicted at all times; he understood the importance of strict regulations in time of actual war but hoped that, "in times of profound peace, a little relaxation of military rigour would not, one should hope, be productive of much inconvenience."[65]

Blackstone knew it was well settled in Roman law that desertion in time of war was punished with death, but in times of peace the same crime was handled "more mildly." The Mutiny Acts did not make this distinction, though. It had been English tradition prior to the adoption of the Mutiny Act that militia men who deserted in times of peace were given a much lighter punishment than in times of war. Unfortunately, given that the Mutiny Acts did not articulate this distinction in the law, Blackstone feared the possibility of an "absolute legislative power" in this regard.[66] There would be no end as to what crimes the legislature could create within the Mutiny Act's provisions. Thus, its passage was a "vast and most important trust ... an unlimited power to create crimes, and annex to them any punishments, not extending life or limb!"[67] He only hoped some "future revision of this act" will be to "enact express articles of war for the government of the army" or that some restriction be placed in the constitution as to prevent abuses from the exercise of martial law.[68]

## Martial Law and the American Colonies

While the Mother Country had formulated a multi-functioning system of martial law to handle the problems with the creation of its permanent standing army, the American colonies had no need for one. Even though the notion of a militia was in slow decline within England, the American colonies still found the institution extremely applicable to their needs. The system was not only cost-efficient, but more capable than any other system could have been for the colonists. Their borders were too vast for the use of a standing army to be effective. It was clearly better, tactically speaking, for the colonists to incorporate the militia for their defense. The main benefit being it provided a rapid response force from every settlement. What's more, the primary threat was not the encroachment of their lands from European powers but from disputes with local Indian tribes and the internal threat of slave uprisings. Though European conflicts had spread to the American frontier, these armies generally did not interfere with British colonial America.

Also, since European armies generally operated on the frontier, and therefore outside of colonial settlements, the ideological conflict between martial and common law was not as prominent as it had been in England.[69]

In fact, the issue of whether to try soldiers in times of peace under the common or martial law did not seem to even gain notice until things came to a head with the infamous Boston Massacre. The event was the culmination of tensions between the soldiers and colonists over many serious matters. Most importantly it showed the colonists' disdain for the use of standing armies in any capacity outside of a foreign conflict. For it was commonly deduced by the leading scholars and philosophers that a standing army operating within the jurisdiction of the civilian populous would eventually be used to usurp the civil and common law. Although this never occurred, as many feared it would after the Boston Massacre, colonists still felt the British soldiers would have their actions on that fateful day in Boston excused. The acting governor of Massachusetts, Thomas Hutchinson, ensured this would not be the case by subjecting the soldiers to a civilian trial.

For even though the troops were perpetually under the "strict regulation" of martial law while sent to "restore the public peace," they were also still accountable to the civil authority for their actions.[70] This also did not excuse the civil authority from not granting the soldiers the "right of self-defence." Justice Trowbridge, who presided over the case, explained, "Where any one is, without his own default, reduced to such circumstances that the laws of society cannot avail him, the law considers him as still, in that instance, under the protection of the law of nature."[71] It was important that "this rule extends to soldiers as well as others; nay, while soldiers are in the immediate service of the king, and the regular discharge of their duty, they rather come within the reason of civil officers and their assistants, and so are alike under the peculiar protection of the law."[72]

Many of the colonists who had lived under the cloak of British soldiers did not see how this decision was just. They did not ask for a standing army to be present. To them, the soldiers should be held to a higher and stricter standard than the civilians they protect, thereby making the soldiers accountable for their actions, self-defense or not. These soldiers' intentions were even widely considered malicious. Many civilians could not grasp how it was constitutionally viable that the soldiers were presiding over the very populous they were supposed to protect, with no foreign enemy in sight. Their logic was that the soldier has "no right at all" because he has "committed an outrage, [and] we have an equal right to inflict punishment, or rather revenge."[73] Patriot Josiah Quincy addressed this issue in his speech to the jury, reminding them that the soldiers were citizens too. He stated:

To be reminded of the color of his garb (by being called a "lobster," "bloody back," "coward," etc.), by which he was distinguished by the rest of his fellow citizens; to be compared to the most despicable animal that crawls upon this earth, was touching indeed a tender point. To be stigmatized with having smarted under the lash at the halberd; to be twitted with so infamous an ignomy, which was either wholly undeserve, or a grievance which should never have been repeated: I say, to call upon and awaken sensations of this kind, must sting even to madness. But accouple these words with the succeeding actions — "You dastard — you coward!" A soldier and a coward! This was touching, "the point of honor, and the pride of virtue." But while these are as yet fomenting the passions, and swelling the bosom, the attack is made... Gentlemen of the jury, for heaven's sake, let us put ourselves in the same situation! Would you not spurn at the spiritless institution of society, which should tell you to be a subject at the expense of your manhood? But does a soldier step out of his ranks to seek his revenge? Not a witness pretends it... Does the law allow one member of the community to behave in this manner towards his fellow citizen, and then bid the injured party be calm and moderate?[74]

What Quincy was reminding the people was that the soldiers are also members of the citizenry they are employed to protect. The soldiers too have the same natural rights of the citizens and, therefore, should be held to an equal standard. It is interesting that Quincy stood to protect the rights of a soldiery that he himself disdained. He was an ardent patriot and could have easily stood by and watched the soldiers suffer a fate that would have aided his political cause, but instead he felt the serving of justice was a higher purpose than that of his own ideals.

Quincy had feverishly remarked that he wished the British army "must be removed, or they will in the end overturn and trample on all that we ought to hold valuable and sacred."[75] The situation in America reminded him too much of what happened to the Roman Republic under Caesar or to England under Cromwell. Philosophers such as Algernon Sidney had asserted that armies created out of the state's populous, such as the British army, were superior to any mercenary army. Because these armies were comprised of its own citizens, the "advantages of good success are communicated to all, and everyone bears a part in the losses."[76] Therefore, such an army "makes men generous and industrious and fills their hearts with love to their country." To Sidney, this is how the Roman army was comprised, placing them "above the rest of mankind."[77] Quincy disagreed. He thought this philosophical theory "deceived that an army of natives would not oppress their own countrymen," arguing that it was a delusion because "Caesar and Cromwell, and a hundred others have enslaved their country with such kind of forces."[78]

Quincy's point was simple. It did not matter whether a standing army was comprised of a state's own citizens or of foreign mercenaries. He commented, "No despotick government can ever subsist without the support of that instrument of tyranny and oppression, a standing army." For "all illegal power must ever be supported by the same means by which it was first acquired."[79] Quincy knew there had to be some form of a military force to protect the interests of the state, though. It is here Quincy cited[80] one of the most revered and read philosophers of the Founding Fathers — David Hume.

Hume supported the idea of a militia. Without a militia, Hume felt, "it is vain to think that any free government will ever have security or stability."[81] His idea was not a new one. Much of Hume's *Idea of a Perfect Commonwealth* was taken from James Harrington's *Oceana*, a philosopher also much revered and read by the Founding Fathers. Harrington saw the "arms of Caesar" being what "extinguished liberty" within the Roman Republic.[82] It was Caesar who changed the quasi-militia system of the Republic into a standing army, thus subverting the rights of the people. The answer to the problem was to return to a military structure when the Roman people's liberty flourished — when there was a militia.

Harrington slightly altered the Roman militia system, though, giving the ability to bear arms to all citizens.[83] This allowed the state to have an army in the field whenever needed. While states that maintained professional armies could only draw as many men that had been trained, Harrington's new militia system could draw out of an annual source of 100,000 youths to create marching armies.[84]

The new militia served a higher purpose, as well. Harrington's militia not only increased the number of men to draw upon, but also muddled the old class system. No longer were just the poor freemen to be armed to protect the interests of the lords. Now, the inclusion of all made the "common soldier herein a better man than the general of any monarchial army." The result was that members of the militia gained "that reward which is so much higher as heaven is above the earth" — the "common right" that "he who stands in the vindication of, has used the sword of justice for which he receives the purple of magistracy."[85]

This new militia system would become the basis of the American colonies' defense. Every colony passed laws requiring every able-bodied man to enroll in its service. At multiple times during the year, its members were mustered, drilled, trained, and disciplined under military rules and regulations. This included the men being liable to martial law and all the consequences resulting from its practice. Moreover, given that the militia usually consisted of all men from the ages of sixteen to forty-five years of age, martial law affected the entire American male populous. All were required to be familiar with its components and punishments resulting from a failure to comply. How strict it should be enforced fostered varied opinions. Surely, the performance of militia service had to result in some loss of liberty. Just how much liberty and at what times was up for debate. Nevertheless, martial law's function was essential in regulating the "right to keep and bear arms." As the New York militia law of 1746 explained, martial law was essential to create the "due & Proper regulation" required for the "Security & Defence" of the province.[86]

Josiah Quincy stood with the English philosophers before him. Quincy would have argued against martial law's full application to the militia unless out of necessity. He understood the theory that martial law needed to be enforced upon the militia to ensure its discipline, but he feared them becoming too disciplined because it would make them a standing army. He wrote:

> In regard to Public Liberty, armies if best disciplined are not less to be dreaded than the worst, but I think more, since their relaxation of discipline takes away from their union and sufficiency; it renders them weaker and less equal to mighty mischief; but where they are strict and united, the highest iniquities are not too big for them. Disorderly troops may rob particulars, ravage towns, and harass a country; but if you would subdue nations, commit universal spoil, and enslave empires, your forces must be under the best regulations... Soldiers know little else but booty, and blind obedience; whatever their interest, or rapacity dictates, they generally will do. It is in their profession to dispute by force, and the sword; they too soon learn their power, and where it is an over-balance for the Civil power, it will always controul the Civil power, and all things.[87]

Quincy's fear was universally shared among the Founding Fathers. They did not support England's sending of British troops to be stationed among the populous because the king and Parliament "would then do as the Roman Emperors did." It was feared that Britain "would make use of that power or force which corruption had before furnished with them, and pretences would be found for removing or destroying all those they found they could not corrupt."[88] Although the Founders would not argue that the king and Parliament had the authority in England, especially under the Mutiny Act, to station a standing army among them, it was believed this should not apply to the colonies. As Thomas Jefferson stated it in a *Summary View*, "every state must judge for itself the number of armed men which they may safely trust among them, of whom they are to consist, and under what restrictions they are to be laid."[89] To the minds of the colonists, these armed men were the militia. It was up to them to determine who the militia was to consist of, but most importantly, under what regulations and restrictions.

In his *Defence of the Constitutions*, John Adams tells the story of how the Roman people ensured its armies were never stationed among them. It had been well established the misery standing armies could impose. Thus, a law was passed preventing any soldier from marching with arms over the river of Rubicon. If a soldier ever chose to disobey this law, he would be declared a public enemy. To remind the soldiers of this duty, an inscription was erected by the river. It read: "If any general, or soldier, or tyrant in arms, whosoever thou be, stand, quit thy standard, and lay aside thy arms, or else cross not this river."[90] The story is notable because it effectively displays the attitude the Founders had regarding martial law. For a soldier to cross the Rubicon and re-enter the ranks of the populous, he must remove his arms and return to the civil order. Showing one's civic role was superior to one's military duty. Although the two were undoubtedly intertwined as a means to protect the nation, the military aspect of society was not to be imposed on the entire populous except out of necessity.

This is the basis upon which the American militia system operated. Much like the Roman Republic's armies, it was every man's duty to enroll and serve in the colonial militias. Every man was required to be well trained and disciplined in the military arts as a means to serve the nation; like in Rome, every citizen was a soldier and every soldier a citizen. During times of war and necessity, the citizen was to become a soldier. Once the war or necessity ended, the soldier was to remove his arms and return to his role as a citizen. It is this principle that the story so effectively demonstrates. If a soldier wanted to return to Italy, he was to remove his arms and return to his role as a citizen. Only when it was his duty to become a soldier again, may he bear arms by re-crossing the Rubicon.

## Martial Law During the American Revolution — The Articles of War

After the Battles of Lexington & Concord, an English civil war was upon the colonists. Within a matter of weeks nearly 16,000 militia assembled in the Boston peninsula. They hailed from all over New England, including Massachusetts, Rhode Island, Connecticut, New Hampshire, Pennsylvania, New York, and New Jersey. It was the first time such a large militia force had congregated in the colonies. It was also the first time these men had assembled for military duty without being subject to the British military rules and regulations.

Artemas Ward was the first to take command of this unorganized mass of armed men. Most of them assembled upon hearing the alarm, arriving with nothing but the clothes they had been wearing while at work in the fields. After chasing the British to Boston, many felt their work had been completed.[91] Men came and went as they pleased, in and out of camp, under no liability for their actions. While patriotism might have brought them to the siege ready to risk life and death in the conflict, it did not help their military discipline.

The discipline within the militia ranks was severely lacking for many reasons. First, most militia only mustered for two to four times a year. This offered very little opportunity for the men to become accustomed to the rigors and strict discipline of a military campaign. Second, without enforcement of the British Articles of War, there were no general military guidelines for all militia. Each colony had its own rules and regulations. The actions of an individual in a Pennsylvania company might be liable to punishment under its martial law, but the same action might be deemed appropriate or outside the authority of another colony's martial law. Third, most of the officers who enforced the discipline were not appointed, but voted by the men of the company to serve as the commanding officer.

While this last precedent had been put in place as a means to ensure commanders did not overstep the limits of their authority, it contradicted the enforcement of strict military discipline. Any officer who was too strict on his men might find it impossible to fill his beating order, thus losing his eligibility for commission.[92] Lastly, there did not exist any universal training method for the troops. It was not until 1777 that Baron von Steuben created his rules of military instruction. This meant that every company's methods of firing and maneuvering differed slightly from one another and, without any military continuity in this regard, there could be no military discipline.

Ward did his best to try to bring military order and discipline to the patriot force. However, even his efforts, and the utmost efforts of other officers, could not alter the sway of political and democratic preferences of the militia. Brigadier General Nathanael Greene was certainly frustrated with the issue. Greene had "made several regulations for introducing order, and composing their murmurs." Nevertheless it was "very difficult [for him] to limit people who had had so much latitude without throwing them into disorder."[93] There were just too many political obstacles to overcome to get every colony's militia on the same page. Enforcement was difficult and soldiers were fully aware that there was no longer any court or government within Massachusetts. It was understood that the Massachusetts Provincial Congress might appoint committees or make recommendations, but any orders issued had no legal authority. It is not to say the soldiers were unwilling to serve the cause and country. It was just that, as historian Charles Martyn described the situation, the soldiers just did not "intend to submit to anybody's arbitrary regulations, nor be censured or punished for violations of rules to which they had not agreed and which nobody else had the right to make."[94]

Upon Washington's arrival to take charge of the army, he would write to Congress he had a "sincere Pleasure in observing that there are Materials for a good Army, a great Number of able-bodied Men, active zealous in the Cause & of unquestionable Courage." Nothing could be further from the truth. The great thing about Washington's character was that he knew how to address Congress to make a situation seem as optimistic as possible. Only in his writing to his fellow generals and friends did Washington ever exert his true feelings on the subject. The grim reality was what he wrote to his friend Richard Henry Lee, stating, "Between you and me I think we are in an exceedingly dangerous situation."[95]

The problems were too numerous to count, but the greatest difficulty was to what extent the soldiers should be punished for violations of martial law. Washington was a staunch disciplinarian when it came to soldiering. He felt martial law served many purposes, including the creation of an obedient, effective fighting force, enforced daily discipline and order, added to the distinctions in rank, and furthered the subordination of soldiers.[96] Washington's army was much different than anything on the European continent, though. The professional British and Prussian forces did not have the problem of short-term enlistments. Those armies were comprised of men serving for long periods. Short-term volunteer enlistments meant Washington and Congress would have to enact a more lenient system of martial law if they were to maintain their fighting force and gain enlistments. The compromise was the creation of the Continental Army. It allowed Washington to have a more permanent fighting force than that of the militia. Furthermore, the force was considered to be legally separate and distinct to the colonies' governments. In effect, the army was constrained to a more stringent form or martial law than the colonial militias.

The creation of the Continental Army was no easy task. There was a general fear of a standing army, and now Congress was about to create just that. The creation of the Continental Army contradicted almost everything the Founders had argued against. The act must have been especially puzzling to Britain's Parliament and Tories who had heard the repeated cries from the colonists for the removal of British troops. Moreover, it had been commonly believed by the Founders that a militia was superior to any standing army. Military urgency and exigent circumstances had now altered their thinking. A standing army was now necessary to subdue another standing army, and with this came the necessity of Articles of War and a universal martial law system.

It was the great legal subordination that martial law imposed that had troubled Englishmen for centuries. There was concern that too much discipline and too many rules would only add to the potential threat that standing armies imposed on liberty.[97] Philosopher John Trenchard was against making any separation in rules between the civil and military because it separated the interests into two classes, instead of promoting one. To Trenchard, liberty was only secure when "the Interest of the Governors and Governed" were the same.[98] Blackstone also perceived this potential danger to liberty. He observed that, when men are "reduced to a state of servitude in the midst of a nation of freemen," they were a danger because they lived "in a state of perpetual envy and hatred towards the rest of the community."[99]

The same concerns resided in Congress. Here the dilemma was twofold. On the one hand, it was necessary to subvert the status of free men because subordination and discipline were essential to the creation and maintenance of a fighting force. This would mean a soldier's body was literally no longer his own, and at the discretion of the commanding officer. On the other hand, it was feared they could not subordinate the soldiers so much as to warp their mind into a different philosophy of liberty.[100]

Not all shared this fear. Those who were accustomed to the differing forms of justice between martial and common law saw it as a normal occurrence. William Tudor, the first judge advocate of the Continental Army simply viewed the situation as: "when a man assumes a Soldier, he lays aside the Citizen, & must be content to submit to a temporary relinquishment of some of his civil Rights."[101] The fear was that this line of thinking was a contradiction of justice. Subordinating an army to a stricter form of law — whose purpose was to secure liberty — was viewed as philosophically awkward. What's more, many saw an additional threat to liberty. By imposing strict obedience to military officers but not the civil authority that organized it, which was really subordinate to whom? This placed the Founders in the same philosophically dilemma that Parliament was in the seventeenth century.

In spite of the contradictions and fears of imposing martial law, ensuring the army was well trained and disciplined was deemed more important than an individual's right to common law justice. The Founders felt it was better that individuals temporarily sacrifice their personal liberties for the benefit of all than to have an unorganized military force. The Founders were not adopting anything new here. Both the Roman Republic and England saw the same sacrifice of individual right as essential. Moreover, prior to the Revolution, the militia had been exposed to the military laws of either the British or their respective colony. It was understood that when one was called into the service of his country, army or militia, they would be exposed to the restrictions military law imposed.

Given that the adopting of martial law provision was deemed a necessity, this left Congress only to consider the punishments that could be inflicted, on whom, and what crimes should be capital.[102] On June 30, 1775, the first Articles of War were passed by Congress. The articles governed everything from behaving indecently during "Divine Worship" to preventing the sale of "any kind of liquors or victuals."[103] Surprisingly, only two articles were under penalty of death. The first, concerning mutinous activity, stated:

> If any commander ... shall be compelled, by the officers or soldiers under his command, to give it up to the enemy, or to abandon it, the commissioned officer, non-commissioned officers, or soldiers, who shall be convicted of having so offended, shall suffer death, or such other punishment as may be inflicted upon them by the sentence of a general court-martial.[104]

The second offense was abandoning or encouraging others to abandon post. Unlike the crime of mutiny, this offense did not offer the option of a general court-martial. Instead it required the guilty party to "suffer death immediately."[105] All other offenses in the Articles of War limited punishment to a general court-martial, regimental court-martial, or to have punishment determined by an individual's commanding officer. At no time were persons subject to court-martial to suffer death, "except in the cases expressly mentioned in the foregoing articles."[106]

The Continental articles were almost taken verbatim from the Massachusetts Articles of War.[107] These latter articles were adopted just two weeks prior to Lexington & Concord.[108] They were vastly different than the British articles.[109] Given the colonists abhorrence for a form of law that could be used to subdue the civilian populous, these articles were viewed as far less stringent. Americans just felt too strongly about "the privileges of the common law and objected to a legal system in which indictment by grand jury and other fundamental rights were unknown."[110] They knew the war they were fighting was itself a protest against arbitrary government. The Massachusetts Articles even articulated this point. For they had been created to combat the "keeping of a Standing Army ... in times of peace."[111] To subject their own people to a form of law that was deemed to be one of the contributing causes of the conflict would make Congress a hypocrite.

The Founders also knew that the "great law of self-preservation may suddenly require" the adoption of martial law. This did not mean that they would not experiment in its practice, however. For the Founders were intending to adopt a more justice-oriented form of the Articles of War — one "without any severe Articles and Rules ... as are usually practiced in Standing Armies." As it was proposed to Benjamin Franklin by the Pennsylvania Committee of Safety, the rules regarding the army should be devised in a manner that would be "generally approv'd by the privates." The committee felt it important that the rules "Approach nearest to that of a free civ[i]l Constitution" because it would "meet with the highest Appropriation."[112] Congress did just that, adopting articles that were "founded in reason, honour, and virtue."[113]

Although lenient by comparison to their British counterpart, the articles' stipulations were not received well by everyone. One anonymous writer by the name of Caractacus was concerned the soldiers would lose the "gentleness and sobriety of citizens." While they might be "our servants" now, too much military discipline and training may "furnish them with the means of becoming our masters." Caractacus reminded his readers that even "officers and soldiers of the best principles and characters have been converted into instruments of tyranny."[114]

Many soldiers also protested to the articles by not signing them. This is because Congress blundered in making the articles a contract of sorts. The First Article stated "if any of the officers or soldiers ... do not subscribe [to] these rules and regulations, then they may be retained in the said army, subject to the rules and regulations under which they entered into the service."[115] Thus, the soldiers could elect to not be subjected to Congress's form of martial law if they so chose. They would simply be held to the military law of their colony's militia laws. Those that did not sign could be discharged at the end of their commitment. It was at Washington's discretion as to whether to retain these individuals.[116] Unfortunately for Washington, he had no choice in the matter. Given his need of troops, Washington was forced to take the soldiers on their terms.[117]

By October 1775, the American's experiment with its lenient Articles of War was coming to an end. It began with the trial of Dr. Benjamin Church. Church had been found to be conspiring with the British and was to be the first individual tried under Article 28. The problem was that Article 28 only offered punishment by general court-martial.[118] Washington felt the punishment was inadequate and referred the case to Congress with the suggestion that some alteration of the law was needed.[119] Not only did the articles' leniency in regards to treasonous activity pose a problem — its entire relaxed character caused disciplining problems.

Upon Washington's arrival, the Judge Advocate General, William Tudor, had initially been optimistic about discipline within the American army. In July he would write to John Adams, before Washington's arrival, that the troops were "lazy, disorderly and dirty," but now the soldiers "strictly and cheerfully executed and obeyed" orders.[120] Tudor also saw a potential problem: He knew the "Freedom, which our Countrymen have always been accustomed to, gives them an Impatience of Controul, and renders it extre[mely] difficult to establish that Discipline so essential in an Army."[121]

His concerns became a reality by the fall of 1775. While Tudor understood why Congress had drafted the articles in a manner that prescribed court-martial proceedings for most offenses, he was quick to learn that this was not an effective way to administer justice upon soldiers. The articles were too reliant upon the "privileges of the common law."[122] Furthermore, punishments were "left too much at [the] discretion" of the jury.[123] This required court-martials to be constantly in session, causing a backlog of cases and a lack of continuity regarding punishments. The articles had to be reorganized.[124]

The first change occurred in November but, even after these changes, issues remained. The articles were still too lenient on crimes. Joseph Reed would write to Congress:

> The military system of government, though much more complete than at first, is yet extremely defective. The mildness of the punishment, even of crimes the most destructive to the Army, such as desertion, burglary, drink, of sleeping on guard, which are capital in all other parts of the world, not to mention mutiny and sedition, which is growing evil, have rather made such crimes known to others that serve as examples. This Army is composed of a greater mixture that nay which has yet been collected, and I am sorry to say we have too many who would equal, if not exceed, the King's troops in all kinds of disorder and irregularity. To men of this stamp thirty-nine lashes is so contemptible a punishment that it is very frequent for them, in the hearing of their comrades, to offer to take much more for a pint of rum. Neither my nature nor education would lead me to unnecessary severity, but I cannot, consistently with the duty and regard I owe the service, avoid giving my clear opinion, that unless some very material alterations in some articles take place, the publick will be greatly defrauded, military duty neglected, and the most dangerous consequences ensue to the American cause.[125]

Washington also felt wary about the dangers of such leniency. It seems the general may have first supported the subjective justice proposed in the articles. When he was giving advice to Colonel William Woodford in commanding troops, Washington wrote that an officer should be "strict in your discipline," but to also "Reward and punish every man according to his merit." To Washington it was important to handle each matter "without partiality or prejudice."[126] Unfortunately, discipline never drastically improved by practicing this form of justice. Washington had tried appealing to the men's patriotism by reminding them of their duty. He even ordered more copies of the articles to be published and required officers to read them to their men weekly — all to no effect.[127]

The general became so frustrated that he would be forced to take matters into his own hands, for he believed a failure in discipline produced "extreme Hazard, Disorder and Confusion."[128] Thus, when the winter of 1776 had caused many men to desert, and thinned the Continental lines, Washington authorized any officer to shoot down any man that shall "skulk, hide himself, or retreat from the enemy."[129] Washington was clearly acting outside the limits of his authority under the Articles of War, but even Judge Advocate Tudor knew the November revision of the articles were "very deficient and in many Instances incompetent to the Purpose."[130]

The proposed solution by the majority of officers was to rewrite the articles so that they were similar to the British articles. As Tudor explained to John Adams, a rewrite was necessary if the cause "would ever have an Army to depend upon."[131] The "Shameless Ravages, and seditious Speeches and mutinous Behavior which prevail throughout [the] Army" were the reason for the "Loudest Language [of] a Reform."[132] Tudor further explained that soldiers without discipline were nothing but "armed Rabble" and to collect numbers of these men would only lead to their eventual slaughter.[133] Therefore Congress must have "Severity in the Government" by adopting a strict Articles of War; if the soldiers' "enthusiasm is fast wearing off, and they are sinking into an Army of mercenaries," they can no longer be "restrained by a Sense of Honour and Duty," but by "a Fear of Punishment."[134]

When Congress revised the Articles of War, they tripled the amount of offenses under penalty of death. Now a soldier could receive the death penalty for assaulting the suppliers of goods, plundering and pillaging, casting away their arms and ammunition, divulging the "watch word to any person who is not entitled to receive it," harboring to protect the enemy, and holding correspondence with the enemy.[135] Although this strict revision of the articles was primarily a result of Washington and Tudor's pleas, America's recent declaring of independence was another.

When Congress had adopted the first Articles of War, they had done so on the presumption that reconciliation would occur. Prior to the Declaration of Independence, they had only been fighting as a means to work out their grievances with England. Now if they lost the conflict, they would assuredly be tried as traitors and hung from the gallows. Thus it was essential to victory that the men who were fighting for independence be given less civil liberties than they had been given in the previous articles. As Nathanael Greene explained, in the interest of "honor, peace and happiness

... we ought to divest ourselves of private motives in our publick conduct where they militate with the publick good." It was important to Greene to remember that although the strict enforcement of martial law was not favorable on its face, "modes Established [that] are calculated to promote the General interest" were "warrantable."[136]

For the remainder of the war, the 1776 articles would remain the basis of the martial law system for the Americans. In 1775 it had been a soldier's option as to whether he would subject himself to the articles' provisions. By the close of 1776 this would drastically change. Volunteer enlistments were no longer a sufficient means to meet troop quotas. Draft lotteries and militia classing systems were put back in place. All able-bodied men were now liable to serve in the revolutionary conflict.[137] No longer would any man have the option as to whether they may be exposed to the restricted liberties and justice that martial law imposed.

## Martial Law and the State Ratifying Conventions

The Second Amendment does not expressly make any reference to martial law. Therefore, it may be argued that martial law is not a condition upon which the "right to keep and bear arms" is based. This assertion serves as a strong textual argument. In fact, throughout the entire Constitution, there is not one mention of "martial law." One argument is that this was intentionally done because the Founders did not want the people exposed to martial law's lack of civil justice. To support this argument one would point to the grievances listed in the Declaration of Independence, two of which expressly make mention of England's use of martial law.

Despite the states' abhorrence for the practice, the phrase "marital law" — in both of its forms — was intentionally left out of the Constitution.[138] The state ratifying conventions prove this. First, the conventions realized the textual dilemma of referring to both the military and civil practice of martial law in one term. When the conventions were referring to martial law in its military legal sense, they referred to it as just that — "martial law." For example, the New York Ratifying Convention proposed, "That the Militia should not be subject to Martial Law except in time of War, Rebellion or Insurrection."[139] Maryland worded its proposed amendment verbatim, reasoning that to expose the militia to martial law in times of peace was "contrary to the Magna Charta" and "the other great fundamental and constitutional laws of Great Britain."[140] Even the Pennsylvania minority chimed in on the topic. They feared the Constitution provided no restriction on the use of martial law, allowing the militia to be "subjected to as strict discipline and government" as a permanent standing army.

With regard to martial law in its other form — when administrative justice usurps individual liberties by replacing the civil system — the Founders were conscious to phrase the law differently. The practice was often referred to as "suspending" the laws. As has already been addressed, the states of Virginia, Massachusetts, and North Carolina all included this terminology in their first constitutions.[141] Out of these three states, only Virginia would propose an amendment checking the use of martial law. Following the wording in their own constitution, it was proposed "that all power of suspending laws or the execution of laws by any authority, without the consent of the representatives of the people in the legislature is injurious to their rights, and ought not to be exercised."[142]

Another manner of referring to martial law can be seen in George Mason's Draft of the Bill of Rights and Maryland's ratifying convention. In both instances there is reference to congressional authority in adopting a mutiny bill. As has already been addressed in England's history of martial law, mutiny bills were the manner by which Parliament enacted martial law statutes. They also prescribed the methods by which Parliament was to use its emergency powers. Their annual passage provided a check on the king and the standing armies; every year, they could make changes to the laws that had not worked out agreeably. Mason and Maryland's proposals were referencing just this kind of check. Mason proposed, "No Mutiny Act shall be passed for any longer Term than Two years." Maryland's convention followed suit, stating, "That no mutiny bill continue in force longer than two years."[143]

Given that the state conventions made proposals to check the employment of martial law, it is clear its omission in the Constitution was intentional. Historians will be quick to jump to the Glorious Revolution and the actions of colonial governors during the American Revolution to object to this. Still, the reality is that by the time the Constitution was being drafted the majority of the Founders had come to understand the necessities of martial law. During the American Revolution it was essential to that conflict's success. Prior to the adoption of the 1776 Articles of War, the Continental forces were without an effective system of discipline. That, coupled with Baron von Steuben's modifications, placed the Continental forces in a position to be a much more efficient fighting force.

Moreover, the events at Shays' Rebellion remained fresh in the Framers' minds. Not only had Congress lacked the ability to assemble a military force to quell the uprising; it also lacked the authority to suspend the laws in

Massachusetts. It was only that state's government that had the power to act. Furthermore, when the Massachusetts government did act, the other states did not look upon it favorably. They felt the terms were too harsh. Thus, the Framers decided it better to not have any express checks on the exercise of martial law. They trusted that Congress would only employ its exercise in extreme circumstances.

Regarding the militia and martial law, the state ratifying conventions' reference to martial law would have infringed on Congressional authority to arm, organize, and discipline the army.[144] Allowing either the New York or Maryland proposals — restricting martial law to times of war — could have severely hindered Congress. Congressional preparation for a potential conflict, outside of a declaration of war, would thus be virtually null and void. For Section 8 of Article I authorized Congress to "execute the Laws of the Union, suppress insurrections and repel invasions."[145] Congress would not be able to "repel invasions" if it could not prepare for them. In addition, Congress could not prepare for invasions if it were unable to hold the militia it called forth to the strict adherence of martial law. Thus, it was important a provision restricting the militia's exposure to martial law during times of war not be adopted.

What's more, Congress never intended on holding those enrolled in the militia to the rules of martial law unless they were mustered or assembled. Up to the adoption of the Constitution, no militia law had been drafted in a manner to impose martial law in such circumstances either. American and English practice shows it was always meant to be limited to when the individual was called upon to perform his militia duty — whenever that may be.

It is important to point out that the penalties under martial law were less severe in times of peace than in times of war. Generally fines were imposed for an individual not complying with the mustering requirements. Even Blackstone noted in England that it was tradition that men who violated martial law in times of peace were handled "more mildly" than in times of conflict.[146] This did not mean that martial law was not in force; for every time the militia was called out, they were held to some standard of martial law. Whether it was penalties or fines, it was some a form of martial law.

## Philosophers and Martial Law

It is well documented that the Founders were learned and well versed in the history, teachings, and philosophy of their predecessors. They often looked to the failings and successes of past governments as a means to aid in the flourishing of America's democratic experiment. This included martial law. For even though the Founders had their qualms with how martial law might be used in an oppressive manner, they also saw its importance.

Hale only briefly touched upon the issue, stating martial law is "neither more nor less than the will of the general who commands the army," and in fact "means no law at all."[147] Blackstone held similar sentiments. Observing that martial law was "built upon no settled principles," it was "entirely arbitrary in its decisions," and "in truth and reality no law."[148] Despite these negative views, Blackstone also admitted martial law served a purpose. Martial law was essential due to the "necessity of order and discipline" within the army. He just hoped the legislature would never misuse this "vast and important trust." Its exercise created an "unlimited power to create crimes and annex to them any punishments not extending life or limb!"[149]

While Hale and Blackstone's opinions of martial law undoubtedly reflect the early concerns of the Founding Fathers, there also existed philosophical sources supporting the almost unfettered use of martial law. For example, an eighteenth-century Swiss philosopher, Emerich de Vattel, provided a significant amount of literature on the subject. None of the Founders would cite Vattel on the issue of martial law, but his works have been shown to be very influential in the formation of the American Republic.

For instance, Vattel's *Law of Nations* supports General Washington and the Continental Congress's adoption of the 1776 Articles of War. Vattel believed "every citizen is bound to serve and defend the state as far as he is capable."[150] In order for a citizen to effectively defend the nation, it was essential that "Good order and subordination" be put in place — what is also known as martial law.[151] Thus, it was given that every man capable of defending the nation had a duty to bear arms in defense of the nation. These men were also under a duty to be subjected to the nation's military regulations.

This did not give the nation unlimited power to use martial law as a means to pursue any ends. Vattel's theory of justice was not supporting an unchecked martial law structure. He felt it was the sovereign or nation's duty to "exactly specify and determine the functions, duties, and rights of military men, i.e., of soldiers, officers, commanders of corps, and generals."[152] Thus, much like English common law, whereby sufficient notice was required for an individual to be held liable for the penalty a statute or law proposed, Vattel was also requiring notice in martial law regulations.

St. Thomas Aquinas also supported the use of martial law in its military context. When Aquinas argued in his *Summa Theologica* that the "end of human life and society" was God, he analogized it to the commander of an army. To him a commander was the supreme authority of the army. Just as the first order of man was to serve God, Aquinas believed the first order of a soldier was to be "subject to the commander." For the soldier to do anything else was considered "most grievous."[153]

Where Aquinas' theory of martial law would have raised the suspicions of the Founders was in his lack of limitations on its power. Aquinas only conditioned it on whether the commander's actions were "directed to the good of the State." While he believed of all the practical sciences that "political science is nobler than the military science," this did not operate, however, as a substantial check on the exercise of martial law. For it only conditioned martial law on whether the commander's actions were for the good of the army. Such a philosophy on martial law virtually left a commander's authority unchecked, allowing any regulation to be deemed in the best interests of the army.

Vattel similarly conditioned martial law on whether it was "relative" to support military functions. He felt a general was required to show that a law supported a military end for it to be justified. Vattel only slightly clarified Aquinas' theory in this area, noting that nothing was more justified than a law that promoted discipline. To Vattel discipline was the whole function of martial law. It was of the "highest importance" to an army. It was essential to "maintain order among the troops, and to enable them to perform their military service with advantage to the state."[154] It was good discipline, Vattel argued, that not only "added to the valour of a free people" but also brought about "those brilliant [Swiss] achievements that astonished all of Europe."[155]

It is here that Aquinas and Vattel's theories conflicted with the Founding Fathers' ideals. For Aquinas and Vattel did not fear that too much military discipline would result in a warring society. Moreover, Vattel was more liberal with the exercise of martial law. He thought the militaristic Prussian example definitively showed "what may be expected from good discipline and assiduous exercise"—that citizen soldiers would become the "most zealous and loyal subjects."[156] Meanwhile, the Founders were generally concerned with creating a soldier class. They believed such a class would consider itself superior to the very citizens they were sworn to protect. Even though the Founders believed every citizen was a soldier and every soldier was a citizen, the role of the citizen was always superior to that of the soldier. This was one of the justifications as to why the Founders supported the use of martial law. Its exercise held the citizen soldier to a higher judicial standard to remind him of his duty to the nation and the populous.

Furthermore, Vattel differed from the Founders' views because he did not fear giving a commander "unlimited" and "absolute" power over the army. The Founders would simply cite the examples of Caesar, James II, Cromwell, and Charles II to argue against Vattel in this regard. It must be remembered that although Washington was the overwhelming majority's favorite to act as commander-in-chief, his selection was primarily a result of his firm belief in political subordination to the civil authority. Even his well intended actions to unify the colonial militias under his command were superseded by Congress.[157] Too prevalent were the fears that permitting extensive authority in one man would undermine the political structure of a republic. Despite these differences in opinion on the exercise of martial law, the Founders still found its exercise to be essential. They just preferred to require more limitations.

It would be unfair to say there did not exist any additional limits on the exercise of martial law under the theories of Vattel and Aquinas. Vattel also conditioned the exercise of martial law on the right of making war. A nation could only make war when it was just or when "nature givens men a right to employ force," such as "when it is necessary for their defence, and for the preservation of their rights."[158] Here the nation only possessed the authority to exercise martial law when a situation of "just war" existed. Only through a "just war" could one derive "all his right from the justice of his cause."[159]

Aquinas never explicitly conditioned one's duty to obey a commander's martial law on the justness of war. He did, nonetheless, define three principles by which a war would be considered just. First, a just war could only be waged by the authority of the sovereign or the nation. Second, a "just cause is required, namely that those who are attacked should be attacked because they deserve it on the account of some fault." Last, it is necessary that when one attacks, that they have "rightful intervention" or that they "intend the advancement of good, or the avoidance of evil."[160]

Vattel's "just war" principles did not differ that much from those of Aquinas. He too limited war to being waged by either the sovereign or nation. He makes no mention of individuals or a body of people waging war against another nation or sovereign. He makes clear that those who made up the military forces could do nothing without the "express or tacit command or their officers."[161] This holds true especially during times of conflict. The individuals that made up the military were to act as nothing more than "instruments at the hands of their commanders." Unless orders were expressly given, an individual was to leave no room for presumption. Given an individual may always act in self-defense,[162] but outside of this one's obligation to the military was to be "strict, as martial law expressly forbids acting without orders."[163]

This was not to say the nation did not have a duty to the citizens that made up its military. Vattel does mention it was unwise for a sovereign or nation to unjustly expose the citizens to the calamities of war. For those who have the power to make war must always consider "its terrible effects, its destructive and unhappy consequences — to only undertake it under the most cogent reasons." It is here that Vattel was reminding the sovereign and the nation of its duty — to do its utmost in looking out for the citizens by carefully making war. He believed just as it was lawful that a sovereign or nation compel its citizens to go to war, it was also lawful for citizens to revolt against a sovereign or nation that "lavished the blood" of the people. To expose the people to the "calamities of war" when the sovereign or nation has the "power to maintain them in the enjoyment of an honourable and salutary peace" was unjust.[164]

Yet individuals could not immediately determine whether a conflict or danger was unjust. The consequences of such a privilege were too large if the people were able to weigh every action of the nation, the justice of its reasons, "and refuse to march to a war which might to them appear unjust."[165] Only until there is "clear and absolute evidence" to the contrary, it was the duty of the people to suppose the actions of the nation "just and wise."[166] If the nation "decides all the disputes of its citizens, represses violence," and checks every attempt of vigilante justice, it possessed the right to use those citizens as a means to protect the whole.[167] Even if the nation does not fully disclose its reasons as to why it is using its people for a conflict, there needs to exist a trust.[168]

This brings us to Aquinas' second principle upon which a just war may be waged. It holds that in order for war to be "just," a nation must be attacked or under threat of attack. Vattel dually supports this, stating the "just" object of war is to "avenge or prevent injury."[169] A defensive war was considered "just" because its purpose was to "protect [people] from injury, by repelling an unjust violence." This did not mean that all defensive wars are "just." A defensive war is only "just" when "made against an unjust aggressor." This is because self-defense is not only a right, but also the "duty of a nation and one of her most sacred duties."[170] Now, if the aggressor has "justice on his side," then there exists no "just" right to make a defensive war — for the aggressor is exerting his "lawful right" by taking arms "to obtain justice which was refused to him." In this circumstance it is actually unjust for the other nation or sovereign to repel by force because the aggressor is acting in "exertion of his right."[171]

Meanwhile, an offensive war is considered as "just" on virtually the same principle. It is "just" when there is "injury, either done or threatened."[172]

When actual injury has been "done" is much easier to determine than when injury out of "threat" occurs. There is no question injury that is "done" could become the subject of debate, but traditionally international rules and standards have governed this area. Therefore, injury that is "done" need not be further addressed. Moreover, when injury is "done" there can be no question about the use of martial law on an assembled militia. The militia is being assembled to repel a physical threat or injury.

It is when injury is threatened that it may become a philosophical and moral concern. For threat alone does not make offensive war "just." Vattel addresses this concern by stipulating injury by "threat" on two conditions. Not only must the nation have "good grounds to think [itself] threatened," it must also be "accompanied by the will."[173] In other words, the "threat" must be immediate and certain. This does not mean the nation is prevented from making preparations for a threat. The nation can always raise and maintain forces "as long as it thinks necessary."[174] Also, insofar that "every citizen is bound to serve and defend the nation as far as he is capable," it is for the nation to determine whom shall be exempt.[175]

In sum, according to Vattel and Aquinas, it is for the nation to determine who shall and who shall not be subject to the regulations of martial law. It was always good policy for the nation to "distribute posts and employments in such manner, that [it] may be most effectually served in all its affairs."[176] Individuals in positions such as the clergy, administration, or justice generally better served the nation's interests outside of military service. Nevertheless, such a determination is supposed to be always left for the nation. Although the people are free to usurp unjust government, there needs to be an initial trust — a trust that government is acting for the benefit of the people as a whole. In the case of the United States, the federal government embodies this notion of trust. It is acting to protect the people through its legislative, judicial, and executive authority. This makes it the duty of the people to defend the same government that protects them. In order to best accomplish this, the people must be formed into an organized military force or, as the Framers' intended, a well-organized and disciplined militia. With this comes government ordered military regulations, what was known in the eighteenth century as martial law.

This is what the Framers were referring to when they drafted the phrase, "A well-regulated militia necessary to the security of a free State." A "well-regulated militia" cannot exist without martial law. Almost every legal commentator, both prior to and after the adoption of the Constitution, attested to that certainty. While there clearly existed some fear among the Founders that too much military regulation creates a militaristic society, there also developed a virtual consensus that martial law was imperative. As the American Revolution perfectly shows, the Founders initially attempted to make their martial law regulations comparative to the common law jury system. This experiment utterly failed. Inevitably, strict military discipline and regulation became paramount to success in the conflict with England. There is no denying that American militias had been exposed to the British Articles of War prior to the conflict. It was just initially hoped such strict regulation would not be needed, something the Founders quickly came to realize as being naive. For without martial law the military was useless.

# CHAPTER FIVE

# "In Defence of Themselves and the State"

The Supreme Court majority claimed it was heavily influenced in coming to its individual right interpretation from contemporary "bear arms" provisions in state constitutions. Their main argument revolves around the fact that nine states' "bear arms" constitutional provisions — written between the eighteenth and the first two decades of the nineteenth century — included either the right of the people to "bear arms in defence of themselves and the State" or "bear arms in defence of himself and the State." The majority stated that this fact makes it clear that the Second Amendment protects more than the right to carry a weapon in an organized military unit, not an inaccurate assumption. The majority failed to do any research on the states' "bear arms" provisions and so, in effect, were purely making unsupported and speculative inferences. If they had done any research, the majority would have came to a different interpretation altogether.

In particular the majority came to the conclusion that the Second Amendment protects a right to self-defense from these state provisions. It argued that the phrases "defence of themselves" or "defence of himself" denote an individual's right to use a firearm for self-defense. There is no debating the phrase "defence of themselves and the State" was contemporaneous with the Second Amendment. By 1802, the Pennsylvania,[1] Vermont,[2] Kentucky,[3] and Ohio[4] Constitutions had all adopted this language. It is the "defence of himself and the State" provisions that are questionable in understanding the Second Amendment. These provisions did not come along until 1817 with the inception of the Mississippi[5] Constitution. Connecticut[6] and Alabama[7] would follow suit by adopting similar wording in their respective constitutions, but these provisions were not drafted until thirty years after the adoption of the Second Amendment. Therefore, these "bear arms" provisions can hardly be called contemporaneous with the Second Amendment.

Furthermore, it is important that each state's constitutional provision be given individual consideration. It is just too dangerous to lump together these provisions without understanding the rights they were drafted to protect. It is a huge judicial error to assume the states' that incorporated the "defence of himself and the State" provisions protect an individual's right to own and use a gun for self-defense. One must look into the respective state's statutory provisions, legal history, drafting debates, and other legislative history surrounding its right to "bear arms." It is particularly surprising that any justice on the Supreme Court, let alone five of its members, would simplistically assume what these state constitutional provisions were meant to protect without even examining them.

One could just as easily assume a more limited interpretation. For example, the "defence of himself and the State" provisions are only protecting the right to "bear arms." Therefore, it could be just as easily inferred that the usage of "right to bear arms" in these states was limited to a military connotation. While this interpretation makes sense to collective right interpreters, to infer what that right was meant to protect without examining its history is not judicially viable. In order to make an accurate interpretation, it is always necessary to examine the provision's history.

The Supreme Court majority was certainly right to give some deference to the phrase "defence of themselves and the State." The phrase was unquestionably incorporated in contemporaneous state constitutional provisions. Both Pennsylvania and Vermont had incorporated the phrase in their "bear arms" provisions prior to the adoption of the Constitution. Kentucky and Ohio also would include the phrase in their respective constitutions within the next fifteen years. Unfortunately, the Supreme Court majority made errors in their interpretation, assuming the words "defence of themselves and the State" was referring to an individual's natural right to self-defense. There exists no statutory history to support this assertion. In fact if anything, the statutory history disproves it. Nothing explains this better than the history of Ohio's "bear arms" provision.

Ohio's "bear arms" provision is particularly important because Ohio was at the forefront of the United States' western settlement. Its frontier was virtually uninhabited and posed many threats to new settlers. One would have to be constantly on the defensive for hostile Indian attacks, outlaws, wildlife, not to mention the western British garrisons. They were threats that Justice Kennedy brought up on multiple occasions during oral arguments. It seems that Kennedy was the swing vote in this regard. For he, like many individual right supporters, believed that the Second Amendment was partially drafted to protect settlers on the frontier. Yet a textual reading of the Second Amendment makes such an assertion ludicrous.

Nevertheless, Kennedy seemed convinced that the Second Amendment protected settlers on the frontier for self-defense purposes. When questioning Walter Dellinger, who was representing the District of Columbia, Kennedy asked if the Second Amendment "had nothing not do with the concern of the remote settler to defend himself and his family against hostile Indian tribes, outlaws, wolves and bears and grizzlies and things like that." Dellinger properly responded that this discourse was not part of the right to "keep and bear arms." This did not satisfy Kennedy, nor did it deter him from asking Paul Clement, who was representing the United States, a similar question. Clement was asked whether he was of the view that "this amendment has nothing to do with the right of the people living in the wilderness to protect themselves, despite an attempt by the Federal Government ... to take away their weapons?" Clement responded by saying, "I wouldn't say that it has no application there," but he provided no supporting evidence. This is exactly what Kennedy wanted to hear. He had even stated in oral arguments that *Miller* was insufficient in describing "the interests that must have been foremost in the framers' minds." Kennedy believed the Framers of the Second Amendment "were concerned about guns being taken away from the people who needed them for their defense."

The problem with Kennedy's line of thinking is that he assumes the Second Amendment was drafted to protect the natural right of self-defense. There is nothing in the debates or ratification proceedings that support this assertion. There is no disagreeing that the federal government promoted individual firearm ownership to protect the Western frontier, but there is nothing to insinuate this was the purpose of the Second Amendment. The strongest argument against this assertion is that the Second Amendment inadvertently was meant to protect the rights that Ohio's "bear arms" provision affords. It is argued that the history of Ohio's settlement, coupled with its "right to bear arms in defence of themselves and the State," shows the Second Amendment was intended to protect individual firearm use as a defense of an individual's safety and property. As will be shown, this too constitutes a historical and legal assumption, and nothing in this history supports such an assertion.

## Article I, Section 4, of the 1802 Ohio Constitution

Out of the first seventeen state constitutions, up to 1802, only Ohio and three others incorporated a provision that protected the "right to bear arms in defence of themselves and the state." The other states include Vermont, Pennsylvania, and Kentucky. Out of the remaining thirteen states up to that time, only three others protected some form of the "right to bear arms." These states included Tennessee,[8] North Carolina,[9] and Massachusetts.[10] These latter states' "right to bear arms" provision was different from the Ohio and the preceding three in that they only protected that right in the "defence of the State" or in the "common defence." There was no mention of the word "themselves" in any of these states' provisions. Therefore, through a natural reading it has been assumed that these latter states' provisions offer slightly less of a constitutional protection to "bear arms" than those such as Ohio.

Meanwhile, up to 1802, the remaining ten states chose not to adopt such a provision. Georgia,[11] New York,[12] and New Jersey[13] opted out because they each chose not to adopt a bill of rights in their respective constitutions. Meanwhile, the states of Delaware,[14] New Hampshire,[15] Maryland,[16] South Carolina,[17] and Virginia[18] did have bills of rights, with Rhode Island and Connecticut[19] choosing to adopt no constitution at all. Thus, when their constitution was adopted in 1802, Ohio was in the minority. It was one of only seven states that gave its citizens the "right to bear arms," and in order to understand exactly what this right was meant to afford, a historical and textual analysis is of vital importance.

Now, while only three of United States original thirteen states adopted a "right to bear arms" provision in their respective constitutions up to 1802, it is interesting that the next four states to be incorporated, including Ohio, would all make an inclusion. Accordingly, out of the next five states to be incorporated into the Union, four would also adopt such a provision.[20] It is uncertain as to why this "right to bear arms" movement in new state constitutions began, but it is not surprising that Ohio incorporated such a provision. The framers of the Ohio Constitution drafted the document in less than a month. Time was of the essence to reach statehood. Instead of drafting their own constitution, which would have taken up a substantial amount of time, the Ohio framers chose to adopt other states' constitutional provisions. They were particularly influenced by the structure and provisions within the Tennessee and Kentucky constitutions. Given both of these states chose to include a "right to bear arms," it is not unexpected that Ohio's Constitution included it as well. In fact, Ohio adopted their provisions verbatim. Unfortunately for historians and legal scholars there is no other evidence suggesting why the "right to bear arms" in Ohio was adopted. One would hope the journal of the 1802 Ohio Constitutional Convention would offer some insight into answering this question. Although this is not the case, there are methods that can help answer what the "right to bear arms" in Ohio was meant to afford — the most plausible being a textual and statutory analysis.

Just like the United States Constitution, the Ohio Constitution was a legal document that established the structure of government while providing individual safeguards to the people. What's more, just as a textual and statutory analysis of the Second Amendment affirms the "right to keep and bear Arms" was not intended to protect individual firearm ownership, the same holds true regarding Ohio's 1802 provision protecting the "right to bear arms for the defense of themselves and the State." Comparing the two side by side, Ohio's provision lacks the right to "keep" arms, but unlike the Second Amendment it defines under what circumstances one may "bear arms." It is the circumstances "for defense of themselves and the state" which have been interpreted by individual right theorists and the Supreme Court majority as constitutionally protecting individual gun ownership. This point notwithstanding, these words have little meaning outside of the protection the Second Amendment affords.

This is because the operating phrase, "bear arms," does not equate in definition to "ownership" or "possession." If the Ohio "right to bear arms" provision was meant to be defined as such, its framers would have incorporated the words "furnish," "provide," "own," or "possess" to denote individual protection to gun ownership. Furthermore, there is no evidence to suggest the Ohio framers meant "bear" to be synonymous with "carry." Thus, outside of any evidence that supports the individual right theory in Ohio, it is clear that "bear arms" does not equate in meaning to individual gun ownership. Lastly, even the Supreme Court majority admits "the Constitution was written to be understood by the voters; its words and phrases were used in their normal and ordinary usage as distinguished from technical meaning."[21] The normal meaning of "bear arms" was originally to use arms in a military capacity in defense of their person and the state when emergencies shall arise. There is no evidence to counter this interpretation; every man was aware of his duty to serve in the militia and aware of his duty to read and comply with their state's militia laws. That is the normal and ordinary meaning.

Just as "bear arms" had not been used in any of the preceding sixteen states' laws to denote anything except for the use of arms in military or militia service, the same holds true in the case of Ohio. Up to the 1851 — the year of the Ohio Constitutional Convention — where the "right to bear arms" provision would be altered for the first and final time, the use of guns was commonly regulated in Ohio's statutes governing crimes and punishments, hunting, and gun laws. As will be shown in each of these regulatory areas, there is nothing that substantiates that the meaning of "bear arms" equates to "carry arms" or a right to individual gun ownership.

## Crimes and Punishments

In 1788, the first act governing "crimes and punishments" was adopted by the Ohio legislature.[22] Not only would it be the basis for every eighteenth and nineteenth-century Ohio statute governing the subject, but it also provides insight in understanding what would become Article VIII, Section 20, of the 1802 Ohio Constitution. First, in describing the crimes involving the use of weapons or arms, at no time is the word "bear" incorporated. Thus, when one uses or carries weapons during the commission of a crime, it can be inferred that one is not "bearing arms." For example, in describing what constitutes robbery, the law reads "[w]hoever shall commit such robbery with personal abuse or violence, or be armed at the time with any dangerous weapon or weapons so as clearly to indicate an intention of violence, he, she or they so offending" is guilty of the "second instance of burglary."[23]

Second, the act's description of what constituted self-defense did not incorporate the word "bear." It stated, "if any person in the just and necessary defence of his own life, or the life of any other person, shall kill or slay another person [who] attempted to rob or murder in the field or highway, or to break into a dwelling house, if he cannot with safety to himself otherwise take the felon or assailant, or bring him to justice, he shall be holden guiltless."[24] The Ohio legislature would have incorporated "bear" in this act to denote protection of "themselves" if Article VIII, Section 20, was meant to protect such a right. It was clearly not, however. The reason "bear" was not included in this act or any subsequent acts on self-defense was because one did not "bear arms" when carrying out this right of common law.

Lastly, the act's description of what constituted treason did not incorporate the word "bear" either. This section of the act corresponds with the preceding sixteen states' use of what words were used to denote acquisition, ownership or possession or arms — "provide" and "furnish." It stated that, if anyone shall be found "furnishing ... enemies with arms, ammunition, or provisions, or any articles for their aid or comfort," they shall be deemed guilty of treason.[25] As with the preceding two examples in this law, there is no evidence to suggest "bear arms" was used to describe any other act but using arms in a military or militia service.

Over the next sixty-three years, the legislature adopted no significant changes in the description of any of these crimes nor substituted the word "bear" in later drafts.[26] In fact, the legislature would expand its list of what constituted as crimes in later drafts, some of which are notable to dismiss the individual right belief that "bear" was synonymous with "carry" or "ownership" when referring to firearms. In 1805, the legislature included the crime "assault with intent to commit rape" to its list. It read if "any person shall, with force and arms, and actual violence ... assault ... the body of any female with the intent to commit rape," they would be imprisoned for two years.[27] The act also included a law against dueling.[28] It stipulated "if any person shall willfully or knowingly carry or deliver any written challenge, or verbally deliver any message purporting to a challenge, or be present at fighting a duel," such person could be found guilty of dueling.[29] In 1815, the legislature included an act against shooting or stabbing with the intent to kill. It stated, "if any person shall shoot, stab, or shoot at any other person with intent to kill, wound or maim, every person" shall be convicted thereof.[30]

Much like the preceding three examples concerning robbery, self-defense, and treason, the laws concerning rape, dueling, and shooting, or maiming did not incorporate the word "bear," nor would they in any subsequent publications. Thus from the totality of examples regarding the use of arms in crimes — including self-defense, one could never claim any person was "bearing arms" in the commission of a crime or in protecting one's self.

### Hunting

As has already been addressed in examining "bear arms" in the Second Amendment, it was common practice for every state to regulate hunting within their respective territories. Ohio's first act to address the subject was adopted in 1799. Like other states that chose to make Sundays a day of religious observance, Ohio made it illegal for any person "to be found reveling, fighting, or quarreling, doing or performing any worldly employment or business, whatsoever."[31] The act also addressed hunting, stipulating that no one "shall be found hunting or shooting."[32] Subsequent acts regulating hunting on Sundays would all use similar language.[33] In none of these acts was the word "bear" incorporated to describe the act of hunting. Therefore, just as none of the previous sixteen states' legislatures had described the act of hunting or shooting as a form of "bearing arms," Ohio's legislature followed suit.

### Ohio's First Gun Law

Ohio's first gun law was passed by the legislature in 1790 and was included in a multifaceted act entitled *An act for suppressing and prohibiting*

*every species of gaming for money or other property, and for making void all con-*
*tracts and payments made in consequence thereof, and also for restraining the*
*disorderly practice of discharging fire arms at certain hours and places.* As the
act implies in its title, it addressed the negligent discharging of firearms in
populated areas such as "streets and [in the] vicinity of cities, towns, villages, and stations," but it also made it illegal to discharge firearms in such
places at night.[34]

The purpose of the act was to ensure the safety of Ohio's citizens, since
the negligent use of arms could result in the loss of life. It stipulated:

> That if any person shall presume to discharge or fire, or cause to be discharged
> or fired, any gun or other fire-arms at any mark or object, or upon any pre-
> tence whatever, unless he or she shall at the same time be with such gun or
> fire-arms at the distance of at least one quarter of a mile from the nearest
> building of any such city, town, village or station, such person shall for every
> such offence, forfeit and pay to use of the county in which the same shall be
> committed, a sum not exceeding five dollars, nor less than one dollar. And if
> any person being within a quarter of a mile of any city, town, village or station
> as aforesaid, shall at the same time willfully discharge or fire any gun or fire-
> arms, or cause to procure the same to be discharged or fired, at any time after
> the setting of the sum and before the rising of the same, he or she so offend-
> ing, shall in like manner pay to the use aforesaid, a sum not exceeding five dol-
> lars, nor less than one dollar....[35]

At no time in this provision was the word "bear" incorporated. Individual right supporters will be sure to point out this act did not address the
"carrying" or "ownership" of arms, and therefore "bear" would need not be
incorporated. Although this argument would seem valid on its face, it loses
any standing in the act's next provision. The act's drafters were sure to protect certain types of firearm discharges by stipulating:

> That nothing herein contained shall be deemed or construed to extend to any
> person lawfully using fire-arms as offensive or defensive weapons, in annoying,
> or opposing a common enemy, or defending his or her person or property, or
> the person or property of any other, against the invasions or depredations of an
> enemy, or in support of the laws and government; or against the attacks of
> rebels, highwaymen, robbers, thieves, or other unlawfully assailing him or her,
> or in any other manner where such opposition, defence, or resistance is
> allowed by the law of the land.[36]

This provision makes it clear that the act did not intend to prevent the
lawful use of arms under the common law, such as in defense of one's person or property. Also notice its use of the word "lawfully." At no time does
it describe the use of firearms as a constitutional or natural right. The use
of "lawfully" implies that it was for the lawmakers to determine what was

allowable. There is not any mention of the kinds a firearm usage that would allegedly be constitutionally protected. More importantly, the act also makes it clear that the drafters did not use the word "bear" in describing any of the lawful actions one may employ when using firearms. If using one's arms in defense of their person or property denoted "bearing arms," the drafters of this act would have worded it as such. However, that was not the case, because "bearing arms" did not extend to actions such as self-defense or in protection of their property. Thus, just as each of the other examples have shown, Ohio's first gun law illustrates "bearing arms" was limited in scope, that is, it only applied to one's ability and duty to perform military or militia service to the State.

## The Ohio Militia in Understanding the "Right to Bear Arms"

When the original thirteen colonies of the United States began establishing their respective militias, each had to face many obstacles and go through numerous changes in its laws in order make the system remotely effective. Ohio's militia was no different. Its first militia law did not even address who was to provide or furnish the required arms and accoutrements. It only required "all male inhabitants of the age of sixteen and upwards" to be "armed, equipped and accoutered" with a "musket and bayonet, or rifle."[37] It was an oversight the legislature quickly corrected. Five months later it established a fine for those men that neglected to "furnish himself with arms, accoutrements and ammunition, agreeably to the requirements of the said law."[38] The new law not only established different fines for failing to provide certain arms and accoutrements, but it also established a system by which inspections of such arms and equipment was to occur.[39] Steadily, Ohio was making efforts to transform its citizenry into an efficient fighting force.

Although Ohio's first militia law was rudimentary compared to the laws of the other states in the Union, it does provide us with the Ohio framers' philosophy as to why a militia was paramount to the success of the young state. Hence, the forming, training, and disciplining of the Ohio militia was deemed significant because it "conduces to health, civilization, and morality." More importantly, it was thought that "assembling without arms in a newly settled country may be attended with danger."[40] Given the new country's Western border, Ohio was in perpetual danger of invasion by either the French, British or Indians. It made sense that not only Ohio's militia be in a constant state of readiness but also be properly armed and accoutered to handle any threat. Owing to Ohio's need to be properly armed to fend off potential dangers, it seemed to be a plausible argument that Article VIII, Section 20, of Ohio's 1802 Constitution was drafted as a means to ensure the safety of the territory by protecting individual arms ownership. While this argument may seem historically valid on its face, it (1) does not explain why "bear" was incorporated instead of "own," "possess," "furnish," or "provide," and (2) upon a closer examination of Ohio's militia it can be seen there is no evidence to suggest that the legislature's early desire that every man "furnish himself" with the proper arms and accoutrements was anything more than a security policy of the state.

Since the first argument as to why Article VIII, Section 20, does not protect individual firearm ownership has already been addressed, an historical analysis of Ohio's militia will only need to be provided. Many contemporary courts, including the Supreme Court majority in *Heller*, have interpreted the 1792 National Militia Act as superseding all of the states' militia laws. They are not alone. For even a small minority of early nineteenth-century politicians thought this way. These individuals believed the state militia laws could not vary from their federal counterpart. This was not true, though. As Mr. Varnum communicated to Congress in 1803 after much debate on whether the 1792 National Militia Act should be altered, it was only "calculated to ensure a complete national defence, if carried into effect by the State Governments, agreeably to the power reserved to the States respectively."[41] What Varnum was stating was national defense was something every state must take steps to contribute to. The federal government was only authorized to "lay the foundation of a militia system, on the broad basis prescribed by the constitution."[42] Any deficiencies in "organization, arming, and discipline of the militia" was not from "any defect in that part of the system which [was] under the control of Congress, but from the omission on the part of State Governments."[43]

In 1806, the problem would resurface. A contingent of states was in favor of restructuring the militia into a class system. This time it was proposed that the burden to serve in the militia should fall primarily upon the male population between the ages of eighteen and twenty-six years.[44] It was proposed because one of the main problems the states faced in complying with the 1792 National Militia Act was getting their citizens to provide the proper arms and accoutrements. It had become too burdensome for every man to furnish and keep the required items serviceable. Again, Mr. Varnum communicated to Congress the inconsistencies of changing the current system in favor of a program that burdened only a distinct class of its citizens. Not only would such a program "be deemed a departure from the principle of distributive justice," but he also reminded his fellow delegates the problem did not rest with the federal government, but with the states.[45] For the "powers necessary to produce an efficient militia are divided between the General Government and the State Governments."[46]

By 1810, states that had not altered or supplemented their respective militia laws to fine individuals for non-attendance during musters once again appealed to the federal government for something to be done. It was believed Congress or the president would finally step in to correct the deficiency. This time a committee of the president reported to the Senate, but the end result did not change. Mr. Smith delivered the report, stating "no authority is delegated to Congress to regulate fines for non attendance." If the states were "anxious for an effective militia, to them belong the power, and to them too belong the means of rendering the militia truly our bulwark in war, and our safeguard in peace."[47] For whatever reason, the state legislatures did not act accordingly. The issue would remain unsettled. It would not be until certain events took place during the War of 1812 that it would be finally resolved.

Prior to the British attacking in that conflict, there was a disagreement between the States of Massachusetts, Connecticut, Rhode Island[48] and the President as to when the latter could call the states' militia into service. Massachusetts argued that, if the people of a state "appear to be under no apprehension of an invasion," it did not have to assemble its militia in defense of the national government.[49] The matter was so serious that three Supreme Court Justices would write to the Massachusetts governor on the subject. Justices Parsons, Sewall, and Parker would inform the governor that the Constitution not only granted the president to be commander-in-chief of the army of the United States, but that he also is "declared to be Commander-in-Chief of the militia of the several States."[50] The Justices' rationale was that, although the power to determine when "exigencies do in fact exist" to call upon the militia is not delegated by the Constitution "nor prohibited by it, to the States, it is reserved to the States respectively; and, from the nature of the power, it must be exercised by those with whom the States have ... entrusted the chief command of the militia."[51] Implicit here is that since the states had granted the power of commander-in-chief to the president, the latter had the authority to determine under what emergencies he may call upon the states' militias.

Following the war, another event gives insight into the powers the states had over the organization and governing of its militia. This time there were debates regarding when the president may call in the militia for the national defense, and if the president could command, or delegate command of, the states' militias when not actually in the field of battle.[52] This time, Secretary of War James Monroe gave his decision on federal versus states' rights over the militia.

Monroe opened by informing the state governments that he had always respected the rights of the individual states, "believing that the preservation of those rights, in their full extent, according to the just construction of the principles of our constitution, is necessary to the existence of our Union, and of free government in these States."[53] He reminded the states that the federal government may only govern "such part of them as may be employed in the service of the United States."[54] When these instances occurred, they were specified in the Constitution[55] and it is undoubtedly a "complete" and "unconditional" power granted to the federal government.[56] To interpret the Constitution otherwise "would be to force the United States to resort to standing armies for all national purposes." Such a "policy so fraught with mischief, and so absurd, ought not to be imputed to a free people in this enlightened age."[57]

Monroe's decision on the matter seemed to give the states very little autonomy, if any, over the functioning of their militias, but his final remarks reminded all concerned of the concurrent power between the federal and the state governments. Monroe only interpreted the Constitution as the federal government controlling the militia when "employed in the service of the United States,"[58] with no exceptions. For there was a reason the Union was divided into states, or in reference to the militia — military districts. Military districts were intentionally defined boundaries "for the purpose of prescribing a limit to the civil duties, if they may be so called, rather than the military."[59] What Monroe was articulating was every state had its own militia to handle its own internal threats. It was when there was an "invasion by a large force" that "all limitations of boundary ... would cease," hence requiring the intervention of the federal government.

Joseph Pearson summed up the issue best when he wrote, "The constitution gives to the general government no control over the militia of the several states, except in three cases viz — to repel invasion, suppress insurrections, and aid in the execution of the laws of the U[nited] States."[60] Pearson could not be more on point because he was almost directly citing the Constitution. For Article I, Section 8, only provided Congress with the power to call forth the militia to "execute the Laws of the Union, suppress insurrections and repel invasions."[61]

This legislative history as to whether the state and federal government may each exercise power over the states' militias is largely significant. It shows there existed concurrent power between the state and federal government. While Congress may pass legislation for organizing and disciplining the federal militia, the state would be operating within its constitutional power if it chose to organize its militia to operate in a manner much different than what Congress prescribed. For example, a state may decide its militia will only consist of men between the ages of twenty-one and twenty-six or decide that its militia be equipped with arms different than those required by the National Militia Act of 1792. It also may decide all the militia's arms be provided by the state. None of these examples would violate the Constitution nor impede on congressional authority over the federal militia system. This is because the state would be operating on the premise of its police power which had been traditionally reserved to it. Where a conflict in power may only occur is if the state did not conform to congressional militia laws when it was required to assemble a militia in defense of the United States. It is under this condition in which the states' militias would have to draft and organize according to the federal standard.

The majority of states chose not to deviate from the federal standard, however, and it was for good reason. This is because operating a militia different than the federal government prescribed would prove expensive and confusing to a state's constituents. In fact, after 1792, most states actually reorganized their militia laws to conform to the federal standard. Needless to say, this did not mean every state failed to adopt its own unique laws. For example, some states took efforts to supply their militia with the required arms and accoutrements, while others chose to stay true to the National Militia Act and require each man enrolled to furnish his own. Furthermore, some states passed laws to supply poor persons with arms. The differences are significant because it shows the states had their own militia laws outside the federal prescribed standard.

This concurrent power is especially significant in understanding the "right to bear arms" in Ohio. In order to understand the rights afforded by Article VIII, Section 20, of the 1802 Ohio Constitution, one need not look further than Ohio's militia laws. Herein the Ohio legislature was free to offer whatever restrictions or protections to its militia, its citizens "right to bear arms," and determine how expansive that right may be. More importantly, just as individual right supporters have wrongfully argued the National Militia Act's requirement that every man enrolled provide his own arms was evidence that the Second Amendment protected individual gun ownership, the same could be argued regarding Ohio's militia laws. Therefore, Ohio's militia laws need to be examined to determine whether such an argument would have any validity in understanding Ohio's "right to bear arms." As will be shown, just as the National Militia Act's arming requirement was nothing more than a reflection of the nation's security policy, Ohio's militia laws, which initially also required individuals provide their own arms, similarly served to promote nothing more than the state's security.

What was unique about Ohio's early militia laws was that its provisions required all men enrolled, that assembled for public worship, to "arm and equip himself according to law in the same manner as if he were marching to engage the enemy."[62] It was the first militia law in the entire United States since Georgia's 1757 law[63] that required the militia to bring its arms to worship. While Georgia's philosophy behind such a law was to deter slave insurrections, Ohio had outlawed the institution of slave ownership but had a similar rationale for the act's adoption. Just as Southerners believed times of worship were opportune times for slave insurrections, Ohioans believed times of worship were opportune times for Indian attacks. Accordingly, the law's purpose was to have its citizenry required to be armed during its most vulnerable state. Moreover, with much of Ohio's population scattered throughout the countryside, it proved difficult to muster and train the militia without interfering with one's day-to-day business. As a result, and given most men would already be attending Sunday worship, it made sense that this would also be an opportune time to train and discipline the militia as well. While it was illegal for men to conduct business on Sunday, the legislature was sure to provide an exception to militia training. Ohio's first gun law reminded its citizenry that although it was illegal to discharge firearms within the vicinity of villages, cities, and towns, nonetheless "that nothing herein contained shall be construed or extend to prevent the necessary military exercise."[64]

The law requiring the militia to arm and equip at worship was not to be taken lightly. Winthrop Sargent, the first secretary of the Northwestern Territory, commented that the law should be attended "with most serious and melancholy consequences." This was because it "presents the opportunity to an enemy of the smallest degree of enterprise to effect such fatal impression upon our infant settlement as posterity might long in vain lament."[65] In fact, the entire militia system was something Ohio politicians did not take lightly, especially the Jeffersonian republicans. When the republicans were doing their utmost to remove Arthur St. Clair as governor, one of their grievances referred to the militia. It stated St. Clair had "[neglected and thereby] obstructed the organization and disciplining of a militia for the defense of the Territory, by withholding the appointment of officers eighteen months after a law had passed establishing them."[66]

Thomas Worthington had even commented to President Jefferson on the issue. He alleged St. Clair was an "open and avowed enemy to a republican form of government ... [and was] also an open and declared enemy to militia regulations, which declaration his practice hitherto has confirmed, as the militia in the Territory are without organization."[67] Jefferson took the charges seriously and had Albert Gallatin, the secretary of the treasury, and James Madison,[68] the secretary of state, look into the allegations. Regarding the militia, Gallatin found that although the acts "evince proper impartiality," the charge did "not seem to afford alone, sufficient grounds for removal."[69] Madison agreed, finding the charge to be "not established."[70]

What further raised Jefferson's suspicions against St. Clair was that the republicans had informed the president that the Ohio governor had been an outspoken critic of the militia, a system the president openly supported. St. Clair replied to these charges by admitting that he "did not treat our militia system very respectfully," but denied that he had not taken the proper measures for insuring they were properly armed, officered, and trained.[71] What's more, St. Clair admitted he had made some criticisms regarding the inadequate use of the militia. Where there was disagreement between St. Clair and the Jeffersonian republicans was where the latter claimed St. Clair had openly supported a standing army. St. Clair knew from where the charge was "deduced," but he had never outright stated the source. To clear his name, St. Clair requested George Todd, who had overheard his political rants, to affirm not "one disrespectful word of the President passed my lips."[72]

The charges that St. Clair had neglected the militia were completely unfounded. Just three years earlier, in 1799, the legislature had adopted a new militia law nearly six times as expansive as the first.[73] Notable changes included (1) changing the age minimum for enrollment from sixteen to eighteen years,[74] (2) exempting all arms and accoutrements provided from "all suits, distresses, executions or sales for debt,"[75] (3) increasing the fine for not appearing properly armed from fifty cents to "no less than one dollar and fifty cents,"[76] (4) requiring all fathers and guardians to be responsible for all arms, accoutrements, and fines for men enrolled under the age of twenty-one years,[77] (5) establishing a class system by which men enrolled would be drafted into service,[78] (6) providing the first detailed Articles of War for Ohio,[79] and, most importantly, regarding the use of arms, (7) incorporating the first poor person provision. This last change exempted individuals who were "unable to furnish and equip" themselves by remitting the fine until such person shall be able to "furnish and equip himself agreeably to law."[80] Three years later, in 1802, Ohio would include its first "scrupulous of bearing arms" provision. It allowed any person who took an oath stating they were "scrupulous of bearing arms or performing military duty" to pay a sum of "one dollar and twenty-five cents" to be exempted for a year.[81] No substantial alterations to the laws would be made over the next seven years.[82]

In 1809, the legislature made a few alterations. The state was now liable for all "arms, accoutrements, horses, and equipage" that individuals brought to the field with them. After such property was appraised, a certificate was granted with the amount of appraisement. If any of this property was ever lost, the state was required by law to provide compensation.[83] In addition to having one's property insured, the militia was also liable to have such articles impressed in times of need.[84] In 1813, another notable law appeared — rules regarding the use of public arms provided by the state and federal government. The law stipulated what actions the quarter-master general may take to ensure "all the public arms, ammunition, accoutrements, camp equipage and military stores were to be managed."[85]

The use of public arms would become essential to the defense and security of Ohio, especially given the state's serious lack of them. This lack of preparedness became more and more apparent and would eventually cause the federal government to intervene and establish a system that adequately supplied arms to all states deficient in them. When Jefferson assumed the presidency, he did so as a staunch supporter of the militia system. He would receive his first national returns of the militia in 1803. Given the returns had not included every state,[86] the results did not alarm him. A year later, though, when the majority of states had made their returns, he would write to the Senate and Congress "[their] incompleteness is much to be regretted, and its remedy may at some future time be a subject worthy the attention of Congress."[87] According to the report, out of the nearly 429,200 privates enrolled in the militia only 223,218 muskets and rifles were available.[88] That meant only 52 percent of the entire United States militia could be properly armed at any time. Furthermore, these returns did not include the states of Delaware, Maryland, and Tennessee — the last two states being known for lack of arms and accoutrements available for their respective militias. What were even more deplorable were the apparent deficiencies in the state of Ohio. Out of the nearly 4,900 men enrolled in its militia, only 2,171 muskets and rifles were available.[89]

Congress quickly inquired into the matter. Asking Secretary of War Henry Dearborn to submit a return of all the arms fit for use that was the property of the United States, the return showed 117,167 muskets and rifles,[90] still leaving the national government in a precarious situation. Although this raised the number of available rifles and muskets to 340,385, this would still leave 88,815 militiamen unarmed in case of war. In 1806 the numbers improved slightly. Out of the nearly 471,590 privates there existed 249,182 stands of arms — increasing the percentage of armed militia from 52 percent to 52.8 percent.[91] In Ohio, both the amount enrolled in the militia (8,031 privates) and the amount of arms (3,515) increased significantly as a result of westward expansion.[92] Unfortunately, the percentage of men enrolled with arms dropped slightly from 44.3 percent in 1804 to 43.7 percent in 1806.

A congressional committee looked into the matter to determine what was responsible for such a deficiency in arms. It was determined the issue was not that individuals were too poor or were unwilling to purchase the required arms by law; on the contrary, the problem laid in the fact that firearms were not readily available for sale.[93] By 1808, things had not improved. Maryland had only 1,200 arms available for its 39,047 militiamen; Virginia had only 13,500 arms for its 65,767 militia; with Massachusetts being statistically the best armed — 48,100 arms for its 70,323 militia.[94] Neither had Ohio's situation improved. The returns showed Ohio had only 5,869 arms for its 13,345 militia privates, meaning it had sustained growth of arms acquired per man enrolled — 44 percent.[95] Overall, the United States had 252,384 arms for the 636,386 militia, equating to only 39.7 percent of the federal militia [that] could be armed at any given time.[96]

Congress first acted by passing a bill authorizing the president[97] to procure more arms for the defense of the United States.[98] Mr. Burwell had brought forth the bill on the belief that "if this country possessed a sufficient number of arms, we are perfectly safe against the world."[99] He felt that "every country which anticipates attack should possess more arms than necessary to army any particular number of men that are likely to be called out at one time."[100] A month later, Congress would pass an additional arms act that was similar to the 1798 Arms for Militia Act.[101] Nevertheless, the problem remained that many of the states could not even purchase arms within their own country, for the federal government had already contracted with all the major armories, making it impossible for the armories to take on new contracts. This left the only option available to the states to purchase arms from foreign nations.[102] Such contracts were expensive and time-consuming, though. To resolve this problem Congress passed the Sale of Public Arms Act. It authorized the president to sell to the individual states "any arms now owned by the United States, and which may be parted without any injury to the public."[103]

The most important act[104] regarding arming the militia would be enacted just weeks after the Sale of Public Arms Act. The Arming the Whole Militia Act appropriated an annual sum of $200,000 for the "purpose of providing arms and military equipments for the whole body of the militia of the United States."[105] While the 1798 Arms for Militia Act and the recent Sale of Public Arms Act merely sold arms acquired by the federal government to individuals and the states, the new 1808 provision did not place the arms up for sale. Instead, the law authorized the president to purchase more sites to build weapon arsenals. The law also stipulated the amount of arms able to be procured by the annual sum[106] allotted was to be distributed "to each state and territory respectively, in proportion to the number effective militia in each state and territory."[107] It was left up to each state to devise the rules by which such arms were to be kept and distributed.[108]

Edwin Gray of Virginia was enthusiastic about the act's prospects. He would write, "Standing armies, everywhere destructive to liberty, must be peculiarly so in a country and government like ours, when the great mass of militia is left unarmed." It was important that Congress "place arms in the hands of all the people, dispersed over the face of the country, and [then] we can have little to fear from Foreign invasion of Domestic treason."[109]

Still, the act was the subject of much debate prior to being passed. The debates provide great insight into understanding the Second Amendment and the states' "right to bear arms" provisions. Similar to the eighteenth-century Congressional debates on the issue, the 1808 debates did not address the Second Amendment either. Mr. Randolph led the debates believing the bill would bring "permanency" to the people's freedom. He felt "it was not possible that a nation free and armed could have their liberties taken from them."[110] Notice Randolph does not cite the Second Amendment. He does not state the Arming the Whole Militia Act will ensure that the Second Amendment will be promoted. Neither does he nor did any other person up to that period in American history state that the Second Amendment was adopted to protect the other rights in the Bill of Rights. This is because the Second Amendment was never about individual gun ownership.

Randolph thought that only one issue remained to be debated on the Arming the Whole Militia Act — how the arms were to be distributed. While some thought that the states should distribute "these arms to the militia individually, others had said they could not consent to make them the property of individuals."[111] Whatever was decided, Randolph had "no objection to reimburse those citizens who have, under the laws of the respective States, provided their own arms."[112]

The first objection to having the states and federal government hold this new allotment of public arms was by Mr. Smilie. He argued that "to disarm the people at pleasure," whenever the government thought prudent, "would be an armed government still, but not an armed people."[113] He felt the people should want to arm so as to protect themselves and their property. Thus, the government should only provide arms for sale to the people.[114] Mr. Macon agreed with Smilie in principle but disagreed as to their distribution. Macon had long felt "it is the duty of the nation to arm the militia" because it is "wrong to make the poor man contribute the same mite towards the general protection as the rich man."[115] He would neither make the arms public property nor sell them to the people. He thought it best the government give the arms to every individual who would bear them "so that, whether a man moves from Maine to Georgia, or whether he shall always remain in the same place, the arms given to him shall be his absolute property."[116]

Mr. Findley objected to Macon's idea. Findley turned to the Pennsylvania militia as his example. He reminded the delegates that Pennsylvania had already been practicing the use of public arms to arm the militia, but the experiment had proved a failure. Thousands of public arms were lost, stolen, or no longer fit for service. Giving arms to individuals who have "no interest in taking care of them when their tour of duty is over" would only be a waste of spending.[117]

Mr. Randolph disagreed. To him, the purpose of giving individuals arms was so they may use and become familiar their functioning. It was paramount to have a militia that was properly trained, and how could an individual be properly trained in the use of arms if he did not possess them. Randolph urged his fellow delegates to "[p]ut arms in the hands of your militia" because if the arms are "worn out by use they may be replaced." The important thing was the "militiaman will have acquired experience at the expense of a musket, which I would not give for the tuition of all drill-sergeants in Europe."[118]

Mr. Lloyd saw the bill as "an evil" since it would be asking the people to give up the arms of the government after they had been distributed. He asked Congress, do you suppose "the people would be so unmindful of their own liberties that they would give up their arms at the discretion of the United States?" He further commented that once you arm the people, "they will not be so pusillanimous as to give up these arms, if they are to be converted to their own destruction."[119] Certainly Lloyd had a strong point. It was suspicious for the federal government to give and take away arms to the people at its pleasure—for this was the basis by which people feared the establishment of standing armies.

Mr. Holland was the only delegate to make a constitutional argument regarding the bill. He thought the bill should be dismissed. Holland knew the Constitution stated the militia "should be armed" when called into service, but "not that they should be supplied with arms."[120] The argument received no attention by the other members. In fact, Macon's earlier comment that it was the "duty of the nation to arm the militia" was more popular.[121] Mr. Rowan would comment even further, stating the "General Government should direct and control the use of arms." He could not see how their "efficiency will not be less derived from the General Government, than if they were purchased individually by the people."[122] Mr. Blackledge agreed. Although he had his quarrels with the bill, he stated, "In voting for this bill, I do it to recognize the principle that the General Government is to arm the militia."[123] At the end of the debates, the bill passed easily with 54 yeas and 33 nays.[124]

The Congressional act proved crucial in supplying arms for the Ohio militias. In January of that year the Ohio Legislature had already appealed to Congress for a loan of 7,000 arms.[125] Now the Arming the Whole Militia Act relieved them of this request. Actually if it was not for Ohio, and the frontier's need for arms, the act might not have passed. During the debates of the 1808 Purchase of Arms Act,[126] Mr. Burwell had reminded Congress "that we have an exposed frontier, liable to the attack of nations on our borders, and it is indispensably necessary that the inhabitants on our frontiers be armed."[127] Thus, many delegates saw Ohio and its frontier as essential in securing the United States from outside threats.

Unfortunately, although the public arms provision provided Ohio with arms by an act of Congress, this was nothing more than a piece of paper. The federal government had loaned Ohio 1,500 stands of arms in 1808,[128] but it would take almost a decade for the armories to manufacture the arms needed to secure the frontier. For the moment Ohio's territory would virtually remain unprotected. In 1811, Thomas Worthington would comment on the issue, including on the inefficiency of the Ohio militia. Worthington wrote to Sam Finley that Ohio was in a "very defenceless condition; without arms — without discipline, indeed without every resource except numbers; but what will numbers avail without arms unless in the possession of them."[129] How were men to be "brought to a knowledge of military duty by the use of Clubs and Cornstalks, which you know to the usual Substitutes in the Muster field." He felt if only the men had arms in their hands "they might be instructed — Measures might be adopted to enforce discipline."[130] Unfortunately, with "the arms being gone," Worthington knew "the interior is left defenceless."[131]

Much like the other states in the Union, Ohio's militia was primarily composed of men of the poorer classes. Men of wealth could simply recruit substitutes[132] to go in their place. It did not help that these men of poorer classes could not provide the required arms. There was no law requiring the person paying the substitute to provide arms and accoutrements for him as well.

By the eve of the War of 1812,[133] nearly four years after the passage of the Arming the Whole Militia Act, the returns of the militia's arms had not improved. It was reported to Worthington that the "deficiency of Arms &

accoutrements" is "very great, and those on hand being so various in their make & bore as to present but an indifferent barrier to an Invading Enemy." The author of this report was sure to remind Worthington that "this among other things is no doubt a great cause of alarm, not only along the frontier, but even in the Interior."[134] Duncan MacArthur would comment there existed "neither tents, blankets, axes, arms or ammunition" for use by the army let alone the militia.[135] In reality, their observations were correct. Out of the 29,183 men enrolled in 1812, only 14,673 arms were available.[136] The Ohio militia's problems ran much deeper than the need for arms and accoutrements, though, with the majority of the blame resting on the lack of an efficient militia law. While MacArthur was confident the Ohio legislature could fix the problem,[137] Sam Finley felt the problem rested in Congress. Finley felt if Congress spent less time on their speeches, and more time on the appropriate expenditures of the treasury, there might be arms to be distributed so the militia may become the "bulwark of our Country."[138] At one point Colonel Lew Cass suggested that the government should purchase the entire militia's arms and equipments as a "fair valuation." This would allow the arms to be "distributed among the community, to answer any valuable purpose of national defence."[139]

By 1813, something had to be done by the Ohio legislature. MacArthur had even commented to Worthington that the "credit of the militia is now destroyed."[140] Complaints were rampant and the campaigns were turning for the worse. John Sloane felt Ohio and the Northwestern Army was "doomed to experience nothing but disaster and disgrace where ever our arms are turned."[141] The Ohio legislature responded with the 1813 *An act for disciplining the militia.* It was the most expansive and detailed militia law to date and would be the basis of the next eighteen years of militia law.[142]

In the years to come, Ohio began adopting its public arms provisions as required by the Arming the Whole Militia Act. The first being adopted in 1815, required all persons holding such public arms to return them immediately.[143] In 1823, a law was passed that required the arms were to be only delivered to the militia "on days of training." At the close of such training, the arms were to be "returned and safely deposited."[144] Four years later, the legislature would request the arms be re-proportioned to the towns of Ripley, New Lisbon, and Mansfield. It was also encouraged that the commandants of the public arms inspect them "as often as they deem expedient."[145] By 1828, the public arms law had doubled in size.[146] More importantly it would ultimately give rise to an important change in the militia laws in the years to come — an elimination of the provision that every man furnish himself with his own rifle or musket.[147]

For nearly fifty years Ohio had required every person enrolled to furnish their own musket or rifle. The 1831 law changed this by only stipulating that "each non-commissioned officer and private, shall arm himself with a good and sufficient musket, rifle or fusee."[148] Although this wording suggests that every person was required to provide their own arms, for the first time the words "provide" or "furnish" were intentionally left out. This is evidenced by what was required by persons of all ranks in the cavalry. These individuals were required to "furnish" themselves with certain equipment, but only required to be "armed" with a "good and sufficient sword, a pair of pistols, and a cartridge box."[149] Nevertheless, the law still implied every man was required to provide the required arms. This is because a private was still liable to be fined twenty-five cents "for not attending muster with the proper arms and accoutrements."[150] This fine was miniscule, though, when comparing it to the maximum of six dollars, to the minimum one dollar and fifty cents, one was liable to be fined in 1799.[151] What's more, the fine could be easily dropped if the private could convince his commanding officer he was too poor to "furnish and equip himself agreeably."[152]

By 1844, it was decided that the "rank and file militia ... be dispensed with."[153] Every male inhabitant was still required to enroll,[154] but the State had decided to turn its defense over to volunteer militias. The militia system was not purely volunteer though, because every person that did not enroll in a volunteer company was required to either pay, in times of peace,[155] a fifty cents annual fee "as commutation for military duty" or perform "two days extra labor on some public highway in the road district in which he may reside."[156] In regards to arming, there was no provision requiring a private to furnish his own rifle or musket.[157] Although there was a fine of two to three dollars for "refusing to appear armed and equipped," this penalty was instituted for the "refusing to appear," not so much for the "fully armed and equipped" reference.[158] This is because the quartermaster general was responsible for distributing the public arms to "supply the volunteer militia."[159]

Thus, by 1844, Ohio had become the sole provider of arms for the defense of its borders. This would not be the only significant change regarding the Ohio militia. Even though, Ohio's own William Henry Harrison had stated in Congress in 1817 that the "safety of a republic depends as much on upon the equality in the use of arms amongst its citizens as upon the equality of rights" and "nothing can be more dangerous ... than to have a knowledge of the military art confined to a part of the people,"[160] he supported a select militia. Ohio soon would follow suit when its legislature began to do just this by classifying its militia. In 1831, while the state still required every man between the ages of eighteen and forty-five to enroll in the militia, those who had reached the age of thirty-five were exempt from mustering and training in times of peace.[161] By 1843, Ohio further classified its militia by exempting all persons under the age of twenty-one years from performance in the militia in times of peace.[162]

In summary, just as the history of the 1792 National Militia Act's clearly shows its arming requirement was nothing more than a national security policy, it is clear that Ohio's militia laws and history also illustrate its arming requirement served to promote nothing more than the state's security. It was Ohio's frontier that needed to be protected. Although Ohio and Congress clearly advocated that arms be readily available to all Ohioans, this was done as a defensive measure — not to promote Article VIII, Section 20, of the Ohio Constitution nor the Second Amendment. Given there are no historical, statutory, or legislative records indicating that Article VIII, Section 20, was meant to protect the right for an individual to own a firearm, any such interpretation is without proper foundation.

## The Protection That the "Right to Bear Arms" in the 1802 Constitution Affords

While the Supreme Court majority in *Heller* inferred the 1802 Ohio Constitution's "right to bear arms" provision promotes their individual right stance, nothing can be further from the truth. First it is important to address one of reasons the majority discarded the theory that Second Amendment was limited to protecting one's service in the militia. The majority argued if the Second Amendment only protected the right to serve in the militia, then Congress had the "plenary authority to exclude them," contending that the Second Amendment would be null and void under Congress's power to organize, arm, and discipline the militia. Congress would then have the power to create a select militia and supersede the "right to keep and bear arms."

The *Heller* majority's logic is unsupported. What the majority failed to examine and mention is the states' militias made up the federal militia. And it was the states' militias that were the bulwark of liberty. The majority had no trouble pointing out that the Constitution implies the militia was already in existence. There is no doubting it is an institution that predated the Constitution. They did not examine the concurrent powers between state and federal government, though. For if they had, it would have been made clear that at no point does the Constitution give the federal government the power to interfere with state militias, their intrastate function, or their militia laws. As Joseph Pearson so eloquently put it, "The constitution gives to the general government no control over the militia of the several states, except in three cases viz — to repel invasion, suppress insurrections, and aid in the execution of the laws of the United States."[163]

The truth is Congress only regulated the militia in service to the United States, and at no other times. It was even admitted by the leaders of federal government on multiple occasions that Congress had no authority to fine, imprison, or discipline individuals enrolled in the militia unless they were in actual service of the country at that time. To the states "belong the power, and to them too belong the means of rendering the militia truly our bulwark in war, and our safeguard in peace."[164] This was the significance of the Second Amendment. It aided in preventing the federal government from interfering with the function of state militias. It was important that the federal government not infringe the ability for the states to defend themselves. Because if the states were each unable to defend themselves, the Union would be defenseless.

Regarding the 1802 Ohio Constitution, the Supreme Court majority provides no evidence to suggest the phrase "bear arms" equated to anything but using arms in the military or militia service of the state. Of all the Ohio statutes up to 1851, only the militia laws ever used the phrase "bear arms."[165] Not in one instance did it appear in any other Ohio law nor is their evidence that the phrase "bear arms" had ever been used in any context outside of the manner equating to using arms in the military or militia service. This is because "bear arms" was understood to be a selective phrase, used only in the military or militia context.

Individual right advocates will point out the phrase that follows "bear arms" in the 1802 provision, which states "in defence of themselves and the State," supports "bear arms" was not intended to be limited to military service. For it is argued the word "themselves" was included to mean one may own and use arms for self-defense. As has already been pointed out in laws governing involuntary manslaughter and self-defense, the word "bear" or the phrase "bear arms" had never been used to describe such an act. Nevertheless, the Ohio courts have interpreted "defence of themselves and the state" as protecting such a right. Until the courts can provide a single example of any Ohio law stipulating the use of "bear" or the phrase "bear arms" in such an instance, Article VIII, Section 20, cannot be historically or textually interpreted to have protected such a right. This leaves open the question: "What does the 'right to bear arms' provision of the 1802 Ohio Constitution protect, and if it does not protect individual arm ownership is there a provision that does?"

In short, the 1802 "right to bear arms" provision does not protect individual firearm ownership. As has been shown through each of the states' laws, including Ohio's, an individual did not need to possess arms in order to "bear" them. Although it was believed by the Framers it was good practice to have arms in the hands of individuals who constituted the militia as a means to keep them well-trained and disciplined to their use, it was not a necessity for one to "bear arms." Arms being owned by the state could just as easily be borne as an individuals or as Mr. Rowan so eloquently put it, "efficiency [in arms] will not be less derived form the General Government, than if they were purchased individually by the people."[166]

In regards to the words "in defence of themselves and the State," when one was "bearing arms," they were doing just that, using arms in a military capacity to defend their liberties as well as the interests of the state that protected them. If the 1802 provision was meant to incorporate anything else, would not the drafters have worded the provision similar to Thomas Jefferson's three drafts of the 1776 Virginia Declaration of Rights — the third draft stipulating that "No freeman shall be debarred the use of arms [within his own lands or tenements]"?[167] It follows that if "bear" was meant to denote anything but the use of arms in military service, would not the Ohio framers have drafted the provision to read "furnish," "own," or "possess" instead of "bear"? Would not the framers have drafted the provision that read "in defence of themselves and the State" to read "in defence of themselves [or] the State"? Given none of these examples are the case, the 1802 "right to bear arms" provision cannot be given anything other than its textual meaning — the right to use arms to protect one's person, one's liberties, and the interests of the state in only a military or militia capacity.

Individual right supporters and the Ohio courts also have failed in interpreting the provision as not restricting the "right to bear arms" in a militia or military capacity because the word "militia" does not appear in it as it does in the Second Amendment.[168] Immediately following the "right to bear arms" rests the following, "and as standing armies in time of peace are dangerous to liberty, they shall not be kept up; and the military shall be kept under strict subordination to the civil power."[169] Although the "right to bear arms" in Ohio does not textually include the word "militia," this subsequent paragraph shows its drafters' purpose behind including the right in the 1802 Constitution: that the people need to have the right to use arms in a military capacity as a means to protect their person and liberties, the interests of the state, and to prevent the need for a standing army in times of peace. This last condition — to prevent the need for standing army in times of peace — is crucial in understanding the preceding "right to bear arms," for it represents the whole basis behind why that right was created to begin with, and until the courts and individual right advocates can show evidence to the contrary, this is not the case. By providing substantiated evidence to prove otherwise, Article VIII, Section 20, cannot be interpreted as meaning anything else.

This still leaves another question, "Is there any provision in the 1802 Constitution that protects or implies that Ohio citizens have the right to own firearms?" One argument can be made for the latter portion of Article VIII, Section 1, which states the people "at all times have the power to alter, reform, or abolish their government, whenever they may deem necessary."[170] It may be argued that the people have a constitutional right to be armed as a check on an abusive or oppressive government. Ever since the Glorious Revolution of 1689, it was a commonly held belief that the people have a right to usurp an unjust government — by force if need be. While the Ohio Constitution undoubtedly is reiterating the principle that unjust government should be abolished, in no way is it referring to force as the means to do so. In countless provisions, even before the drafting of the 1802 constitution, the legislature had passed acts making it illegal to assemble with arms, commit war or treason upon the state.[171]

This leaves the only remaining plausible argument — that one has a right to own firearms under the 1802 constitution, in the guarantee that "all men are born equally free and independent, and have certain natural, inherent, and unalienable rights; amongst which are ... acquiring, possessing, and protecting property."[172] This section provides the strongest argument for firearm ownership supporters. Unfortunately, given the state may regulate property to promote the wellness and safety of its citizenry, such ownership may be restricted. In fact, under the state's police power, it may even permanently prohibit firearm ownership as long as it followed Article VIII, Section 4, which stipulates, "private property ought and shall ever be held inviolate, but always subservient to the public welfare, provided a compensation in money be made to the owner."[173] Thus, prohibiting firearm ownership would not infringe upon the "right to bear arms" because an individual need not own arms to "bear" them.

Moreover, the state and federal government provided such arms at their discretion. Of course, a complete ban on firearms was never considered during the time the 1802 constitution was in effect. Such action would be deemed politically dangerous to the new republic and its safety. It would be a mistake to infer that the government could not have instituted such a ban. In fact, there is not one instance in the debates of Congress or Ohio, regarding arming the militia, where a delegate argued the taking away of the citizens' arms would be unconstitutional. During the debates there were instances where people saw such an action us unsavory or inadvisable, but never unconstitutional. It was just deemed politically improper to take away the citizens' arms, for such an action would heighten suspicions towards the danger of the government raising a standing army to suppress the populous.

## CHAPTER SIX

# Bearing Arms in the Ohio Constitution

Until the Second Amendment becomes incorporated under the Fourteenth Amendment, the states do not need to give the Supreme Court's holding in *Heller* any consideration. Certainly there will be state courts that interpret their respective "right to bear arms" provisions as synonymous with what the Supreme Court majority has held. Such borrowing of constitutional interpretation has been common practice, as is shown to be particularly true when comparing federal and state constitutional protections. This does not have to be the case, though.

It is significant that each state gives its constitution's "right to bear arms" provision its due force. Many states' provisions are unique. Many have revised the protections on multiple occasions, and in other instances the terms have become the subject of public policy debate. Moreover, the Supreme Court majority's analysis of the Second Amendment was nothing more than politics in adjudication. Their selective incorporation of all the historical sources is a testament to this. Most importantly however, the majority's analysis did not examine each state's "right to bear arms" provision. Instead the majority grouped the provisions, determining that every state's constitution up to 1820 protected a right to individual gun ownership. Needless to say, this may be the boldest and most far-reaching assumption the modern day Supreme Court has ever made.

It is also important that state courts do not give the decision in *Heller* any consideration for another reason: to determine whether their respective "right to bear arms" provisions has a broader protective scope than the Second Amendment. It is well established that some of the state constitutions may afford more civil liberties than the United States Constitution. Even Thomas Jefferson described the state governments and their constitutions as "the true barriers of our liberty in this country." It is the same notion the Supreme Court has reiterated in cases such as *Kelo v. City of New London*. This being the United States Constitution only offers so much protection against the intrusion of state and local government. If the people want broader protections, they must look to their state constitutions; the wording in state constitutional provisions may be textually constructed in a manner that enlarges a right already protected in the United States Constitution.

The same holds true for states' "right to bear arms" provisions, particularly in Ohio. Given that the current text of the Ohio Constitution's "bear arms" provision would appear, on its face, to encompass a broader protection than the Second Amendment, Ohio may become the next legal battleground for gun advocates. Article I, Section 4, of the Ohio Constitution states, "The people have a right to bear arms for their defense and security; but standing armies, in times of peace, are dangerous to liberty, and shall not be kept up; and the military shall be in strict subordination to the civil power."[1] It is this provision's use of the phrase "for their defense and security" that may become the issue of much debate.

Just as the Supreme Court majority misinterpreted the Second Amendment, the Ohio courts have also erred in interpreting the Ohio Constitution — holding that Ohio's "right to bear arms" protects every individual to own a firearm. Unfortunately for gun advocates, the Ohio Supreme Court has consistently held that although their interpretation of Ohio's right to bear arms is a "fundamental" and an "individual one," it is "not absolute."[2] In effect, therefore, the Ohio legislature may limit one's ability to carry arms under its police power so long as it does not conflict with this "fundamental right." Yet, no Ohio court has elaborated on the nature of this "fundamental right." This is because there exists no evidence defining individual gun ownership as a fundamental right. Essentially, it is something the Ohio courts have made up with no documentation, primary sources, or ratification and legislative history. The Ohio courts could have made up a definition but have chosen not to — and for good reason. For if the Ohio courts defined this fundamental right to own guns, it would impede the Ohio legislature's ability to regulate firearms.

## The 1802 Ohio Constitution's Right to Carry Firearms in the Courts

During the 1850–51 constitutional convention the Ohio "right to bear arms" provision was slightly altered and incorporated into the 1851 Ohio

Constitution. Surprisingly, not one case concerning the constitutionality of the 1802 constitution's "right to bear arms" provision was ever brought. The only case that seemed to have addressed that document's "right to bear arms" occurred when the constitutional convention was actually in session. In July 1850, the court of common pleas of Hamilton County decided *Ohio v. Walker*.[3] In the case, the defendant, Walker, pleaded self-defense when he stabbed two unannounced police officers with a concealed Bowie knife who had assaulted his person. As a result of the wound one of officers perished, leaving this case before the court.[4]

Although the case primarily dealt with the issue of self-defense, it also was the first case to briefly address the constitutionality of "carrying" weapons. The defendant argued that when considering whether he acted with "malice" and "preparation" in stabbing the officers, the court ought to take in consideration that in Ohio "every man has a constitutional right to carry weapons for self-defense; and hence there is no presumption of malice from the carrying of a weapon such as a knife."[5] The court responded by stating Ohio "had done well in securing to each citizen such a right."[6] The court further provided "it will be a dangerous hour" if it is "taken away" by "whatever reforms" the legislature may adopt to limit that right.[7] It seems by the wording of this decision the presiding justice knew that a law against the carrying of concealed weapons was eminent[8] and might have been trying to prevent it from ever being considered. It is significant to note that the majority of Ohio's closest neighbor States — Indiana,[9] Kentucky,[10] Tennessee,[11] and Virginia[12] — had all adopted laws against the carrying of concealed weapons. This left Ohio as the only state in the Northwest Territory not to have adopted such a law. Thus it is plausible that the court was making an effort to prevent the legislature from ever considering it, but it is impossible to know for sure.

The same can be said of exactly which constitutional provision the court was referring to as "securing to each citizen" a "constitutional" right to carry weapons. It is impossible to know for sure. It can reasonably inferred that the defendant was alluding to Article VIII, Section 20, but given the court neither cites nor quotes what part of the Ohio Constitution it is referring to, one can only assume. Needless to say, unlike the remainder of the decision in *Walker*, the court offered no reasoning as to why it held that carrying weapons for self-defense was a constitutional right. If the judge was referring to the "right to bear arms," he certainly was unfamiliar with the fact that the phrase "bear arms" had never been incorporated into any self-defense statute or law. Therefore, if this case had been reviewed under a textual and statutory analysis regarding the right to "self-defense" and the "right to bear arms," the court would not have defined "carrying weapons" as a "constitutional right," and instead would have considered it as a statutory protection.

## A Textual and Historical Analysis of the 1851 Ohio Constitution's "Right to Bear Arms"

The 1850–51 Ohio Constitutional Convention was the first and last time the "right to bear arms" provision was altered. The new provision altered the phrase "people have a right to bear arms for the defence of themselves and the State"[13] to read the "people have the right to bear arms for their defense and security."[14] Thus, the phrase "for their defense and security" was substituted in lieu of "for defence of themselves and the State." The change is noteworthy because it could legitimately be argued that the new phrase, on its face, and apart from the operating phrase "bear arms," would appear to imply that the people have a constitutional right to self-defense.

Moreover, it could be argued that the phrase "bear arms" had changed in meaning by the time of the 1850–51 Ohio Constitutional Convention as to enlarge its protective scope to include all forms of arms use — i.e. hunting, recreational, and self-defense. Although these arguments seem logically sound, there is not one shred of evidence to support this conclusion. As will be shown, the debates of the 1850–51 Ohio Constitutional Convention and other historical sources do not support Article I, Section 4, of the 1851 Ohio Constitution changed the meaning of the rights afforded by Article VIII, Section 20, of the 1802 Ohio Constitution.

## The 1851 Bill of Rights and Its Committee on the Preamble and Bill of Rights

On May 10, 1850, the convention resolved that a seven member committee[15] on the preamble and bill of rights be created to determine "what changes, alterations or amendments they deem necessary"[16] to be made to the Ohio Constitution's Bill of Rights. Henry Stanbery, who would later be appointed to the said committee, reminded his fellow convention members that the appointment of the committee was a "very important matter." He did not "intend to enlarge upon the subject, as every member saw the importance of it."[17] In the end, the committee would comprise of Elijah Vance, C.J. Orton, Lucius Case, William L. Bates, Simeon Nash, William Groesbeck, and Henry Stanbery[18] — the last three who would become prominent members of the legal profession.

The same day the committee was appointed, Mr. Cutler submitted a resolution reminding them of the duty of their task. Given that the eighth article of the 1802 constitution embraced "the well settled and long established principles of self-government, defining clearly the rights of persons and property, and securing to all the largest liberty consistent with the public good, accords, it is principles." Cutler proposed that these rights be continued "without material alteration."[19] He felt "these general principles" had been "embraced" by the "great majority of the people."[20] Therefore, Cutler desired that "it not to be changed." As with many of the members of the convention, there existed some confusion as to whether they were to amend the 1802 constitution or to rewrite it as an entirely new document. If the latter be the case, Cutler was strongly for maintaining the protections, wording, and structure of eighth article of the 1802 constitution because it was the "safer course."[21] For he felt "the less we do" with what would become the bill of rights of the new constitution, "the better."[22]

There were no objections, concerns, or amendments to Cutler's resolution. This gives great weight to the argument that the meanings of the "bear arms" provisions of both the 1802 and 1851 constitutions were intended to be synonymous unless there can be shown to exist any legislative history to prove otherwise. In fact, if anything regarding the collective rights of the people from the 1802 constitution to the 1851 constitution is to be immediately noticed, it is that the new bill of rights' provisions were drafted in a manner that was shorter and more concise. The twenty-eight rights guaranteed in Article VIII of the 1802 constitution would be restructured to only include twenty rights in the 1851 constitution.

Throughout the convention, very little was debated about the new constitution's bill of rights. The records show unequivocally that the first draft[23] submitted by the committee on the preamble and bill of rights was almost taken in its entirety except for a few exceptions. In regards to the "bear arms" provision, the first draft enclosed it as reading: "The people shall have the right to bear arms for their defence and security, but standing armies in time of peace are dangerous to liberty and shall not be kept up, and the military shall be in strict subordination to the civil power."[24] The new provision only came up for debate twice — January 15 and February 3. On both dates it was proposed that the word "shall" in the first line be removed, which was agreed to.[25] The only other amendment requested was made by Mr. Leidy. He proposed to strike out the word "peace" and place in lieu thereof the words "shall be regulated as may be provided by law."[26] That proposed amendment failed.

Thus, although the phrase "for their defence and security" would seem to have altered the 1802 Ohio Constitution's "right to bear arms" provision, there exists no legislative history to support its drafters or framers gave the new provision an expanded protective scope or different interpretation. If anything, given the drafters had made many changes in the 1802 constitution's bill of rights in order to make it shorter, more concise, and easier to interpret, the phrase "for their defence and security" was meant to do nothing more than just that.

Nevertheless, one cannot rule out that there may be other secondary historical and legislative materials to show that the drafters of the 1851 "right to bear arms" provision intended it have a more protective scope. Thus, an examination of each member of the committee of the preamble and bill of rights is necessary. Out of the seven members, only three — Henry Stanbery, Simeon Nash, and William S. Groesbeck — have left us with any correspondence or materials which we may infer how they interpreted Article I, Section 4. One must examine their opinions on individual rights, property, and self-defense.

### Henry Stanbery

The Honorable Henry Stanbery was born in New York City on February 20, 1803, and would later die in that city on June 26, 1881. A well respected lawyer in his own right, Stanbery eventually settled in Columbus upon his election to attorney general of Ohio in 1846. In 1850 he was elected to the constitutional convention, upon which in 1852 he moved his practice to Cincinnati. Within the next decade he would come to join the forces of the Republican Party, and became a huge supporter of the Lincoln administration. In 1866, he was rewarded by President Johnson with an appointment to attorney general of the United States. Moreover, Stanbery would receive a nomination to serve on the Supreme Court, but given his presiding as Johnson's counsel in the latter's impeachment proceedings, he was never appointed.[27]

Stanbery would even write a book on the constitutions of the United States, entitled *Manual of the Constitutions of All the United States, in Which the Various Provisions and Departments of Power Are Arranged Under Distinct Heads*,[28] but it does not provide any information regarding the "right to bear arms." Unfortunately, neither his papers nor his decisions while attorney general of both Ohio and the United States[29] offer any insight on the "right to bear arms." In his opinions as the attorney general of Ohio, there are many decisions regarding the militia laws, but they only support what we already know to be true: By 1844 the Ohio militia was comprised of volunteer companies and the old training requirement that all men appear armed and accoutered was no longer applicable.[30] Thus, given that Stanbery's decisions do not discuss the "right to bear arms," nor his opinions on personal property nor self-defense, we are left uncertain as to exactly what his opinion was on the Article I, Section 4, of the Ohio Constitution.

### William Groesbeck

William Slocum Groesbeck, like Stanbery, was born in the state of New York in 1815, but within the first year of his life, he and his family would be among the first of the early settlers of Ohio. In 1836 he was admitted to the Ohio bar and quickly became one of the leading young members in the profession. Even at his early age, he became well known for his advocacy and speeches which led to his election to the Ohio Constitutional Convention. Following the submission of the 1851 Ohio Constitution to the people, he wrote an extended series of articles explaining its provisions.[31] Although it would be hoped he would have focused one of his speeches on the "right to bear arms," unfortunately he did not, but there are other sources which may give some insight into his opinion on that right.

In 1855, Groesbeck would publish an essay entitled *An Address on the True Scope of Human Governments.*[32] In it he supported government because "men have certain inalienable rights, among which are the enjoying and defending life and liberty, acquiring, possessing and protecting property, and pursuing and obtaining happiness and safety."[33] As a means to "secure these rights," government must be instituted.[34] He reminded his readers that, prior to government, "life was but a miserable alteration of hope and fear" because "all their personal rights were but poorly enjoyed, if not brutally outraged." Especially threatening was their protection to property or as Groesbeck termed it, "the means of life and external comfort."[35] Therefore to "secure these rights," they instituted a government "for the equal benefit of all."[36]

In order to secure rights of all, though, one must first ensure the general defense of the government that protects them, so that "doers of wrong" and "the plunderers of the wilderness" will be put in check.[37] For government to accomplish this, a "combination for the general defense and protection has been formed which they cannot withstand" — the establishment of laws. It is only from laws, as a society, which we may go from a "stupid and cheerless barbarism" to a "brilliant and prosperous civilization."[38] Here it is clear that Groesbeck was an advocate for government and its instituting of laws to protect the people from harm. For although he believed that "a good and industrious community requires very little law making," he also knew "an honest, upright, well-meaning man never consults the statute book to know how he should live from day to day."[39] His argument was simple — if one does what is right in your conscience, he will never have to worry about breaking the law. It was the "murderers, house burners, burglars, thieves, and all manner of evil-doers" who only concerned themselves in knowing what is crime.[40] Thus, under this line of reasoning, Groesbeck was in favor of the adoption of any law that protected the people, and most assuredly would have been an advocate for any law protecting the right to self-defense or property. Unfortunately, his essay did not discuss that right directly nor the "right to bear arms." Therefore, it is uncertain how Groesbeck felt the government may regulate the people's safety. While he was for the axiom "government which is best, governs least," this still doesn't answer whether firearms could ever be restricted or regulated or whether the Ohio Constitution protected their possession.

Following the end of the Civil War, Groesbeck would give a speech supporting the adoption of the Fourteenth and Fifteenth Amendments. It too gives some insight regarding Groesbeck's mindset on the liberties and rights of men under government, but again is not conclusive. Herein, he felt that the "sovereignty of the State" meant "the State has exclusive authority and power to manage its own internal affairs ... [n]othing more than this, but nothing less."[41] Regarding what rights thought to be "sacred," he included the "liberty of the person, freedom of speech, and the like."[42] Thus, much like his *An Address on the True Scope of Human Governments*, the speech shows Groesbeck was a staunch supporter of states' rights and the protections it may afford its citizens. Where again he falls short is being more descriptive as to what he felt were the "sacred rights" that the U.S. Constitution has always "commanded respect" to.[43] He only refers to the "freedom of speech" specifically, leaving us to assume what rights were actually meant to be incorporated in his reference to "the like."

### Simeon Nash

The writings of Simeon Nash probably provide the deepest insight into understanding whether the "right to bear arms" was intended to be an individual right or provide a constitutional right to self-defense. Nash wrote two important treatises regarding the relationship between the law and legal theory — *Morality and the State*[44] and *Crime and the Family*.[45] The latter treatise examined the different duties that should be prescribed to the family and the state in ensuring young persons do not become criminally involved. It provides little insight on the "right to bear arms," but it is the former work on morality whereby he examined the duties of the state and the individuals that comprise it. Its contents are helpful.

Nash certainly believed the state's duty was to "protect men in the enjoyment of their inalienable rights."[46] He defined "inalienable rights" as those "rights with which God has clothed them in order to enable each to discharge his whole duty."[47] The state was just as much under a duty to obey the laws as the individuals that composed it. Therefore the state could not violate these rights without "transcending its authority and jurisdiction ... thus becoming in its turn an usurpation, an illegality."[48] Although Nash did not list what these "inalienable rights" were, he would later write a list of acts the state could not "lawfully do." For even the state was under certain "limitations and restrictions."[49] They include that the state may not (1) interfere with an individual's right to form moral judgments, (2) allow individuals to be in state of servitude, even if one chooses to do so voluntarily, (3) interfere with an individual's right to labor, (4) interfere with an individual's right to marry or with the socialization process of raising one's family, (5) interfere with one's right to education, and most importantly, (6) interfere or infringe upon an individual's right to own, contract, or acquire property.[50]

At no point in Nash's *Morality and the State* does he make reference to the inalienable, natural, or social right to own, use, or carry firearms. In fact, he makes no mention of arms at all. The closest reference made to Article I, Section 4, is when Nash talks about self-defense. It was self-defense that the court in *Walker* held was a "constitutional right" which afforded one the entitlement to carry weapons.[51] Nash's philosophy in this area conflicts with that court's determination. Nash did not feel self-defense was a "constitutional right," but a "conditional right."[52] This is because one may only employ self-defense when a "condition arises" such as when one party is "assailed."[53] "[H]ence, there can be no right to combine in advance to resist an attack which may never be made."[54] It would seem as if Nash was directly responding to the holding in *Walker*. Under Nash's interpretation of the right to self-defense, one cannot "combine in advance" the preparation of self-defense by carrying a weapon to "resist an attack which may never be made." Thus, it can be clearly seen that if Nash had been deciding *Walker*, it would have resulted in a totally different outcome.

Although Nash did not support "self-defense," as the *Walker* court understood it, or the carrying of arms to deter attacks as a constitutional guarantee, and does not even mention the right to own, use, or possess firearms as a natural, constitutional, or social right, he is undoubtedly a supporter of one's right to property. Just as it has been shown through an historical and textual analysis that the 1802 Ohio Constitution's best protection for individual firearm ownership was the Article VIII, Section I, right to property, Nash's treatise supports the same conclusion.

To Nash, property was a "general right" that could not be limited in time.[55] It was "not an end; it [was] a mean[s] to a greater end; hence the acquiring, transferring and inheriting it must be matters of expediency."[56] It was up to the state to protect these rights by not only protecting against "wrongs to the right of private property, but it must also point out and regulate the mode of its acquisition, transfer, and descent."[57] This is not to say the state could not regulate property to protect other citizens as well. After all, it was the duty of every individual to "sacrifice his personal interests at times to protect those of the State."[58]

## "Bearing Arms" at the 1850–51 Ohio Constitutional Convention

While the Ohio Constitutional Convention did not debate what would become Article I, Section 4, of the new constitution, there is a substantial amount of legislative history on how the framers used and interpreted "bearing arms." It was during the debates for what would become the article for the militia that the phrase "bear arms" was used consistently to denote an individual's use of arms for military service.

Just as the Ohio militia laws were evolving up to 1850, they were also slowly eroding the eighteenth-century version of a militia — mandatory musters, training, and the old requirement that every man furnish his own arms and accoutrements — had all become obsolete. The convention's debate on the issue only further supports this history that the militia system was eroding. Mr. Hitchcock gave the best statement as to what the opinion of the delegates was regarding the militia when he stated:

> I will say ... that the constitution should say as little on the subject of the militia as possible. I believe that we have one of the best militia systems in this State that there is in the Union; and practically that is none at all.[59]

Mr. Hitchcock's statement was followed with immediate laughter,[60] and was not the only statement to be found humorous. The propositions regarding the enrollment of women and blacks provided similar entertainment for some, but for the delegates proposing them they were serious issues. There was no debating that the militia system had become a joke. Mr. Curry described the militia trainings as "useless, expensive, and in some degree, demoralizing assemblages."[61] Mr. Smith agreed, and also described the training as "useless, if not demoralizing in their character."[62] Meanwhile, Mr. Robertson could not see the reason why they continued such training at all. He regretted that "so little interest is manifested for the preservation of a correct military spirit among the mass of our people" that the militia system had become the "butt of ridicule and burlesque."[63]

In reality, there was only one issue up for serious debate regarding the militia — which white males should be required to enroll in the militia? It is in this debate we come to understand how the framers of the 1851 Ohio Constitution understood what "bearing arms" meant to encompass; on June 15, Mr. Stanton would propose the militia article contain the following provision: "No person or persons conscientiously scrupulous of bearing arms shall be compelled to do military duty, in time of peace."[64] The proposition was initially adopted by a vote of 39 yeas to 29 nays,[65] but within the days to follow would not survive the final draft of the constitution.

In fact, later that day the provision came under attack by Mr. Hawkins. He was concerned as to whether the provision implied that "conscientiously scrupulous of bearing arms" would have to "contribute nothing to the support of the war, either by service or money — whether they are thereby to be wholly excepted?"[66] Meanwhile, Mr. Smith was worried about whether the provision would conflict with the United States' power on the subject since it had not passed such a law.[67] He knew New York had passed such a law excusing all individuals' "scruples of conscience [that] may be averse to bearing arms," but hoped his fellow delegates could elaborate on the matter.[68]

Mr. Loudon chose to respond by using a different route than what Mr. Smith had proposed, by appealing to their patriotism. He considered the scrupulous issue one of "grave principle," since he knew every man, such as himself, who had seen military service, believed the militia was one of the "bulwarks of our liberty" and should never be altered as to allow a standing army to take over.[69] Loudon was so adamant against the scrupulous provision that he actually preferred to allow blacks to serve, "than to make such a distinction between white men" that exempted them from being "called upon to defend the rights of their country from invasion on every side."[70]

Mr. Morris replied to Loudon, to appeal to the delegates that the militia was a financial burden on the people and that George Washington himself would have supported the principle that "no man should be compelled to do military duty against his will."[71] However, this argument would fall upon deaf ears. The argument that would ultimately win out was initiated by Mr. Lidey. He reminded the delegates that — if militia enrollment were to decrease — they might lose a substantial portion of their public arms quota.[72] Lidey had no objection to exempting men from mustering in times of peace. He just did not believe they should be exempt from enrollment, for he and the other delegates knew the enrollment statistics were the measure by which the federal government proportioned its public arms.

Obviously, the "conscientiously scrupulous of bearing arms" provision did not pass, but the convention's use of the phrase "bear arms" throughout the debate shows it was meant to denote service in a militia or military context. The provision would be debated again at the constitutional convention of 1873–74.[73] Similar to the convention of 1850–51, it would be the only instance when "bearing arms" or "bear arms" was debated, thus further showing the phrase was limited in definition to militia or military service.

## Ohio's First Concealed Weapon Law in Understanding "Bear Arms"

While the *Walker* court seemed to be sending a message to the Ohio legislature against the adoption of a concealed weapons law, it certainly had no effect. On March 18, 1859, it was resolved that "whoever shall carry a weapon or weapons, concealed on or about his person, such as a pistol, bowie-knife, dirk, or any other dangerous weapon, shall be deemed guilty of a misdemeanor."[74] The accused may be acquitted if it shall be proven to the jury "that at the time of carrying any of the weapon or weapons aforesaid" they were "engaged in the pursuit of any lawful business, calling, or employment" so as to "justify a prudent man in carrying the weapon."[75] Herein the law acted as a strict liability offense until the accused could prove he was carrying the weapon for a legitimate purpose.

As has already been discussed, there seemed to have been a growing movement for concealed weapon laws during the nineteenth century. The first mention of such a law that would appear in a Cleveland newspaper was a Louisiana law passed in 1855. The event only took up a small paragraph of the newspaper, but its author surely was not a supporter of the carrying of concealed weapons. He commented that although the carrying of concealed weapons might justify most of their homicides such action "might be more justifiable in a slaveholding than in a free community."[76] Although Ohio would not follow suit for four more years, in 1856 Cleveland passed an ordinance against the use of firearms within the city limits.[77] On ten instances, nine of which occurred in June, the *Plain Dealer* reported individuals who were fined a dollar for violating the ordinance.[78]

When the concealed weapon law was finally passed by the Ohio legislature, the *Plain Dealer* cheered its adoption as "proper." It further described the act of carrying a concealed weapon as "a most cowardly as well as murderous practice anywhere."[79] Thus, it would seem that the Cleveland people of 1859 never questioned its constitutionality. Moreover, there is no evidence in the *House*[80] or *Senate*[81] *Journal* to suggest the legislature ever considered it infringing upon one's right to "bear arms" in Ohio for, as the historical evidence has shown, to "bear arms" was not to "carry arms." The two were not synonymous. One may "carry arms" while never bearing them, but it was impossible for one to "bear arms" without carrying them.

The act itself even stipulates against the "carrying" of concealed weapons, not the "bearing" of concealed weapons. The legislature was not acting in a manner to limit one's right to "bear arms"; they were acting to limit one's ability to "carry arms." Of real significance is the lack of any evidence that shows Ohio's lawmakers deemed the two phrases as being equal. Therefore, given that there is no legislative record or history to even suggest that the Ohio legislature was attempting to limit the 1851 constitution's "right to bear arms for their defence and security," individual right supporters need to cease equating "bear" with "carry," "own," or "possess."

## Article I, Section 4, and the Ohio Courts

While it is within the power of every state's judiciary to determine the protective scope of its constitutional provisions, the Ohio courts' analysis of Article I, Section 4, has been rudimentary, and the sources which they rely on are historically unsupported. In fact, it would not be until 2003, in *Klein v. Leis*,[82] that the Ohio Supreme Court even made a minimal effort to look at the history on the issue. Up to that point, every Ohio court decision on the "right to bear arms" had relied purely on case law, offering very minimal insight into what that right was truly meant to afford.

Two years removed from the decision in *Walker*, in 1852 the Ohio Supreme Court would take up its first case in which the "right to bear arms" was mentioned, and also the first such case since the 1851 change in the provision. Similar to *Walker*, the case of *Stewart v. Ohio*[83] would address the constitutionality of self-defense. The accused asked the court on appeal to reinstruct the jury as to whether "in this State any man has a constitutional right to carry weapons for self-defense, and hence there is no presumption of malice from the carrying of a weapon such as the knife" with which he killed.[84] This appeal was different from the lower court's jury charge because it had also added the stipulation "that the jury may and ought to take into consideration the manner by which, and purposes for which the prisoner had possession of the knife in question."[85] The court saw no error in the modification. Thus the appeal ultimately failed in this regard. Nevertheless, although the Ohio Supreme Court did not modify the jury instruction to aid the accused, they also did not question the lower court's understanding that carrying weapons was a constitutional right. Moreover, the jury instruction was synonymously worded with the *Walker* court's opinion, showing that case would have a significant impact in understanding what the "right to bear arms" in Ohio was meant to encompass in the years to come.

It would not be until 1900 that the supreme court would again take up the protective scope of Article I, Section 4, in *State v. Hogan*.[86] The issue before the court was whether a law that imprisoned "tramps" that are found to be "carrying a firearm, or other dangerous weapon" was unconstitutional.[87] Like *Walker* and *Stewart*, the court incorrectly assumed "carrying arms" equated to "bearing arms" when it stated a "man may carry a gun for any lawful purpose, business or amusement, but he cannot go about with that or any other dangerous weapon to terrify and alarm a peaceful people."[88] The court was not completely inept about what the "right to bear arms" afforded, though. It was correct to note that it secures to the people a right that cannot be deprived, but it also "enjoins a duty in execution of which that right is to be exercised."[89] Thus, the court was correct in noting that the "right to bear arms" was a conditional right. This is because the people are only permitted to "bear arms" when they do so for the "protection of [their] country." There can be no "vindication in the bill of rights" when one uses arms for the "annoyance and terror and danger of its citizens."[90]

*State v. Nieto* would be the next significant case to address the constitutionality of "bearing arms" in Ohio.[91] The issue was whether the state could prohibit the carrying of concealed arms in one's home.[92] This court, too, found "carrying arms" synonymous with "bearing arms" when it noted that the statute in question did not act as a "prohibition against carrying weapons but as a regulation of the manner of carrying them."[93] It did not see how the maxim that "every man's house is his castle" prevented the legislature from passing a law that operated within an individual's home, thus upholding the statute's constitutionality.[94] Moreover, much like the cases before it, *Nieto* upheld that the "right to bear arms" afforded individuals the right of self-defense to protect their person and property.[95]

For the next fifty years, the Ohio courts' stance on the right virtually remained a non-issue. It was well settled that the state may regulate the manner of carrying arms "under the police power, provided that the regulation is reasonable."[96] In fact, the courts would step further and further away from Simeon Nash's stance of what constituted self-defense. For example, in 1972, the Akron Municipal Court held that the language in Article I, Section 4, directly "speaks of the citizen's self-defense and security to his right to attain those ends by bearing arms."[97] Unfortunately for gun advocates, this court did not see any manner by which the legislature could fail to regulate the "bearing of arms except to defend one's self or one's family,"[98] but even this interpretation is inaccurate for Article I, Section 4, does not protect a right to self-defense of one's self, family or property.

During the 1850–51 convention, when the *Walker* court convened, it held that "every man has a constitutional right to carry weapons for self-defense," thus inferring "self-defense"[99] was a constitutional right when one used arms to accomplish that objective. The *Walker* court did not cite Article VIII, Section 20's "right to bear arms" protection, but it can be assumed it was specifically what the court was referring to. This means that the phrase "defence of themselves and the State" was interpreted to include "self-defense." As subsequent decisions have shown, further Ohio court decisions would not deviate from this interpretation. This became much clearer when, in 1851, "defence of themselves and the State" was replaced by "for their defence and security."

While the courts have inferred "self-defense" was what the drafters were referring to in the phrase "their defence and security," the evidence actually points to the contrary. There is no denying "self-defense" is a right protected under the common law, or that it had been included within Ohio's statutes on crimes and punishment. Yet, as Simeon Nash noted, this was a conditional right. One could only exercise this right on the condition that a situation presented itself in which it may be applied. The delegates of the Ohio convention did not deviate from this point of view.

The issue of "self-defense" presented itself during the convention's debate over the removal of capital punishment as a penalty for capital offenses. On December 7, Mr. Quigley objected to eliminating capital punishment because he believed in the "sacred principle" that "punishment must be proportionate to the crime."[100] He used the example of "self-defence" to illustrate his point. He argued if capital punishment was not permitted for capital crimes such as burglary or robbery, then criminals being "armed and you unarmed would prevent their arrest in the great majority of cases, especially if the robber or murderer of fact that you dare not take his life."[101] Quigley feared the "great law of self-defence"—what he believed to be a "natural right"—would be undermined by eliminating capital punishment.[102] No one responded to Quigley's argument in this regard. Not one member cited, referred, inferred, or even mentioned that the "right to bear arms" protected what Quigley feared would result from the elimination of capital punishment.

Besides, Quigley himself did not refer to the "right to bear arms." He certainly hoped every man would go "just so far as necessary for protection" and "defence of [his] family, self and property," but he never termed or inferred that such an action was constitutionally protected. Thus, it is not logical that the "right to bear arms for their defence and security" was drafted to include a right to use guns for "self-defense" in protection of one's person, family or property — if Quigley thought "self-defense" would be undermined by excluding capital punishment as a penalty. Would the supporters of capital punishment not have pointed out to Quigley that his "self-defense" analogy was constitutionally inept if the "right to bear arms" protected one to use a gun as a means to protect his person, family or property?

Mr. Mason was the only other member to take up the issue of Mr. Quigley's concern. He was in favor of capital punishment because "society has the right to take the life of the murderer on the same principle that the individual has the right to take the life of a man who assails him with murderous intent."[103] This was so because the right of self-defense exists not only "in state of nature, but in a state of society."[104] This brought on the following debate:

MR. MASON: "And, whenever society is assailed in the person of one of its members with the intent to take the life of that member, society may take the life of the assailant, the individual assailed having failed successfully to assert the right of nature in that given case. No one doubts this. No one doubts but that I have the right to take the life of the man who assails me with the intent of depriving me of my life — that I have a right to repel force with force, and with such an amount of force as will overcome the resistance with which I am met."

MR. BATES: "I will ask the gentleman if a man attacked him, and he overcame the assailer, and had him in his power, tied down, would he have the right to take his life?"

MR. MASON: "I suppose the argument's successful if we establish the fact that the person assailed has the right to take the life of the assailant. And if there be an exception, I would ask the gentleman if an exception to a general rule has the effect to overthrow a general principle?"

MR. BATES: "The exception does not apply. You must have a man in your possession, thoroughly secured, before you hang him."

MR. MASON: "Then the argument is that when you have a man in your power after murdering another, you are to spare his life."

MR. BATES: "That is it."

MR. MASON: "I said that the right of self-defence is not surrendered by entering into society, for in a state of society, if assailed, it is my admitted right to resist the assailant to the extent of taking his life, if necessary to save my own. I am faultless — he is guilty — one or the other must suffer in the struggle — the life of the one or other must be forfeited. The theory of justice and of truth says that the life of the guilty ought in such case to be taken, and the life of the innocent party preserved. The rights of every individual in a state of nature revert to the society of which he is a member; and whatever individuals can do, society can do-otherwise society affords a less degree of protection for the rights of individuals than a state of nature."[105]

Like Mr. Quigley's reference to "self-defense," both Mr. Mason and Mr. Bates agreed it was a natural right. They just disagreed at how far natural right may be regulated. What's more, at no point did either man make any reference to the Ohio Constitution for "self-defense." This clearly proves that the delegates of the 1850–51 Ohio Constitutional Convention did not intend Article I, Section 4, to serve as a constitutional protection for "self-defense." That being so, the phrase "for their security and defence" should not be interpreted as such.

It would not be until 1993 that the Supreme Court of Ohio would take up the "right to bear arms" issue again in *Arnold v. City of Cleveland.*[106] Between 1972 and up to this point, the Ohio lower court consistently and rightfully held "it is a well established principle that there is no absolute constitutional right of an individual to possess a firearm, either under the Second Amendment ... or under Section 4, Article I of the Ohio Constitution."[107] In *Arnold,* a challenge was brought regarding the municipality's ordinance prohibiting the possession or sale of assault weapons. Regarding the "right to bear arms," the *Arnold* court held it to be "fundamental" and an "individual one," but not "absolute."[108] It rightfully determined that the "right to bear arms is not an unlimited right and subject to reasonable regulation,"[109] although not for the proper reasons. While it is certainly within the state's right to regulate the "right to bear arms" under its militia laws — such as regulating age, training, enrollment, musters, arms, and equipment — the *Arnold* court wrongfully asserted "bearing arms" equated to "carrying arms," and was thus referring to the state's "reasonable exercise" of its police power.[110]

That court was in error when it held that Article I, Section 4, was "implemented to allow a person to posses certain firearms for defense of self and property."[111] The court came to this determination because it believed there was "no reported debate" over "the right-to-bear-arms" language as used in either the 1802 or 1851 versions of the Ohio Constitution.[112] Although the court is technically correct that Article I, Section 4, itself was not the subject of much debate, the use of the phrase "bear arms" was used extensively during the debate over the "scrupulous" to "bearing arms" provision. That debate clearly shows how the phrase "bear arms" was meant to be construed by the framers of the 1851 Ohio Constitution, and it should not be interpreted otherwise.

Moreover, the court cited *Hogan*,[113] holding that the "right to bear arms" was implemented to protect property.[114] It is uncertain as to why the court in *Hogan* ever came to such determination because, like the *Walker* court regarding self-defense, the *Hogan* court did not cite any source, nor does Article I, Section 4, include the word "property." The interpretation is nothing more than a judicial apparition. It could be inferred that the court was combining the protection for property in Article I, Section 1, with the "right to bear arms," but it is hardly clear-cut. Perhaps the court was inferring that the Founding Fathers bore arms against Britain in the Revolutionary War to protect their property, but again such an inference is historically inaccurate. When Congress adopted the *Declaration of Causes and Necessity For Taking Up Arms* in 1775 it did not identify protection of property as one of the reasons they bore arms, so there exists no sufficient historical evidence to suggest property was ever constitutionally or fundamentally considered a valid reason for "bearing arms."

Even if we are to consider "taxes" as property — a significant factor in the start of the American Revolution — it must be remembered that the colonists never bore arms over the issue. In fact, the Founding Fathers only considered taxes a grievance. They had been consistently working towards reconciliation until certain events took place up to 1776.[115] It was the Battles of Lexington and Concord that caused over 20,000 men to arrive at Boston armed in the summer of 1775 — not property. Furthermore, even if we were to consider property as the reason the Founding Fathers were "bearing arms" against Britain, they did so as a collective people — not as individual banditti. The "right to bear arms" for the defense of property was only to be exercised as a collective right.

Lastly, the *Arnold* court wrongfully inferred there was no debate on Article I, Section 4, at the 1851 convention because "the right to possess and use certain arms under certain circumstances was widely recognized and uncontroversial."[116] Arms possession was actually very controversial and an issue of much debate in the United States Congress. As has already been addressed, ensuring that individuals possessed arms for the defense of the nation was a matter of national security. While early efforts were made to ensure every man provide his own firearm, it was later deemed more expedient that the federal government and states provide them. At no time during this alteration — from individual arms possession to arms owned and secured by the government — was there ever any debate as to whether such a move interfered with one's "right to bear arms." It was essentially deemed more efficient for the people to "bear arms" if the government provided them.

The most recent Ohio Supreme Court case to consider the scope of the "right to bear arms" was *Klein v. Leis*.[117] While the *Klein* court would make the most methodical and historical approach to date, it also assumed "bear arms" was synonymous with "carry arms." It did, however, accurately address that after the adoption of Ohio's first concealed weapon statute, there was no questioning whether the state could pass laws governing the manner one might carry a weapon until 1920.[118] Unfortunately, it assumed this was the case because the state could regulate the manner one may "bear arms." If only the *Klein* court had looked further into the history on this issue, it would have found this was not the valid justification for the concealed weapon statute being in accordance with the Ohio Constitution. The statute was not passed because the "right to bear arms" can be regulated, but because there was no constitutional guarantee to "carry arms." There was only a guarantee to use arms in the militia or military context — not to own them.

## The Protection That the "Right to Bear Arms" in the 1851 Ohio Constitution Affords

An original and textual construction of the Second Amendment and Article I, Section 4, of the Ohio Constitution does not support the individual right interpretation. While there is certainly a colorful historical and textual argument to be made that the right to "bear arms" provision in both constitutional provisions protects every individual's right to own firearms, such an interpretation is not part of its protective scope.

Just like the Second Amendment, there is no substantiating evidence to support the "right to bear arms" in the Ohio Constitution protects the right to personally own, use, or carry firearms outside a militia or military context. There is not one instance of the phrase "bear arms" having been used in any other manner but for the military or militia context. Besides, there does not exist one Ohio self-defense, hunting, firearm, or crime law that describes the act of using or carrying arms as "bearing arms." As the militia and legislative history shows, "bearing arms" was only used to describe the act of using arms in service of the state or country.

Lastly, even after the 1851 constitution's change of wording from "for defence of themselves and the State" to "for their defence and security," the subsequent language remained virtually the same as originally drafted. The Ohio "right to bear arms" provision was still a means to prevent the maintenance of a standing army in times of peace. To be sure, the only way to ensure this protection was to maintain the militia. It was through the militia that Ohio's citizens had the right to "bear arms," but nothing was stipulated as to who was to own them. The state could just as easily possess the arms for "bearing" as the individual. The history of the militia laws and public arms attests to this fact. Thus, until substantial and direct historical data can be compiled to prove otherwise, the Ohio Supreme Court should overturn its previous decisions and limit the "right to bear arms" to be used in the military or militia context.

It is not to say the Ohio Supreme Court is in error in asserting the "right to bear arms" is a right that may be regulated. It is just that the right is not used in the manner in which the court has determined. The "right to bear arms" may be regulated through the militia laws, despite the lack of a guarantee as to whom is to provide the arms or the articles governing their use in Article I, Section 4. There exists only the guarantee that the people be allowed to "bear arms," but even this right in conditional. It is conditional on the fact that individuals who "bear arms" support a just government and are doing so for the state's interests and not their own.

# Chapter Notes

## Introduction

1. *District of Columbia v. Heller*, 128, S.Ct. 2783, 2821–22 (2008).

2. U.S. Const, Amend II.

3. They challenged *D.C. Code § 7-2502.02* (a) (4), which generally bars the registration of handguns (with an exception for retired D.C. police officers); *D.C. Code § 22-4504*, which prohibits carrying a pistol without a license, insofar as that provision would prevent a registrant from moving a gun from one room to another within his or her home; and *D.C. Code § 7-2507.02*, requiring that all lawfully owned firearms be kept unloaded and disassembled or bound by a trigger lock or similar device. Shelly Parker, Tracey Ambeau, Tom G. Palmer, and George Lyon want to possess handguns in their respective homes for self-defense. Gillian St. Lawrence owns a registered shotgun, but wishes to keep it assembled and unhindered by a trigger lock or similar device. Finally, Dick Heller, who is a District of Columbia special police officer permitted to carry a handgun on duty as a guard at the Federal Judicial Center, wishes to possess one at his home. Heller applied for and was denied a registration certificate to own a handgun." *Parker v. District of Columbia*, 478, F.3d 370, 373–74 (2007).

4. *Parker v. District of Columbia*, 311, F. Supp.2d 103, 109 (D.C. Cir., 2004).

5. *Parker*, 478, F. 3d at 376.

6. *Ibid.*, 374.

7. *Ibid.*, 395.

8. *Parker v. District of Columbia*, 478, F.3d 370, *petition for cert. filed*, 76 USLW 3083 (U.S. Sep 04, 2007) (No. 07-290).

9. *Ibid.*, *petition for cert. filed*, 76, USLW 3095 (U.S. Sep 10, 2007) (No. 07-335).

10. The first court was *United States v. Emerson*, 270, F.3d 203 (5th Cir., 2001). The *Emerson* court held the Second Amendment "protects the rights of individuals, including those not then actually a member of any militia or engaged in active military service or training, to privately possess and bear their own firearms ... that are suitable as personal, individual weapons and are not of the general kind or type excluded by *Miller*." *Ibid.*, 260.

11. Those courts that have adopted the "pure collective right" model argue the right to keep and bear arms protects only the right of state governments to preserve and arm their militia. This model has been adopted by the Fourth, Sixth, Seventh, and Ninth Circuits. *Love v. Pepersack*, 47, F.3d 120 (4th Cir. 1995); *United States v. Warin*, 530, F.2d 103 (6th Cir., 1976); *Gillespie v. City of Indianapolis*, 185, F.3d 693 (7th Cir., 1999); *Hickman v. Block*, 81, F.3d 98 (9th Cir., 1996). Meanwhile, the other courts have prescribed to the "sophisticated collective right" model. The First, Third, Eighth, Tenth, and Eleventh Circuits have prescribed to the "sophisticated collective right" model. *Cases v. United States*, 131, F.2d 916 (1st Cir., 1942); *United States v. Rybar*, 103, F.3d 273 (3d Cir., 1996); *United States v. Hale*, 978, F.2d 1016 (8th Cir., 1992); *United States v. Oakes*, 564, F.2d 384 (10th Cir., 1977); *United States v. Wright*, 117, F.3d 1265 (11th Cir., 1997). This model has several variations, acknowledging individuals could raise Second Amendment claims, but limit the right as a purely civic provision that offers no protection for the private ownership or use of arms. *Parker*, 478, F.3d at 379.

12. *Presser v. Illinois*, 116, U.S. 252 (1886); *United States v. Cruikshank*, 92, U.S. 542 (1875) (per curium) (holding that the Second Amendment is an amendment that serves no purpose other than to restrict the powers of the federal government); *Miller v. Texas*, 153, U.S. 535 (1894) (per curium) (holding that the Second and Fourth Amendments operate only on the

179

federal power, and have no effect to the proceedings in state courts).

13. This has caused a divide among state courts regarding the interpretation of the Second Amendment. Seven state courts have held the Second Amendment protects an individual right. *Hilberg v. F.W. Woolworth Co.*, 761, P.2d 236 (Colo. Ct. App., 1988); *Brewer v. Commonwealth*, 206, S.W.3d 343 (Ky., 2006); *State v. Blanchard*, 776, So. 2d 1165 (La., 2001); *State v. Nickerson*, 247, P.2d 188 (Mont., 1952); *Stillwell v. Stillwell*, 2001, WL 862620 (Tenn. Ct. App., 2001); *State v. Anderson*, 2000, WL 122218 (Tenn. Crim. App., 2000); *State v. Williams*, 158, Wash. 2d 904 (Wash. , 2006); *Rohrbaugh v. State*, 216, W. Va. 298 (W. Va., 2004). Meanwhile, at least ten state courts have held the Second Amendment protects a collective right: *Sandidge v. United States*, 520, A.2d 1057 (D.C., 1987); *Commonwealth v. Davis*, 369, Mass. 886 (Mass., 1976); *In re Atkinson*, 291, N.W.2d 396 (Minn., 1980); *Burton v. Sills*, 53, N.J. 86 (N.J., 1968); *In re Cassidy*, 268, A.D. 282 (N.Y. App. Div., 1944); *State v. Fennell*, 95, N.C. App. 140 (N.C. Ct. App., 1989); *Mosher v. City of Dayton*, 48, Ohio St. 2d 243 (Ohio, 1976); *Masters v. State*, 653, S.W.2d 944 (Tex. App., 1983); *State v. Vlacil*, 645, P.2d 677 (Utah, 1982); *Kalodimos v. Village of Morton Grove*, 103, Ill. 2d 483 (Ill., 1984).

14. It is believed the Equal Protection Clause of the 14th Amendment would extend the militia's right to bear arms to every citizen. The Equal Protection Clause is in Section 1 of the 14th Amendment. It states, "All persons born or naturalized in the United States, and subject to the jurisdiction thereof, are citizens of the United States and of the state wherein they reside. No state shall make or enforce any law which shall abridge the privileges or immunities of citizens of the United States; nor shall any state deprive any person of life, liberty, or property, without due process of law; nor deny to any person within its jurisdiction the equal protection of the laws." U.S. Const, Amend XIV.

15. 307 U.S. 174 (1939).

16. *Ibid.*, 176.

17. 282 U.S. 716, 731 (1931).

18. *District of Columbia v. Heller*, 128, S.Ct. at 2790.

19. *District of Columbia v. Heller*, 128, S.Ct. at 2816–17.

20. *Ibid.*, 2817–18.

21. U.S. Const, Amend XIV.

22. *McDonald v. City of Chicago*, No. 08-C-3645 (N.D.Ill. June 27, 2008) (complaint, June 26, 2008).

23. *Ibid.* (answer, July 16, 2008).

24. Stephen P. Halbrook, *The Founder's Second Amendment: Origins of the Right to Bear Arms*, 9–28 (2008).

25. *Ibid.*, 29-124. One of Halbrook's most unfounded contentions occurs when he claims the Native Americans' concerns about being supplied with weapons links the right to "keep and bear arms" to colonists hunting. Halbrook writes, "The ministry's aim to 'prevent us from having guns,' whether through such actions as the import ban or direct seizure, had the purpose of allowing the British to deprive the colonists of their liberty and property. But it had a further pernicious effect, which the Mohawk would have understood better than the urban white man — depriving the people of guns interfered with subsistence hunting. As General Gage had noted years before, Native Americans 'are disused to the Bow, and can neither hunt nor make war, without FireArms, Powder and Lead.' For many rural whites, too, firearms were used to put food on the table. Adams' above message made clear that the colonists saw hunting as a significant purpose behind the right to keep and bear arms." *Ibid.*, 93. Halbrook's assumes too much with very little historical research to support his contention. For those who are familiar with the history of the Native American tribes in the American Revolution know this to be unfounded. The colonists, and the British for that matter, used the supplying of arms as a means to recruit each tribe to either side or to remain neutral. And during their recruiting, at no time, did either side convey that the confiscating of the other's arms (whether it be the colonists depriving loyalists or the Ministry depriving the colonists) as an infringement on their right to keep and bear arms. *See* Patrick J. Charles, *Irreconcilable Grievances: The Events that Shaped the Declaration of Independence*, 213–72 (2008).

26. *Ibid.*, 126-68.

27. David E. Young, *The Founders View of the Right to Bear Arms*, 12–26 (2007). Young's book is poorly sourced. It only provides citations for the first 225 notes, but the book goes up to 746 notes. Moreover, these notes are often out of sequence. For example, on page 212, it jumps from note 746 to 744 and then to 221. Lastly, looking at the notes Young does provide, his examination of all the revolutionary sources is miniscule compared to other scholars in this area. Unlike his *Origins of the Second Amendment*, which provides copies of primary sources to examine, Young's *The Founders View of the Right to Bear Arms* is a source that should not be heavily relied upon.

# Chapter One

1. The First Amendment states, "Congress shall make no law respecting an establishment

of religion, or prohibiting the free exercise thereof; or abridging the freedom of speech, or of the press; or the right of the people peaceably to assemble, and to petition the government for a redress of grievances." U.S. Const, Amend I.

2. *The Origin of the Second Amendment: A Documentary History of the Bill of Rights,* 723 (David F. Young ed., 2d ed., 1995).

3. *West Virginia v. Barnette,* 319, U.S. 624 (1943).

4. Article One stated, "After the first enumeration required by the first article of the constitution, there shall be one Representative for every thirty thousand, until the number shall amount to one hundred, after which the proportion shall be so regulated by Congress, that there shall be not less than one hundred Representatives nor less than one Representative for every forty thousand persons, until the number of Representatives shall amount to two hundred; after which the proportion shall be so regulated by Congress, that there shall not be less than two hundred Representatives, nor more than one Representative for every fifty thousand persons." *The Origin of the Second Amendment: A Documentary History of the Bill of Rights* at 743.

5. Article Two stated, "No law varying the compensation for the services of the Senators and Representatives shall take effect, until an election of Representatives shall have intervened." *Ibid.*

6. *Ibid.*

7. The First and Second Articles were the only two articles not adopted within the Bill of Rights. Article One was adopted by ten of the fourteen states: New Hampshire, Vermont, Rhode Island, New York, New Jersey, Pennsylvania, Maryland, Virginia, North Carolina, and South Carolina. It only missed ratification by one vote. The Second Article was only adopted by six of the fourteen States: Vermont, Delaware, Maryland, Virginia, North Carolina, and South Carolina. *Ibid.*

8. *Parker,* 478, F.3d at 383.

9. *Ibid.*

10. *Ibid.*

11. *An Act to oblige the Male white Persons in the Province of Georgia to carry Fire-arms to all Places of publick Worship* (Ga., 1757).

12. *Ibid.* South Carolina passed a similar law in 1743. It required that "every white male" that "is or liable to bear arms in the militia" and "shall not carry with him a gun or pair of horse pistols in good order, and fit for service, with at least 6 charges of gun powder and ball, and shall not carry the same into church … every person shall forfeit and pay the sum of 20s." *An Act for the better Security of this Province against the Insurrections and other wicked Attempts of*

*Negroes, and other Slaves; and for reviving and continuing, an Act of the General Assembly of this Province, entitled an Act for the better Ordering and Governing of Negroes and other Slaves in this Province* (S.C., 1743). This act shows that there was a clear distinction in the use of the words "bear" and "carry." Notice how the word "bear" was incorporated with the words "arms in the militia," while the word "carry" was used to denote possession. South Carolina also used the word "carry" instead of the word "bear" in its slave patrol laws. It required white inhabitants to "carry with him on his patrol for service one good gun or pistol in order." *An Act for the better establishing and regulating of Patrols in this Province,* Sec. 4 (S.C., 1746).

13. *An Act for the speedy trial of criminals, and ascertaining their punishment in the county courts when prosecuted there, and for payment of fees due from criminal persons,* Sec. 7 (Md., 1715).

14. *An Act to prevent the firing of Guns and other Fire-Arms within this Colony* (N.Y., 1773).

15. *An Act to suppress the disorderly practice of firing guns, & c. on the times therein mentioned* (Pa., 1774).

16. *An Act for the better Ordering and Governing of Negroes and other Slaves in this Province,* Sec. XLI (S.C., 1740).

17. *An Act to prevent Routs, Riots, and tumultuous Assemblies, and the evil Consequences thereof* (Mass., 1786).

18. *An Act to prevent Routs, Riots and tumultuous Assemblies* (N.J., 1797).

19. *An Act against riots and rioters* (Pa., 1705).

20. *An Act to restrain Tavern-keepers and others from selling strong Liquors to Servants, Negroes and Mulatto Slaves, and to prevent Negroes and Mulatto Slaves, from meeting in large Companies, from running about at Nights, and from hunting or carrying a Gun on the Lord's Day,* Sec. 4 (N.J., 1751).

21. 3 "Statutes of Large of Pennsylvania," 255 (1721), quoted in Smith, *The Constitutional Right to Keep and Bear Arms,* 46.

22. 1 "Laws of the State of North Carolina," 164 (1741), quoted in Smith, *The Constitutional Right to Keep and Bear Arms* at 47.

23. *An Act for the trial of Negroes,* Sec. 6 (Del., 1700).

24. "Digest of the Laws of the State of Georgia," 776 (1768), quoted in Smith, *The Constitutional Right to Keep and Bear Arms* at 47.

25. 6 William H. Hening, *The Statutes at Large of Virginia,* 109 (1823). Similar wording was used in Virginia's 1723 law. See 5 Hening at 131. For other Virginia slave laws preventing the carrying of weapons, see 2 Hening at 481; 3 Hening at 459.

26. Patrick Charles, *Washington's Decision: The Story of George Washington's Decision to Reac-*

*cept Black Enlistments in the Continental Army, December 31, 1775*, 3, 6 (2006). There were exceptions to slaves bearing arms in some of the colonies, but this only occurred in dire times of need, such as war.

27. 1 *Dictionary of the English Language*, 107 (4th ed., Timothy Cunningham ed., 1773).

28. 1 1797 Delaware Laws, 104, Sec. 6 (*An Act for the trial of Negroes*).

29. For examples, see *An Act for the Preservation of the Breed of Wild Deer* (Md., 1729); *An Act for the more effectual preservation of the breed of deer* (Md., 1773); *An Act for the preservation of the breed of wild deer, and for other purposes therein* (Md., 1789); *An Act to Prevent the Killing of Wild Deer, at Unreasonable Times* (N.H., 1758); *An Act to prevent Killing of Deer out of Season and against Carrying Guns and Hunting by Persons not Qualified* Sec. 4, 6 (N.J., 1722); *A Supplementary Act to the act entitled, An Act to prevent the killing of Deer out of Season and against carrying of Guns, and hunting by persons not qualified*, Sec. 7 (N.J., 1751); *An Act to prevent hunting with Fire-Arms in the City of New-York, and the Liberties thereof*, Sec. 1 (N.Y., 1763); *An additional act to an act, entitled, An act to prevent killing deer at unreasonable times and for putting a stop to many abuses committed by white persons, under pretence of hunting* (N.C., 1745); *An act to amend an act entitled "An additional act to an act, entitled, an act to prevent killing deer at unreasonable times and for putting a stop to many abuses committed by white persons under pretence of hunting"* (N.C., 1768); *An Act for the Preservation of Deer, and to prevent the Mischiefs arising from Hunting at unreasonable Times* (S.C., 1769); *An Ordinance for the Preservation of Deer, and to prevent the Mischiefs arising from Fire-Hunting* (S.C., 1785).

30. *Parker*, 478 F.3d at 395.

31. 2 *The Papers of Thomas Jefferson*, 443, 444 (J.P. Boyd ed., 1950).

32. See 1 Hening at 199, 228, 248, 294, 300–01, 437; 2 Hening at 96–97; 3 Hening at 69, 180, 328, 462–63; 4 Hening at 425; 5 Hening at 61–63, 430; 7 Hening at 412–13; 8 Hening at 591–93.

33. *The Complete Bill of Rights: The Drafts, Debates, Sources, and Origins*, 182 (Neil H. Cogan, ed., 1997).

34. *The Origin of the Second Amendment: A Documentary History of the Bill of Rights 1787–1792* at 154–75.

35. Don B. Kates inaccurately depicts the minority as a "substantial portion of Pennsylvania delegates that broke away on this issue." Don B. Kates, *Handgun Prohibition and the Original Meaning of the Second Amendment*, 82, Mich. L. Rev. 204, 222 (1983). There is no indication just how many dissented on this issue

alone. To place the document in its proper historical context, it must be remembered, in political declarations like this, that a complete list of grievances was always compiled. This was done not only to make the argument concise and circular but was felt to be politically essential when declarations were issued. See Pauline Maier, *American Scripture: Making the Declaration of Independence*, 105, 123 (1998).

36. The hunting amendment was listed as the Eighth Amendment, coming right behind the "right to bear arms" amendment. It read, "The inhabitants of several states shall have the liberty to fowl and hunt in seasonable times, on the lands they hold, and on all other lands in the United States not enclosed, and in like manner to fish in all navigable waters, and other not private property, without being restrained therein by any laws to be passed by the legislature of the United States. *Ibid.* at160.

37. For examples, see *An Act to prevent the hunting of deer, and other wild beasts, beyond the limits of the lands purchased of the Indians by the Proprieties of this province, and against killing deer out of season*, Sec. 5–6 (Pa., 1760); *An Act to prevent the killing of Deer out of Season, and against carrying of Guns or Hunting, by Persons not qualified* (Pa., 1721).

38. Niccolo Machiavelli, *The Prince and Discourses*, 48 (Max Lerner ed., 1950).

39. Algernon Sidney, *Discourses Concerning Government*, 205 (Thomas G. West ed., 1990).

40. *Ideal Commonwealths*, 256, 317 (Henry Morley ed., 1901).

41. *Parker*, 478 F.3d. at 384.

42. The O.E.D. shows the definition of "bear" may include that of a military sense, but only one definition is specific to arms. The broader use of this definition referred generally to weapons, and not just to military service. Clayton E. Cramer, *For Defense of Themselves and the State: The Original Intent and Judicial Interpretation of the Right to Keep and Bear Arms*, 7 (1994).

43. Noah Webster's first edition of *An American Dictionary of the English Language* was published in 1928. The edition showed several variations of the use of the verb "bear" in the sense of "carry" or "wear," but there was nothing specific to military service in the definition. *Ibid.*, 6. Webster's definition of "bear" reads, "[t]o wear; to bear as a mark of authority or distinction, as, to bear a sword, a badge, a name; to bear arms in a coat." *An American Dictionary of the English Language*, (at keep) (1st ed., 1828).

44. *Parker*, 478 F.3d at 384.

45. *Ibid.*

46. *An Act for the better ordering the Militia of this Province*, Sec. 15 (Ga., 1765).

47. *An Act for the Regulating the Militia*, Sec.

1 (N.H., 1718). *See also An Act for the Regulating the Militia,* Sec. 1 (N.H., 1759).

48. *An Act for the better regulating the Militia,* Sec. 1 (N.J., 1777). Section 4 of this act also incorporates the phrase "bear arms." It stated, "That every Person above directed to be enrolled shall bear Arms, attend Musters, and in all Things be comfortable to the Rules and Orders herein mentioned." *Ibid.,* Sec. 4.

49. The first person to do research supporting this point was James M. Smith. In his thesis, Smith argues the use of the phrase "bear arms" in anything other than a military sense was very rare, and was not seen after 1700. Although, he says the use of the word "bear" to mean "carry" was used before 1700. Smith cites four examples, all of which the use of the word "bear" is supposed to mean "to carry." All of these examples were incorporated in militia laws, and have been interpreted incorrectly by Smith. All these examples were using the term in the military sense. James M. Smith, "The Constitutional Right to Keep and Bear Arms," 42–47 (1959) (unpublished J.D. thesis, Harvard University) (on file with the Harvard University Law Library).

50. Reacting to the universal fear that Congressional control over militia might be misused, James Madison originally proposed the following be instated into Article I, Section 8, of the Constitution: "The right of the people to keep and bear arms shall not be infringed, a well armed and well regulated militia being the best security of a free country; but no person religiously scrupulous of bearing arms shall be compelled to render military service in person." 1 *Annals of Congress,* 451, (1789). A committee of eleven, composed of Madison and representatives from the other states met six weeks later. They revised Madison's original recommendation to now read: "A well regulated militia, composed of the body of the people, being the best security of a free state, the right of the people to keep and bear arms shall be not infringed." Cress at 36. Historian Pauline Maier has found Madison planned on "including freedom of religion, of speech, and of the press, the rights of assembly and of petition, and the right to bear arms — in Article I, Section 8, among other restrictions on Congress." Maier, *American Scripture: Making the Declaration of Independence* at 195–96.

51. U.S. Const, Art I, § 8, cl. 16.

52. These fears were addressed in speeches by George Mason, Patrick Henry, and William Grayson. 1 *The Papers of John Marshall,* 254 (Herbert A. Johnson ed., 1974).

53. *Ibid.,* 274.

54. *Ibid.*

55. Clayton E. Cramer and Joseph Edward

Olson, "What Did 'Bear Arms' Mean in the Second Amendment?" 6 *Georgetown Journal of Law & Pub.* Pol'y, No. 2 (2008).

56. 2 John Adams, *A Defence of the Constitutions of Government of the United States of America,* 422 (London, John Stockdale, 1794).

57. *Ibid.,* 422–23.

58. *District of Columbia v. Heller,* 128 S.Ct. at 2805.

59. *An Act for establishing a Militia within this State,* Sec. 6 (Del., 1782).

60. *A Supplement to the act entitled, An act to regulate and discipline the militia of this state,* Sec. 30 (Md., 1799).

61. 4 Hening at 121. See also, 8 Hening at 241–45.

62. 11 Hening at 478–79. See also, 12 Hening at 697.

63. There are instances where militia laws stated those enrolled "shall always keep provided," but "keep" in these sentences was the adverb. Even in these instances "provide" was used to denote ownership or possession. For examples, see *An Act for regulating and governing the Militia of the Commonwealth of Massachusetts, and for repealing all Laws heretofore made for that Purpose; excepting and Act, intitled "An Act for establishing Rules and Articles for governing the Troops stationed in Forts and Garrisons, within this Commonwealth, and also the Militia, when called into actual Service,"* Sec. 18 (Mass. 1793); *An Act for regulating and governing the Militia of the State of Vermont, and for repealing all Laws heretofore passed for that purpose,* Sec. 16 (Vt. 1793).

64. *An Act for the better establishing and regulating of Patrols in this Province,* Sec. 4 (S.C. 1746)

65. New Hampshire also showed a difference in meaning between "keep" and "provide." New Hampshire did not use the word "keep," and instead preferred to "have in constant Readiness." In their militia acts of 1780 and 1786, New Hampshire required "every Non-Commissioned Officer and Soldier, both in the Alar[m] List, and Training Band, shall be provided, and have in constant Readiness, a good Musquet and Bayonet...." *See An Act for forming and regulating the Militia within this State, and for repealing all the Laws heretofore made for that Purpose* (N.H. 1780); *An Act for forming and regulating the Militia within this State, and for repealing the laws heretofore made for that purpose,* Sec. 7 (N.H. 1786). Virginia also noted this distinction in its 1723 militia act. Section eleven stated, "And for the encouragement of every soldier to provide and furnish himself, according to the directions of this act, and his security to keep his horse, arms, and ammunition when provided, *Be it enacted....* That the horses and

furniture, arms and ammunition, provided and kept, in pursuance of this act, be free and exempted at all times from being impressed upon any account whatsoever." 4 Hening at 121. The words "provide and furnish" defined one's duty to own or possess, and "keep" and "kept" showed one's duty to "maintain" or "service."

66. *An Act for establishing a Militia within this State*, Sec. 6 (Del. 1782). In 1793, Delaware required "every citizen enrolled" to "provide himself with the arms, ammunition and accoutrements herein after mentioned," see *An Act for establishing the militia in this state*, Sec. 4 (Del. 1793). See also *An Act for Establishing a Militia within this state*, Sec. 5 (Del. 1778).

67. *An Act for Establishing and regulating Patrols* (Ga. 1757).

68. *An Act to regulate and discipline the militia of this state*, Sec. 1 (Md. 1793).

69. *An Act for forming and regulating the Militia within the Commonwealth of Massachusetts, and for repealing all the Laws heretofore made for that Purpose* (Mass. 1781). See also *An Act for regulating and governing the Militia of the Commonwealth of Massachusetts, and for repealing all Laws heretofore made for that Purpose; excepting and Act, entitled "An Act for establishing Rules and Articles for governing the Troops stationed in Forts and Garrisons, within this Commonwealth, and also the Militia, when called into actual Service,"* Sec. 18 (Mass. 1793). For other examples of the other colonies using the word "provide" in their militia laws, see *An Act for the Regulating the Militia*, Sec. 5 (N.H. 1718); *An Act for Regulating the Militia*, Sec. 1 (N.H. 1759); *An Act for forming and regulating the Militia within the State of New-Hampshire, in New England, and for repealing all the Laws heretofore made for that Purpose*, Sec. 6 (N.H. 1776); *An Act for forming and regulating the Militia within this State, and for repealing all the Laws heretofore made for that Purpose* (N.H. 1780); *An Act for forming and regulating the Militia within this State, and for repealing the laws heretofore made for that purpose*, Sec. 7 (N.H. 1786); *An Act for better settling and regulating the Militia of this Colony of New-Jersey, for the Repelling of Invasions and Suppressing Insurrections and Rebellions*, Sec. 12 (N.J. 1746); *A Supplementary Act to the Act, entitled, An Act for better settling and regulating the Militia of this Colony of New-Jersey, for the repelling Invasions, and suppressing Insurrections and Rebellions; as also for continuing such Parts and Clauses of the said Law as are not altered and amended by this Act*, Sec. 4 (N.J. 1757); *A Supplement to the Act, intitled, "An Act for organizing and training the Militia of this State,"* Sec. 5 (N.J. 1793); *An Act for regulating the Militia of the Colony of New York*, Sec. 4, 8 (N.Y. 1772); *An Act for regulating the militia of the State of*

*New York* (N.Y. 1778); *An Act to regulate the Militia*, Sec. 1 (N.Y. 1786); *An Act to revise and amend the Militia Laws*, Sec. 1 (N.C. 1800); *An Act to regulate the Militia of the Common-Wealth of Pennsylvania*, Sec. 18 (Pa. 1777); *An Act for the regulation of the Militia of the commonwealth of Pennsylvania*, Sec. 5 (1793); 6 Hening at 116; 8 Hening at 241–45; *An Act for the better establishment and regulation of the militia in this state*, Sec. 7 (Tenn. 1798); *An Act for forming and regulating the militia, and for encouragement of military skill, for the better defence of state* (Vt. 1779); *An Act regulating the Militia of this State* (Vt. 1786); *An act regulating the Militia of the State of Vermont* (Vt. 1787); *An Act for regulating and governing the Militia of the State of Vermont, and for repealing all Laws heretofore passed for that purpose*, Sec. 16 (Vt. 1793).

70. 1 *Stat.* 271 (1792).

71. *An Act for the better regulating the Militia*, Sec. 4 (N.J. 1777); *see also An Act for organizing and training the Militia of this State*, Sec. 2 (N.J. 1792); *A Supplement to the Act, intitled, "An Act for organizing and training the Militia of this State,"* Sec. 5 (1793).

72. *An Act for raising troops for the protection of the inhabitants of Davidson county*, Sec. 5 (N.C. 1786).

73. *An Act for embodying and brining into the field Twelve Hundred able-bodied effective Men, of the Militia, to serve within this State for One Month, from the Time of their Rendezvous, and no longer Term, and not to be marched out of the same* (R.I. 1781).

74. 7 Hening at 94. For other examples *see* 9 Hening at 12; 10 Hening at 20–21.

75. *An Act for forming and regulating the Militia within the Commonwealth of Massachusetts, and for repealing all the Laws heretofore made for that Purpose* (Mass. 1781). New Hampshire copied this provision word for word. See *An Act for forming and regulating the Militia within this State, and for repealing all the Laws heretofore made for that Purpose* (N.H. 1780); *An Act for forming and regulating the Militia within this State, and for repealing the laws heretofore made for that purpose*, Sec. 7 (N.H. 1786).

76. *An Act for the regulation of the Militia of the Commonwealth of Pennsylvania*, Sec. 39 (Pa. 1802).

77. *Baron von Steuben and his Regulations*, 119 ( Joseph R. Riling ed., 1966).

78. *Ibid.*, 120.

79. *Ibid.*, 144, 146.

80. *Ibid.*, 148.

81. 478 F.3d at 386.

82. *Holmes v. Jennison*, 39 U.S.540, 570–71 (1840).

83. 1 *Stat.* 271 (1792).

84. U.S. Const, Art. I, § 8, cl. 16.

85. *An Act for establishing a Militia within this State*, Sec. 6 (Del. 1782).

86. *An Act for forming and regulating the Militia within the Commonwealth of Massachusetts, and for repealing all the Laws heretofore made for that Purpose* (Mass. 1781).

87. *An Act to regulate the militia* (N.Y. 1786). For other examples requiring individuals to provide their own arms and accoutrements, see *An Act for Establishing and regulating Patrols* (Ga. 1757); *An act for raising troops for the protection of the inhabitants of Davidson county* (N.C. 1786); *An Act to revise and amend the Militia Laws*, Sec. 2 (N.C. 1800); *An Act for the regulation of the Militia of the commonwealth of Pennsylvania*, Sec. 5 (Pa. 1793); *An Act for embodying and brining into the field Twelve Hundred able-bodied effective Men, of the Militia, to serve within this State for One Month, from the Time of their Rendezvous, and no longer Term, and not to be marched out of the same* (R.I. 1781); 4 Hening at 118–26; *An Act for the Regulation of the Militia of this State* (S.C. 1782); *An Act for forming and regulating the militia, and for encouragement of military skill, for the better defence of the state* (Vt. 1779); *An Act for regulating the Militia of this State* (Vt. 1786); *An act regulating the Militia of the State of Vermont* (Vt. 1787); *An Act for regulating and governing the Militia of the State of Vermont, and for repealing all Laws heretofore passed for that purpose*, Sec. 16 (Vt. 1793).

88. *An Act for establishing a Militia within this State*, Sec. 6 (Del. 1782).

89. *An Act for forming and regulating the Militia within the Commonwealth of Massachusetts, and for repealing all the Laws heretofore made for that Purpose* (Mass. 1781); *An Act for settling the Militia* (N.H. 1687); *An Act for the Regulating the Militia*, Sec. 16 (N.H. 1718); *An Act for forming and regulating the Militia within this State, and for repealing all the Laws heretofore made for that Purpose* (N.H. 1780); *An Act for forming and regulating the Militia within this State, and for repealing the laws heretofore made for that purpose*, Sec. 7 (N.H. 1786); *An Act for forming and regulating the militia within this State, and for repealing all the laws heretofore made for that purpose* (N.H. 1792).

90. *An Act for the better regulating the Militia*, Sec. 13 (N.J. 1777).

91. *An Act for making current Thirty Thousand Pounds, in Bills of Credit, for his Majesty's Service in the Present War*, Sec. 24 (N.J. 1757).

92. *A Supplementary Act, to the Act for the Ordering and Regulating the Militia of this Province for the better Defense and Security thereof* (Md. 1732).

93. *An Act his Majesty's Service, and further Defence and Security of this Province* (Md. 1756).

94. *An Act to regulate the Militia of the Common-Wealth of Pennsylvania*, Sec. 18–19 (Pa. 1777).

95. *An Act to repeal part of the additional supplement to the Acts for the regulation of the Militia of this Commonwealth* (Pa. 1790).

96. 4 Hening at 118–26.

97. 7 Hening at 94.

98. *Ibid.*, 113–14.

99. 9 Hening at 12

100. *Ibid.*, 87.

101. 10 Hening at 20–21; 11 Hening at 132, 174

102. 9 Hening at 87.

103. 11 Hening at 478–79; 12 Hening at 9. The 1784 act required every soldier to have "a good clean musket, carrying an ounce ball, and three feet eight inches long in the barrel, with a good bayonet and iron ramrod well fitted thereto, a cartridge box properly made, to contain and secure twenty cartridges fitted to his musket, a good knapsack and canteen; and … one pound of good powder and four pounds of lead." It was the duty of each private to "constantly keep the aforesaid arms, accoutrements and ammunition ready," but if the private was "so poor that he cannot purchase the arms herein required, such court shall cause them to be purchased out of the money arising from delinquents." 11 Hening at 478–79.

104. 12 Hening at 432.

105. *Ibid.*

106. *Ibid.*

107. 8 Hening at 241–45.

108. *Ibid.*

109. This essay was entitled "Consequences of Hostilities Between the States," published on November 20, 1787, and was written by Alexander Hamilton. The essay did not address the individual right to bear arms, and only addressed the negative consequences if there was a war between the states. See *The Federalist Papers No. 8* (Alexander Hamilton) (consequences of wars between states).

110. This essay was entitled "The Same Subject Continued: The Idea of Restraining the Legislative Authority in Regard to the Common Defense Considered," published on December 26, 1787, and was written by Alexander Hamilton. The essay did not address the individual right to bear arms, but did address the idea of a social contract between the people and their government. The principle developed during the Glorious Revolution of 1689 and was extended in American Revolution. It stated the people have right to usurp rulers or representatives that "betray their constituents." Under such circumstances, the "citizens must rush tumultuously to arms, without concert, without system, without resource, except in their

courage and despair." See *The Federalist No.* 28 (Alexander Hamilton) (a national army and internal security).

111. This essay was entitled "The Influence of the State and Federal Governments Compared," published on January 29, 1788, and was written by James Madison. The essay did not address the individual right to bear arms, but did address the superiority of the American militia system over any standing army. The essay read: "Let a regular army, fully equal to the resources of the country, be formed; and let it be entirely at the devotion of the federal government; still it would not be going too far to say, that the State governments, with the people on their side, would be able to repel the danger. The highest number to which, according to the best computation, a standing army can be carried in any country, does not exceed one hundredth part of the whole number of souls; or one twenty-fifth part of the number able to bear arms. This proportion would not yield, in the United States, an army of more than twenty-five or thirty thousand men. To these would be opposed a militia amounting to near half a million of citizens with arms in their hands, officered by men chosen from among themselves, fighting for their common liberties, and united and conducted by governments possessing their affections and confidence. It may well be doubted, whether a militia thus circumstanced could ever be conquered by such a proportion of regular troops. Those who are best acquainted with the last successful resistance of this country against the British arms, will be most inclined to deny the possibility of it. Besides the advantage of being armed, which the Americans possess over the people of almost every other nation, the existence of subordinate governments, to which the people are attached, and by which the militia officers are appointed, forms a barrier against the enterprises of ambition, more insurmountable than any which a simple government of any form can admit of. Notwithstanding the military establishments in the several kingdoms of Europe, which are carried as far as the public resources will bear, the governments are afraid to trust the people with arms. And it is not certain, that with this aid alone they would not be able to shake off their yokes. But were the people to possess the additional advantages of local governments chosen by themselves, who could collect the national will and direct the national force, and of officers appointed out of the militia, by these governments, and attached both to them and to the militia, it may be affirmed with the greatest assurance, that the throne of every tyranny in Europe would be speedily overturned in spite of the legions which surround it." The essay only addresses the people's right to bear arms in the context of militia service. It was through the militia system that the American people possessed the "advantage of being armed" over the countries of Europe, which had turned to using standing armies. The essay's main point was a standing army would never be capable of usurping the rights of the populace because the militia system afforded a larger military force than any force the government could assemble. The essay does not address any natural or individual right to own arms, because this right was through the militia. See *The Federalist No.* 46 (James Madison) (state and federal power compared).

112. This essay was entitled "Concerning the Power of Congress to Regulate the Election of Members," published on February 22, 1788, and was written by Alexander Hamilton. The essay addressed the potential abuses by the legislative branch of government in controlling its own elections, and did not address any individual right to bear arms. See *The Federalist No.* 59 (Alexander Hamilton) (national regulation of congressional elections).

113. After the Revolution, in December 1790, when Congress was debating the adoption of the National Militia Bill, Mr. Jackson informed the other delegates the importance of a strong and well regulated militia in preventing standing armies. He reminded them of England, whose "militia of late has been neglected — the consequence is a standing army." Thus, "if we neglect the militia," Jackson stated, "a standing army must be introduced." Congress could not do this though because "[i]n a Republic every man out to be a soldier, and be prepared to resist tyranny and usurpation, as well as invasion, and to prevent the greatest of all evils — a standing army." 2 *Annals of Congress*, 1806 (1791). In a later debate on militia, Mr. Jackson is also on record stating, "He should regret the time when this country would depend on a standing army." It was important to discipline the militia because it is "consistent with the strictest principles of republicanism." *Ibid.*, 1816. In April, Mr. Benson commented that "the institution of the militia is to enable the individual States to oppose the encroachments which may be made on them by the General Government!" 3 *Annals of Congress*, 553 (1793)

114. *The Complete Bill of Rights: The Drafts, Debates, Sources, and Origins* at 185–86.

115. *Ibid.*, 186.

116. *Ibid.*, 187. Many other attempts were made that day to have the "religiously scrupulous" section removed. On every occasion the motion was "negatived." *Ibid.*, 188–89.

117. *Ibid.*

118. *Ibid.*, 188.

119. *Ibid.*, 175.

120. *Ibid.*, 190.

121. *Ibid.*

122. *Ibid.*, 191.

123. *Ibid.*, 172.

124. *Ibid.*, 176.

125. *Ibid.*

126. Charles, *Washington's Decision: The Story of George Washington's Decision to Reaccept Black Enlistments in the Continental Army, December 31, 1775* at 113–14.

127. 4 *The Papers of John Adams*, 91 (Robert Taylor ed., 1979).

128. On November 28, 1775, the General wrote to Joseph Reed, "After five, I think, different meetings of the General Officers I have, in a manner, been obliged to give into the humor and whimsies of the people, or get no army." Charles, *Washington's Decision: The Story of George Washington's Decision to Reaccept Black Enlistments in the Continental Army, December 31, 1775* at 111.

129. *Ibid.*, 113–14.

130. 3 *American Archives: Documents of the American Revolution, 1774–1776, Fourth Series*, 1653, 1654 (Peter Force ed., 1853).

131. 3 *The Writings of Samuel Adams*, 229 (Harry Alonzo Cushing ed., 1908).

132. *Ibid.*, 230.

133. 3 *American Archives: Documents of the American Revolution, 1774–1776, Fourth Series* at 255–56.

134. *Ibid.*, 821–22.

135. *Ibid.*, 1945.

136. *The Complete Bill of Rights: The Drafts, Debates, Sources, and Origins* at 200.

137. *Ibid.*

138. *Ibid.*, 193.

139. *Ibid.*, 194

140. *Ibid.*

141. *Ibid.*, 195.

142. *Ibid.*

143. *Ibid.*, 197.

144. *Ibid.*, 199.

145. *Ibid.*

146. *Whether the Second Amendment Secures an Individual Right: Memorandum Opinion for the Attorney General* at 63.

147. It read, "That the people have a right to bear arms for the defense of themselves and their own state, or the United States, or for the purpose of killing game; and no law shall be passed for disarming the people or any of them, unless for crimes committed, or real danger of public injury from individuals; and as standing armies in the time of peace are dangerous to liberty, they ought not to be kept up; and that the military shall be kept under strict subordination to and be governed by the civil powers." *The Complete Bill of Rights: The Drafts, Debates, Sources, and Origins* at 182.

148. The other was, "The inhabitants of the several states shall have the liberty to fowl and hunt in seasonable times, on the lands they hold, and on all other lands in the United States not inclosed, and in like manner to fish in all navigable waters, and others not private property, without being restrained therein by any laws to be passed by the legislature." *Ibid.*

149. 2 *Papers of Thomas Jefferson* at 443–44.

150. See 1 Hening at 199, 228, 248, 294, 300–01, 437; 2 Hening at 96–97; 3 Hening at 69, 180, 328, 462–63; 4 Hening at 425; 5 Hening at 61–63, 430; 7 Hening at 412–13; 8 Hening at 591–93.

151. See *An Act to prevent the hunting of deer, and other wild beasts, beyond the limits of the lands purchased of the Indians by the Proprieties of this province, and against killing deer out of season*, Sec. 5–6 (Pa. 1760); *An Act to prevent the killing of Deer out of Season, and against carrying of Guns or Hunting, by Persons not qualified* (Pa. 1721).

152. Schwartz, 2 *Bill of Rights* at 674–75.

153. Samuel Adams may have also been a small minority in this case. From the outset of hostilities Adams' feared the dangers standing armies posed. He often made comments against the maintenance of the Continental Army and feared giving Congress too much control over the states' militias at the outset of the Revolutionary War. See *The Writings of Samuel Adams* at 250–51 (Harry Alonzo Cushing, ed., 1908).

154. Janice Potter, *The Liberty We Seek: Loyalist Ideology in Colonial New York and Massachusetts* at 32.

155. *Ibid.*, 30.

156. 1 Lorenzo Sabine, *Biographical Sketches of Loyalists of the American Revolution*, 227 (1864).

157. 2 Sabine, *Biographical Sketches of Loyalists of the American Revolution*, 231 (1864).

158. *Ibid.*, 322.

159. *A Fragment of Facts, Disclosing the Conduct of the Maryland Convention, on the Adoption of the Federal Constitution* (1788).

160. *Ibid.*

161. *Ibid.*

162. *Ratification of the Constitution by the State of New Hampshire, June 21, 1788* (1788).

163. See *An Act, describing the Disqualifications to which Persons shall be subjected, who have been, or may be guilty of Treason, or giving Aid or Support to the present Rebellion, and to whom a Pardon may be extended* (Mass. 1787). It reads, "That they shall keep the peace for the term of three years ... and that during that term of time, they shall not serve as Jurors, be eligible to any town office, or any other office under the Government of this Commonwealth, and shall be disqualified from ... giving their votes for the same term of time, for any officer, civil or mil-

itary, within this Commonwealth, unless such persons, or any of them, shall after the first day of May, seventeen hundred and eighty eight, exhibit plenary evidence of their having returned to their allegiance ... That is shall be the duty of the Justice before whom any offender or offenders aforesaid may deliver up their arms, and take and subscribe the oath aforesaid ... and it shall be the duty of the Justice to require such as shall take and subscribe the oath of allegiance, to subjoin their names, their places of abode, and their additions, and if required, to give to each offender who shall deliver up his arms ... a certificate of the same under his seal ... and it shall be the duty of such Major General or commanding officer, to give such directions as he may think necessary, for the safe keeping of such arms, in order that they may be returned to the person or persons who delivered the same, at the expiration of said term of three years, in case such person or persons shall have complied with the conditions above-mentioned, and shall obtain an order for the re-delivery of such arms, from the Governour."

164. *Ibid.*

165. This states, "The Times, Places and Manner of holding Elections for Senators and Representatives, shall be prescribed in each State by the Legislature thereof; but the Congress may at any time by Law make or alter such Regulations, except as to the Places of chusing Senators." U.S. Const., Art. I, Sec. 4 (1789).

166. *Ratification of the Constitution by the State of New Hampshire, June 21, 1788* (1788).

167. *Whether the Second Amendment Secures an Individual Right: Memorandum Opinion for the Attorney General* at 65–66.

168. It read "That a well regulated militia, composed of the body of the people, trained to arms, is the proper, natural, and safe defence of a free state; that standing armies, in time of peace, should be avoided, as dangerous to liberty; and that, in all cases, the military should be under strict subordination to, and governed by, the civil power." Virginia *Declaration of Rights*, Art. XIII (1776).

169. *Ratification of the Constitution by the State of New York* (1788).

## Chapter Two

1. *District of Columbia v. Heller*, 128 S.Ct. at 2805.

2. St. George Tucker, *View of the Constitution of the United with Selected Writings*, 214 (Clyde N. Wilson foreword, 1999).

3. *Ibid.*

4. *Ibid.*

5. *Ibid.*, 215.

6. William Rawle, *A View of the Constitution of the United States of America*, 126 (2nd edition, 1829).

7. *Ibid.*, 125–26.

8. *Ibid.*, 125.

9. *Ibid.*

10. *Ibid.*, 126.

11. *Ibid.*

12. *District of Columbia v. Heller*, 128 S.Ct. at 2806.

13. *Ibid.*, 2806–7.

14. 3 Joseph Story, *Commentaries on the Constitution of the United States*, 747 (1833).

15. *Ibid.*

16. *Ibid.*, 746.

17. *Ibid.*, 745–46.

18. *Ibid.*, 747.

19. It has already been shown that Tucker, Rawle, and Story all had given commentary supporting the right Oliver states.

20. Benjamin Oliver, *The Rights of an American Citizen*, 177 (1832).

21. *Ibid.*, 176.

22. *Houston v. Moore*, 18, U.S. 1, 21 (1820).

23. 3 Story, *Commentaries on the Constitution of the United States* at 745–47.

24. *Houston*, 18, U.S. at 21.

25. *Ibid.*

26. 13 F.Cas., 840 (1833).

27. *Ibid.*, 852.

28. *Ibid.*, 850–51.

29. *Ibid.*, 852.

30. Pa. Const., Art. IX, § 21 (1790).

31. *Aldridge v. Commonwealth*, 2 Va.Cas., 447 (1824).

32. *Ibid.*

33. Va. Const. Declaration of Rights § 13 (1776).

34. 12 Hening at 182.

35. *An act, to amend an Act, entitled an Act for regulating the Navigation of James River, above the Falls of the said River*, Sec. 2 (Va. 1811).

36. *An act farther to amend the penal laws of this commonwealth*, Sec. 3 (Va. 1823).

37. I *U.S. Stat* 271 (1792).

38. 13 Hening at+ 343–55.

39. Charles, *Washington's Decision: The Story of George Washington's Decision to Reaccept Black Enlistments in the Continental Army, December 31, 1775* at 151.

40. *Ibid.*

41. *Waters v. State*, 1 Gill 302 (1843).

42. *An Act relating to Free Negroes and Slaves*, Sec. 6 (1831).

43. *An Act to Enroll, Equip, and Regulate the Militia of this State*, Sec. 1 (1834).

44. *United States v. Sheldon*, 5 Blume Sup.Ct. Trans. 337, 346 (1829).

45. *District of Columbia v. Heller*, 128 S.Ct. at 2802.

46. *Ibid.*, 2808.

47. *United States v. Sheldon*, 5 Blume Sup.Ct. Trans. at 346.

48. *Nunn v. State*, 1 Ga. 243, 251 (1846).

49. *Ibid.*

50. *District of Columbia v. Heller*, 128 S.Ct. at 2809.

51. *Nunn v. State*, 1 Ga. at 251.

52. *Ibid.*

53. *Hill v. State*, 53 Ga. 472 (1874).

54. It reads, "A well regulated militia being necessary to the security of a free state, the right of the people to keep and bear arms shall not be infringed; but the general assembly shall have power to prescribe the manner in which arms may be borne." Ga. Const, Art. I, § 14 (1868). The 1861 Georgia Constitution did protect, "The right of the people to keep and bear arms shall not be infringed." Ga. Const, Art. I, § 6 (1861). This constitution was created when Georgia seceded from the Union, and therefore is null and void.

55. 92 U.S. 542 (1875).

56. 7 *Landmark Briefs and Arguments of the Supreme Court of the United States Constitutional Law*, 291 (Philip B. Kurland ed., 1975) (brief for the United States).

57. *Ibid.*

58. *Ibid.*, 289.

59. *District of Columbia v. Heller*, 128 S.Ct. at 2812–13.

60. *United States v. Cruikshank*, 92 U.S. at 542.

61. See 7 *Landmark Briefs and Arguments of the Supreme Court of the United States Constitutional Law* at 287–314.

62. *Ibid.*, 325–26 (brief for defendants by David S. Byron in *United States v. Cruikshank*).

63. *Ibid.*, 352 (brief for defendants by attorney R.H. Marr).

64. *Ibid.*, 373.

65. *Ibid.*

66. *Ibid.*, 386–87 (brief for defendants by attorney John A. Campbell).

67. *Ibid.*, 387.

68. 116 U.S. 252 (1886).

69. *Ibid.*, 265.

70. 307 U.S. at 176.

71. *Ibid.*, 178.

72. *Printz v. United States*, 521, U.S. 898, 939 FN1 (1997).

73. *Ibid.*, 938.

## Chapter Three

1. U.S. Const, Art. I, § 8, cl. 16.

2. 1 *American State Papers: Military Affairs*, 6 (1832).

3. *Ibid.*

4. Knox's plan called for a militia class system based on a person's age. The Advanced Corps was to consist of all men between the ages of eighteen and twenty-one, and would be the bedrock of the American defense. The Main Corps would have consisted of all men from twenty-one to forty-five years of age, and lastly, the Reserved Corps would consist of men from forty-six to sixty years of age. *Ibid.*, 6–8.

5. 3 *Annals of Congress* at 418.

6. *Ibid.*, 419.

7. *Ibid.*

8. The *Annals of Congress* reported Congressman Sturges argued: "Adverting to the Constitution ... the meaning of organizing ... simply relates to forming, arming, and arranging in a particular way, those materials which are furnished by the militia laws of the several States." *Ibid.*, 420.

9. *Ibid.*

10. Given the lack of uniformity of arms during the American Revolution, and the problems that arose from this, it was thought best that Congress require a uniform weapons for the National Militia. It would seem that this idea gained popularity through Baron von Steuben's *Regulations for the Order and Discipline of the Troops of the United States*, which was originally published in 1779. The very first regulation reads, "The arms and accoutrements of the officers, non-commissioned officers, and soldiers, should be uniform throughout." *Baron von Steuben and his Regulations* at 5.

11. There was a debate over whether minors, poor men, and apprentices should be supplied with arms by the United States. The provision was not accepted because, as Mr. Wadsworth put it, to have the government arm "perhaps one-third" of the militia, and have them "liable to be disarmed" by the same government, "would tend more to excite suspicion and rouse a jealously dangerous to the Union." 2 *Annals of Congress* at 1809.

12. 1 *U.S. Stat*, 271 (1792).

13. In February 1792, when the bill was under debate, Mr. Niles even described the requirement that every man provide his own arms as "operating like a capitation tax." 3 *Annals of Congress* at 421.

14. See Notes 91–107 in Chapter One.

15. See Notes 97–100 in Chapter One.

16. *An Act for regulating the Militia of this Commonwealth* (Ky. 1792).

17. *An Act to regulate and discipline the militia of this state* (Md. 1793).

18. *An Act to organize the militia of this State* (N.Y. 1793).

19. *An Act to Organize the Militia throughout the State of South Carolina, in conformity with the act of Congress* (S.C. 1794).

20. *An Act for the better establishment and regulation of the militia of this state* (Tn. 1798).

21. 13 Hening at 343–55.

22. *An Act for establishing the militia in this state* (Dl. 1793).

23. *An Act for regulating and governing the Militia of the Commonwealth of Massachusetts, and for repealing all Laws heretofore made for that Purpose; excepting and Act, intitled "An Act for establishing Rules and Articles for governing the Troops stationed in Forts and Garrisons, within this Commonwealth, and also the Militia, when called into actual Service*, Sec. 19 (Mass. 1793).

24. *An Act for forming and regulating the militia within this State, and for repealing all the laws heretofore made for that purpose* (N.H. 1792).

25. *A Supplement to the Act, intitled, "An Act for organizing and training the Militia of this State,"* Sec. 5 (N.J. 1793).

26. *An Act for the regulation of the Militia of the commonwealth of Pennsylvania*, Sec. 5 (Pa. 1793).

27. *An Act for regulating and governing the Militia of the State of Vermont, and for repealing all Laws heretofore passed for that purpose*, Sec. 17 (Vt. 1793).

28. 2 Hening at 481; 3 Hening at 459.

29. In 1739, at the Stono River in South Carolina, one hundred slaves staged a rebellion. The slaves, already trained in military tactics, raided a store to procure guns and ammunition, killing two of the shopkeepers. Thinking they would take advantage on the war between Britain and Spain, the armed slaves began their march to Florida for their freedom. Along the march their numbers continued to grow until the royal governor called out the colonial militia to suppress the rebellion. The event was published in newspapers throughout the colonies and struck fear throughout the South. See James Oliver Horton, *Slavery and the Making of America*, 37, 38 (2005).

30. See *An Act for Establishing and regulating Patrols* (Ga. 1757); *An Act to amend and continue an Act, intitled "An Act for establishing and regulating Patrols* (Ga. 1760); *An Act for the better establishing and regulating of Patrols in this Province* (S.C. 1746).

31. *An Act to oblige the Male white Persons in the Province of Georgia to carry Fire-arms to all Places of publick Worship* (Ga. 1757); *An Act for the better Security of this Province against the Insurrections and other wicked Attempts of Negroes, and other Slaves; and for reviving and continuing, and act of the General Assembly of this Province, entitled an Act for the better Ordering and Governing Negroes and other Slaves in this Province* (S.C. 1743).

32. *An Act to oblige the Male white Persons in the Province of Georgia to carry Fire-arms to all Places of publick Worship* (Ga. 1757).

33. On November 20, 1792, a committee was appointed to amend the Militia Act. *See* 3 *Annals of Congress* at 701.

34. *Ibid.*, 419.

35. 1 *American State Papers: Military Affairs* at 69–70.

36. 1 *U.S. Stat*, 271–72 (1792).

37. *An Act for regulating the Militia of this Commonwealth* (Ky. 1792).

38. *An Act to regulate and discipline the militia of this state* (Md. 1793).

39. *An Act for regulating and governing the Militia of the Commonwealth of Massachusetts, and for repealing all Laws heretofore made for that Purpose; excepting and Act, intitled "An Act for establishing Rules and Articles for governing the Troops stationed in Forts and Garrisons, within this Commonwealth, and also the Militia, when called into actual Service* (Mass. 1793).

40. *A Supplement to the Act, intitled, "An Act for organizing and training the Militia of this State,"* Sec. 5 (N.J. 1793).

41. 1 *American State Papers: Military Affairs* at 70.

42. *An Act for the regulation of the Militia of the commonwealth of Pennsylvania* (Pa. 1793).

43. *An Act to Organize the Militia throughout the State of South Carolina, in conformity with the act of Congress* (S.C. 1794).

44. *An Act for the better establishment and regulation of the militia of this state* (Tn. 1798).

45. *An Act for regulating and governing the Militia of the State of Vermont, and for repealing all Laws heretofore passed for that purpose*, Sec. 17 (Vt. 1793).

46. 3 *Annals of Congress* at 708.

47. *Ibid.*

48. *Ibid.*

49. *Ibid.*, 709.

50. *Ibid.*

51. *Ibid.*

52. *Ibid.*, 710.

53. *Ibid.* See also Mr. Jackson's comments on this issue in *Footnote 120*.

54. For examples, see *Ibid.*, 420–22; 6 *Annals of Congress*, 1681 (1849).

55. 3 *Annals of Congress* at 710.

56. The vote was 37 for the bill, 31 against. The bill was eight votes shy of meeting the required two-thirds. *Annals of Congress*, 6 at 1685.

57. *Ibid.*, 1683–84.

58. *Ibid.*, 1684.

59. *Ibid.*, 1685.

60. 8 *Annals of Congress* 1927 (1851).

61. Giles stated the problems "consist in the want of a competent source of supplying the arms; the want of some provision for furnish-

ing persons with arms, who may be deemed unable to furnish themselves; and the want of adequate uniform penalties to enforce a compliance with the requisitions of the existing militia laws." 1 *American State Papers: Military Affairs* at 107.

62. 1 *Circular Letters of Congressmen to Their Constituents, 1789–1829*, 22 (Noble E. Cunningham Jr. ed., 1978).

63. *Ibid.*

64. 3 *Annals of Congress* at 708–712; 6 *Annals of Congress* at 1675–85, 1688–91, 2099, 2224; 8 *Annals of Congress* at 1384–86, 1524–25.

65. *A Supplement to an act, intitled, An Act for establishing the militia in this state* (Dl. 1796).

66. *Ibid.*

67. *A Supplement to the Act, intitled, "An Act for organizing and training the Militia of this State,"* Sec. 5 (N.J. 1793).

68. *Ibid.*

69. 8 *Annals of Congress* at 1930.

70. *An Act to provide for the suppressing an insurrection in the Western Counties of this commonwealth* (Pa. 1794; *An Act to provide arms for the use of the commonwealth* (Pa. 1797).

71. *Ibid.*

72. *Ibid.*

73. 1 *Circular Letters of Congressmen to Their Constituents, 1789–1829*, 99.

74. *Ibid.*

75. 1 *U.S. Stat*, 576 (1798).

76. 8 *Annals of Congress* at 1931.

77. *Ibid.*, 1938.

78. *Ibid.*, 1931.

79. *Ibid.*, 1932–33.

80. *Ibid.*, 1931.

81. *A Supplement to the act entitled, An act to regulate and discipline the militia of this state,* Sec. 28 (Md. 1799).

82. *Ibid.*, Sec. 30.

83. *An Act to alter and amend the Militia Law of this State, and to provide for arming the militia thereof*, Sec. 3 (Ga. 1799).

84. *Ibid.*

85. 1 *U.S. Stat*, 271–72 (1792). Opponents to this provision understood the importance of adopting a uniform arms requirement, but thought it bore too large of an expense on persons enrolled. Aaron Kitchell thought such a provision was "impossible to be complied with." Thomas Sumpter thought it was "almost totally impracticable to carry it into execution" since it "would involve an enormous and unnecessary expense." Meanwhile, Nathaniel Niles considered such a provision was operating as a "capitation tax," and could only be assessed as a tax within the limits of the Constitution. See 3 *Annals of Congress* at 421.

86. *An Act for the speedy trial of criminals, and ascertaining their punishment in the county courts when prosecuted there, and for payment of fees due from criminal persons* (Md. 1715) (required any person that shall shoot, kill, hunt, or seen to carry a gun on another's land to pay one thousand pounds of tobacco); *An Act to prevent Killing of Deer out of Season and against Carrying Guns and Hunting by Persons not Qualified* (N.J. 1722) (required any person that shall carry any gun or hunt on the "improved or inclosed Lands" of another's plantation to pay thirty shillings for each violation); *An Act to prevent hunting with Fire-Arms in the City of New-York, and the Liberties thereof* (N.Y. 1763) (required any person, other than the owner of the land, that shall carry, shoot, or discharge any firearm in the city of New York to forfeit twenty shillings); *An Act to suppress the disorderly practice of firing guns, & c. on the times therein* (Pa. 1774) (required any person that shall fire their guns, rockets, fireworks, or any fire arms on New Years Day to pay forth shillings for each offense); 1 Hening at 401 (any person that shall discharge their firearm was required to pay a fine of 100 pounds of tobacco); *An Act for the better Ordering and Governing Negroes and other Slaves in this Province* (S.C. 1740) (required any person that shall discharge their firearm at night to pay forty shillings).

87. *An Act in Addition to the several Acts already made to the prudent Storage of Gun Powder within the Town of Boston* (Mass. 1783).

88. *Ibid.*

89. *Ibid.*

90. *An Act for the Preservation of Deer and other Game, and to prevent trespassing with Guns,* Sec. 3 (N.J. 1771).

91. *An additional act to an act, entitled, An act to prevent killing deer at unreasonable times and for putting a stop to many abuses committed by white persons, under presence of hunting,* Sec. 5 (N.C. 1745).

92. *Declaration of Independence* [¶ 2] (1776) (quoting) ("whenever any form of government becomes destructive of these ends, it is the right of the people to alter or abolish it, and to institute new government").

93. *Declaration of the Causes and Necessity for Taking Up Arms* [¶ 12] (1775).

94. *Ibid.*, [¶ 10]. South Carolina's Constitution of 1776 also describes the necessity of taking up arms. It reads, "The colonists were therefore driven to the necessity of taking up arms, to repel force by force, and to defend themselves and their properties against lawless invasions and depredations." S. C. Const (1776). The document does not cite their actions as part of a "constitutional" or "natural" right.

95. Also, neither the Olive Branch Petition nor the Declaration of Independence cited the British confiscation of colonial arms as "uncon-

stitutional" or as a violation of their "natural" right.

96. John E. Selby, *The Revolution in Virginia, 1775–1783*, 19 (1988).

97. Lord Dunmore sent a detachment of British seamen to seize the gunpowder in Williamsburg. Under the cover of night the sailors transported the gunpowder to HMS *Magdalen* in the James River. Unknown to the seamen, a spy had witnessed their mission and informed the revolutionary leaders. News of the event spread instantly. The following day "drums were beating, shouting citizens assembling, and the local independent company of gentlemen volunteers following into ranks." The situation turned so violent that Peyton Randolph, the speaker of the Virginia assembly, had to intervene to restore order. He asked the mob to disperse so a governing body could be assembled to address the matter. The assembly members argued that the absence of the gunpowder made the town vulnerable. A rumor had been circulating that a slave insurrection was afoot. Dunmore took advantage of the situation and stated that he, too, had heard of "an insurrection in a neighboring county." 3 *Revolutionary Virginia: The Road to Independence*, 5 (W.J. Van Schreeven ed., 1973). He published that he heard of "an intended insurrection of the Slaves, who had been seen in large numbers in the night time about the Magazine." 2 *American Archives: Documents of the American Revolution, 1774–1776, Fourth Series* at 465. He informed the assembly if they needed the powder it would be made available to them in half an hour. Dunmore's assurance that he had only taken the gunpowder to prevent a possible slave revolt calmed down the colonists. Selby, *Revolutionary Virginia* at 2.

98. Josiah Martin had dismantled the pieces of cannon next to his residence to comply with Lord Dartmouth's orders. Upon doing this, a group of inhabitants from New Bern confronted the governor since "the circumstance had caused alarm, because the Governor of Virginia had lately deprived the People of that Colony of their Ammunition." Martin informed the body of men he had "dismounted the Guns ... because the carriages were entirely rotten and unserviceable, and incapable of bearing the discharge of them on the King's birthday that was at hand." The answer persuaded the men to disperse but even Governor Martin admitted it "was not really one of [his] motives." The real reason Martin had the cannon dismounted was "to make the removal of them more difficult" since he had received "repeated advices of a design concerting ... to seize those guns by force." 1 *Naval Documents of the American Revolution*, 788 (1964).

99. *Declaration of the Causes and Necessity to Take Up Arms* [¶ 8]

100. James H. Stark, *The Loyalists of Massachusetts and the Other Side of the American Revolution*, 51 (1910).

101. It read, "He has waged cruel war against human nature itself, violating its most sacred rights of life and liberty in the persons of a distant people who never offended him, captivating and carrying them into slavery in another hemisphere, or to incur miserable death in their transportation hither. This piratical warfare, the opprobrium of *infidel* powers, is the warfare of the *Christian* king of Great Britain. [determined to keep open a market where MEN should be bought and sold,] he has prostituted his negative for suppressing every legislative attempt to prohibit or to restrain this execrable commerce [determining to keep open a market where MEN should be bought and sold]: and that this assemblage of horrors might want no fact of distinguished die, he is now exciting those very people to rise in arms among us, and to purchase that liberty of which *he* had deprived them, by murdering the people upon whom *he* also obtruded them: thus paying off former crimes committed against the *liberties* of one people, with crimes which he urges them to commit against the *lives* of another." Maier, *American Scripture* at 239.

102. 5 *American Archives: Documents of the American Revolution, 1774–1776, Fourth Series* at 1638.

103. 1 Sabine, *Biographical Sketches of Loyalists of the American Revolution* at 281.

104. *Ibid.*, 309.

105. 4 *The Papers of George Washington: Confederation Series*, 431 (W.W. Abbot ed., 1995).

106. *Ibid.*

107. *Ibid.*

108. *Ibid.*

109. *An Act, describing the Disqualifications to which Persons shall be subjected, who have been, or may be guilty of Treason, or giving Aid or Support to the present Rebellion, and to whom a Pardon may be extended* (Mass. 1787).

110. *Ibid.*

111. Mass. Const. of 1780, *Declaration of Rights*, Art. 17.

112. *An Act for the more speedy and effectual suppression of tumults and insurrections in the commonwealth* (Mass. 1787).

113. *Commonwealth v. Blanding*, 20 Mass., 304, 314 (1825).

114. At the end of this statement, Justice Parker cites a case that was decided by Justice Story, *Dexter v. Spear*, 4 Mason, 115 (1825). In *Dexter*, at no point does Justice Story make any mention of the right to keep arms or a similar analogy. Thus, further showing that Parker was making nothing more than an analogy.

115. *4 The Papers of George Washington: Confederation Series* at 431.

116. *Ibid.*, 432.

117. 29 *Writings of Washington*, 182 (J.C. Fitzpatrick ed.,1939).

118. *Ibid.*

119. *4 The Papers of George Washington: Confederation Series* at 433.

120. 9 *The Papers of James Madison*, 286 (Robert Rutland ed., 1975).

121. *Ibid.*, 307.

122. *Ibid.*, 315.

123. *Ibid.*, 343.

124. *Ibid.*, 395–96, 399.

125. Mass. Const., *Declaration of Rights*, Art. XVII (1780).

126. *Ratification of the Constitution by the State of New Hampshire, June 21, 1788* (1788).

127. *An Act for Regulating the Militia*, Sec. 1 (N.H. 1718).

128. *An Act for the Regulating of the Militia*, Sec. 1 (N.H. 1759); "Bear arms" was also used in its military connotation in the 1702 act entitled *An Act for the Commission of Joseph Dudley as Governor of New Hampshire, Dated April 1, 1702.* It read, "You shall Send an Account to Us, and Our Commissioners for Trade and Plantations, of the present number of Planters and Inhabitants, Men, Women, and Children, as well Masters as Servants, Free and unfree, and of the Slaves in Our said Province, as also a Yearly Account of the Increase and Decrease of them, and how many of them are fit to bear Arms in the Militia of our Said Province." *An Act for the Commission of Joseph Dudley as Governor of New Hampshire, Dated April 1, 1702* (N.H. 1702).

129. For examples see *An Act for establishing a Militia within this State*, Sec. 38 (Del. 1782); *An Act to regulate and discipline the Militia of this Commonwealth, and for other purposes* (Ky. 1792); *An Act to regulate and discipline the militia of this state*, Sec. 1 (Md. 1793); *An Act for regulating and governing the Militia of the Commonwealth of Massachusetts, and for repealing all Laws heretofore made for that Purpose; excepting and Act, intitled "An Act for establishing Rules and Articles for governing the Troops stationed in Forts and Garrisons, within this Commonwealth, and also the Militia, when called into actual Service,"* Sec. 18 (Mass. 1793); *An Act for regulating and governing the Militia of the State of Vermont, and for repealing all Laws heretofore passed for that purpose*, Sec. 16 (Vt. 1793); 1 *Stat.*, 272.

130. 2 *Annals of Congress* at 1806.

131. *Ibid.*

132. *Parker*, 478, F.3d at 387–88.

133. 1 *Stat.*, 271.

134. 10 U.S.C. § 311.

135. *Parker*, 478, F. 3d at 388.

136. *Ibid.*, 389.

137. 1 *Stat.*, 271.

138. 3 *Annals of Congress* at 418–24, 574–80, 701–02, 708–11; 4 *Annals of Congress* at 527–28; 6 *Annals of Congress* at 1675–91, 2223–24; 7 *Annals of Congress* 1384–86, 1524–25, 1772–73.

139. 7 *Annals of Congress*, 1927–33.

140. Va. Const *Declaration of Rights* § 13 (1776). Delaware's 1776 *Declaration of Rights* stated "a well regulated militia is the proper, natural and safe defence of a free government." *The Origin of the Second Amendment* at 752.

141. *Ibid.*

142. It reads, "In all criminal prosecutions, the accused shall enjoy a right to a speedy public trial, by an impartial jury of the State and district wherein the crime shall have been committed...." U.S. Const, Amend. VI.

143. It reads, "The powers not delegated to the United States by the Constitution; nor prohibited by it to the States, are reserved to the States respectively, or to the people." U.S. Const, Amend. X.

144. *Parker*, 478 F.3d at 389.

145. See Vt. Const, *Declaration of Rights*, Art. XV (1777); Vt. Const, *Declaration of Rights*, Art. XVIII (1786); Vt. Const, *Declaration of Rights*, Art. XVI (1793); Pa. Const, *Declaration of Rights*, Art. XIII (1776); Pa. Const, Art. IX, § 21 (1790); Ky. Const, (1792); Ky. Const, Art. X, § 23 (1799); Ohio Const, Art. VIII, § 20 (1802); Tenn. Const, Art. XI, § 26 (1796); N.C. Const, *Declaration of Rights* § 17 (1776); Mass. Const, *Declaration of Rights*, Art. XVII (1780); Conn. Const, Art. I, § 17 (1818).

146. *The Complete Bill of Rights: The Drafts, Debates, Sources, and Origins* at 169.

147. *Parker*, 478 F.3d at 396.

148. 1 Joseph Story § 208.

149. *Parker*, 478 F.3d at 396.

150. *Ibid.*

151. *The Origin of the Second Amendment* at 712.

152. *Ibid.*

## Chapter Four

1. U.S. Const, Art. I, § 9 ¶ 2 (1787).

2. Bernard Bailyn, *The Ordeal of Thomas Hutchinson*, 124 (1974).

3. *Ibid.*, 127.

4. *Ibid.*, 133–4.

5. 1 *Diary and Letters of Thomas Hutchinson*, 78, 79 (Peter Orlando Hutchinson ed., 1884).

6. Bailyn, *The Ordeal of Thomas Hutchinson* at 134.

7. 1 *Diary and Letters of Thomas Hutch-*

*inson* at 80–1; Bailyn, *The Ordeal of Thomas Hutchinson* at 159.

8. 9 *Documents of the American Revolution 1770–1783*, 171 (K.G. Davies ed., 1975).

9. 2 *The Correspondence of Thomas Gage*,183 (Clarence Edwin Carter ed., 1962).

10. *Ibid.*, 193.

11. *Ibid.*, 684.

12. It read, "As I have ever entertained Hopes, that an Accommodation might have taken Place between GREAT-BRITAIN and this Colony, without being compelled by my Duty to this most disagreeable but now absolutely necessary Step, rendered so by a Body of armed Men unlawfully assembled, firing on His MAJESTY'S Tenders, and the formation of an Army, and that Army now on their March to attack his MAJESTY'S Troops and destroy the well disposed subjects of the Colony. To defeat such treasonable Purposes, and that all such Traitors, and their Abettors, may be brought to Justice, and that the Peace, and good Order of this Colony may be again restored, which the ordinary Course of the Civil Law is unable to effect; I have thought fit to issue this my Proclamation, hereby declaring, that until the aforesaid good Purpose can be obtained, I do in Virtue of the Power and Authority to ME given, by His MAJESTY, determine to execute Martial Law, and cause the same to be executed throughout this Colony: and to the Peace and good Order may the sooner be restored, I do require every Person capable of bearing Arms, to resort to His MAJESTY'S STANDARD, or be looked upon as Traitors to His MAJESTY'S Crown and Government, and thereby become liable to the Penalty the Law inflicts upon such Offenses; such as forfeiture of Life, confiscation of Lands, &. &. And I do hereby further declare all indented Servants, Negroes, or others, (appertaining to Rebels,) free that are able and willing to bear Arms, they joining His MAJESTY'S Troops as soon as may be, foe the more speedily reducing this Colony to a proper Sense of their Duty, to His MAJESTY'S Crown and Dignity. I do further order, and require, all His MAJESTY'S Liege Subjects, to retain their Quitrents, or any other Taxes due or that may become due, in their own Custody, till such a Time as Peace may be again restored to this at present most unhappy Country, or demanded of them for their former salutary Purposes, by Officers properly to receive the same."

13. Sylva Frey, *Water from the Rock: Black Resistance in a Revolutionary Age*, 63 (1992).

14. Patrick Charles, *Irreconcilable Grievances: The Events That Shaped the Declaration of Independence*, 90 (2008).

15. The other four reasons were: (1) the Battles of Lexington and Concord, (2) the Battle of Bunker Hill, (3) allegedly inciting slave insurrections, and (4) allegedly allying with the Indians against the colonists. *Declaration of the Causes and Necessity of Taking Up Arms* ¶¶ 8–11 (1775).

16. *Ibid.*, ¶ 12.

17. *Declaration of Independence* ¶¶ 14, 25 (1776).

18. 1 *The Papers of George Mason*, 288 (Robert A. Rutland ed., 1970).

19. Mass. Const, Art. XX (1780).

20. N.C. Const, *Declaration of Rights*, Art. V (1776).

21. *Vegetius: Epitome of Military Science*, 69 (N.P. Milner trans., 1996).

22. *Ibid.*

23. *Ibid.*, 69–70.

24. *Ibid.*, 70.

25. *Ibid.*, 71.

26. *Ibid.*

27. See Dig. 49.16; *Code Just.* 12.36.

28. Dig. 49.16.3.13 (Modestinus, *Concerning Punishments, Book IV*).

29. C.E. Brand, *Roman Military Law*, 120 (1968).

30. Brand, *Roman Military Law* at 43.

31. *Ibid.*

32. *Ibid.*, 117–8.

33. *Ibid.*

34. *Code Just.* 12.36.18 (Emperor Anastasius to John, General of the Army).

35. *Ibid.*

36. *Ibid.*

37. *Code Just.* 12.36.16 (Emperor Leo to Dioscorus).

38. Lindsay Boynton, "Martial Law and the Petition of Right," 79, *Eng. Hist. Rev.*, 255, 258 (1964).

39. *Ibid.*, 266–71.

40. Paul Christianson, "Arguments on Billeting and Marital Law in the Parliament of 1628," 37, *Hist. J.*, 539, 544 (1994).

41. *Ibid.*

42. *Ibid.*, 545.

43. *Ibid.*, 550.

44. *Ibid.*

45. *Ibid.*, 551.

46. *Ibid.*

47. *Ibid.*, 553.

48. *Ibid.*, 554.

49. *Ibid.*, 557.

50. *Ibid.*, 555.

51. *Ibid.*, 560–1.

52. William S. Fields; David T. Hardy, "The Third Amendment and the Issue of the Maintenance of Standing Armies: A Legal History" 35 *Amer. J. L. Hist.* 395, 404 (1991).

53. Lois G. Schwoerer, *The Declaration of Rights, 1689*, 71 (1981).

54. *Ibid.*

55. 1 William Blackstone, *Commentaries,* 413–14.

56. Algernon Sidney, *Discourses Concerning Government,* 199, 200 (Thomas G. West ed., 1990).

57. Lawrence Delbert Cress, "Radical Whiggery on the Role of the Military: Ideological Roots of the American Revolutionary Militia," 40, *J. Hist. Ideas* 47 (1979).

58. *Ibid.,* 48.

59. *Ibid.,* 49.

60. Frederick Bernays Wiener, *Civilians Under Military Justice: The British Practice Since 1689 Especially in North America,* 13, 14 (1967).

61. *Ibid.,* 14. This latter section would later be dropped. By 1716 it had been well established that no soldier could be tried by court-martial in England for murder or other common law crimes committed. While the 1720 "eight day rule" was in effect, though, a group of law officers held that they could now try a soldier for murder absent a civil complaint, thus leading to the "eight day rule" being removed. Nevertheless, the Mutiny Acts sufficiently display the early attitude toward the exercising of martial law during times of peace — it was a form of law that was to be only used in times of necessity. This is not to say that martial law did not apply in areas were the common law was void of punishment, for there still needed to be a system in place to keep the soldiers well trained and disciplined, as well as accountable for their military actions.

62. *Ibid.* 15–31.

63. 1 Blackstone, *Commentaries* at 413.

64. *Ibid.*

65. *Ibid.,* 415.

66. *Ibid.*

67. *Ibid.*

68. *Ibid.,* 416.

69. Fields; Hardy, "The Third Amendment and the Issue of the Maintenance of Standing Armies: A Legal History," 35 *Amer. J. L. Hist.* at 413–5.

70. Peleg W. Chandler, 1 *American Criminal Trials,* 401, 402 (1970).

71. *Ibid.,* 410.

72. *Ibid.*

73. *Ibid.,* 369–70.

74. *Ibid.,* 373–4.

75. *Portrait of a Patriot: The Major Political and Legal Papers of Josiah Quincy Junior,* 74 (Daniel R. Coquillette ed., 2005).

76. Sidney, *Discourses Concerning Government* at 199.

77. *Ibid.*

78. *Portrait of a Patriot: The Major Political and Legal Papers of Josiah Quincy Junior* at 74.

79. *Ibid.,* 102.

80. *Ibid.,* 125.

81. David Hume, *Essays: Moral, Political, and Literary* 525 (Eugene R. Miller ed., 1985).

82. James Harrington, "Oceana," *Ideal Commonwealths* 183 (Henry Morley ed., 1901).

83. *Ibid.,* 256.

84. *Ibid.,* 269.

85. *Ibid.,* 361.

86. Caroline Cox, *A Proper Sense of Honor: Service and Self Sacrifice in George Washington's Army,* 77 (2004).

87. *Portrait of a Patriot: The Major Political and Legal Papers of Josiah Quincy Junior* at 131–2.

88. *Ibid.,* 146.

89. 1 *Papers of Thomas Jefferson,* 134 (Julian Boyd ed., 1950).

90. *The Political Writings of John Adams,* 283 (George W. Carey ed., 2000).

91. Charles Martyn, *The Life of Artemas Ward: The First Commander-In-Chief of the American Revolution,* 94 (1921).

92. *Ibid.,* 96.

93. 1 *The Papers of General Nathanael Greene,* 85 (Richard K. Showman ed., 1976).

94. Martyn, *The Life of Artemas Ward: The First Commander-In-Chief of the American* at 109. Massachusetts actually requested Congress to take control of regulating the armed force outside Boston. They wrote: "We are now compelled to raise an Army, which, with the assistance of the other Colonies, we hope, under the smiles of Heaven, will be able to defend us and all America from the further butcheries and devastations of our implacable enemies. But as the sword should, in all free States, be subservient to the civil powers; and as it is the duty of the Magistrates to support it for the people's necessary defence, we tremble at having an Army (although consisting of our own countrymen) established here, without a civil power to provide for and control them. We are happy in having an opportunity of laying our distressed state before the representative body of the Continent, and humbly hope you will favour us with your most explicit advice respecting the taking up and exercising the powers of civil Government, which we think absolutely necessary for the salvation of our Country; and we shall readily submit to such a general plan as you may direct for the Colonies, or make it our great study to establish such a form of Government here, as shall not only most promote our own advantages, but the union and interest of all America. As the Army now collecting form different Colonies is for the general defence of the rights of America, we would beg leave to suggest to your consideration the propriety of your taking the regulation and general direction of it, that the operations of it may more effectually answer the purposes designed." Peter Force: 2 *American Archives: Fourth Series* 621 (1837–55).

95. Patrick Charles, *Washington's Decision: The Story of George Washington's Decision to Reaccept Black Enlistments in the Continental Army, December 31, 1775*, 105 (2006).

96. Cox, *A Proper Sense of Honor* at 74–5.

97. *Ibid.*, 77. See also Maurer Maurer, "Military Justice Under General Washington," 28 *J. Mil. Aff.* 8, 9 (1964).

98. John Trenchard, *A Short Historie of Standing Armies in England* (1698).

99. 1 Blacksone, *Commentaries* at 572.

100. Cox, *A Proper Sense of Honor* at 78.

101. Force, 3 *American Archives: Fourth Series* at 1164. This quote must have been common among the Founding Fathers. On his June 26, 1775, address to the New York Provincial Congress, Washington would write, "When we assumed the Soldier, we did not lay aside the citizen...." 1 *The Papers of George Washington: Revolutionary Series* 41 (W.W. Abbot ed., 1985). In Caractacus' "Standing Armies" editorial he wrote, "It is impossible to subdue a country of any extent where every citizen is a soldier, and every soldier is a citizen." Force, 3 *American Archives: Fourth Series* at 220.

102. Cox, *A Proper Sense of Honor* at 79.

103. 2 *Journals of the Continental Congress, 1774–89* 111, 111–22 (1905).

104. *Ibid.*, 116.

105. *Ibid.*

106. *Ibid.*, 119.

107. 1 *The Papers of George Washington: Revolutionary Series* at 45. The Continental Articles of War included an additional sixteen articles relating to furloughs, musters and returns, sutlers, pardons, the personal effects of deceased officers and enlisted men, and the signing of the articles by all members of the army. The Continental Articles also defined with more specificity the punishments imposed by court-martials. *Ibid.*, 46 n.3.

108. Maurer, "Military Justice Under General Washington," 28 *J. Mil. Aff.* at 9. For articles, see William Winthrop, *Military Law and Precedents*, 947 (1920).

109. Winthrop, *Military Law and Precedents* at 931–46.

110. Maurer, "Military Justice Under General Washington," 28 *J. Mil. Aff* at 9.

111. Winthrop, *Military Law and Precedents* at 947.

112. *Ibid.*; 22 *The Papers of Benjamin Franklin, 148* (William B. Willcox ed., 1982).

113. *Ibid.*

114. Force, 3 *American Archives: Fourth Series* at 219–20.

115. 1 *The Papers of George Washington: Revolutionary Series* at 278, 279 n.5.

116. *Ibid.*

117. Washington would write to John Hancock: "I have therefore forebore pressing them, as I did not experience any such Inconvenience from their Adherence to their former Rules, as would warrant the Risque of entering into a Contest upon it: More especially as the Restraints necessary for the Establishment of essential Discipline & Subordination, indisposed their minds to every Change, & made it both Duty & Policy to introduce as little Novelty as possible. With the present Army, I fear, such a Subscription is impracticable. But the Difficulty will cease with this Army." 2 *The Papers of George Washington: Revolutionary Series*, 25 (W.W. Abbot ed., 1987).

118. *Ibid.*, 85 n.3. See also 1 *The Papers of Nathanael Greene* at 144–5.

119. Maurer, "Military Justice Under General Washington," 28 *J. Mil. Aff.* at 12. On October 3, 1775, a Council of War determined "the Enormity of the Crime, & the very inadequate Punishment pointed out that it should be referr'd to the General Congress for their special Discretion & that in the mean Time [Church] be closely confined, & no Person visit him but by special Direction." 2 *The Papers of George Washington: Revolutionary Series* at 83. The question of Church's punishment was brought up again during the Proceedings of the Committee of Conference held between the 18 and 24 of October. *Ibid.*, 187.

120. 3 *The Papers of John Adams*, 79 (Robert J. Taylor ed., 1979).

121. *Ibid.*, 79–80.

122. Force, 3 *American Archives: Fourth Series* at 1163.

123. *Ibid.*, 1164. For a complete list of the problems Tudor had with the articles, see 3 *The Papers of John Adams* at 107, 128, 261 n. 7.

124. Washington had sent a circular to his officers inquiring as to what changes should be made to the existing Articles of War. See 2 *The Papers of George Washington: Revolutionary Series* at 194–6, 204; 1 *The Papers of Nathanael Greene* at 130–3; 22 *The Papers of Benjamin Franklin*, 230–4.

125. Peter Force, 1 *American Archives: Fifth Series*, 576 (1837–55).

126. 2 *The Papers of George Washington: Revolutionary Series* at 346.

127. Artemas Ward had only required the articles be read monthly. Washington hoped reinforcing the provisions of the articles would better discipline his troops. 3 *The Papers of George Washington: Revolutionary Series* at 13.

128. 1 *The Papers of George Washington: Revolutionary Series* at 54.

129. 3 *The Papers of George Washington: Revolutionary Series* at 379.

130. 4 *The Papers of John Adams* 367 (Robert J. Taylor ed., 1979).

131. *Ibid.*

132. 5 *The Papers of John Adams* 13 (Robert J. Taylor ed., 1983).

133. *Ibid.*

134. *Ibid.*, 15. Tudor would write a similar letter on September 23, 1776. See *Ibid.*, 36.

135. 5 *Journals of the Continental Congress, 1774–89* 788, 788–807 (1905); Force, 2 *American Archives: Fifth Series* at 1363–73.

136. 1 *The Papers of Nathanael Greene* at 122.

137. This does not include military exemptions, men conscientiously scrupulous to bearing arms, and if a draftee could find a substitute. Even if a soldier found a substitute, the soldier was still liable to some of the provisions in the Articles of War.

138. There is reference to the writ of habeas corpus, but the phrase "martial law" was intentionally left out. U.S. Const, Art. I, §9 ¶ 2 (1787).

139. See *Ratification of the Constitution by the State of New York, July 26, 1788.*

140. See *A Fragment of Facts Disclosing the Conduct of the Maryland Convention, on the Adoption of the Federal Constitution, April 21, 1788.*

141. *See* 1 *The Papers of George Mason* at 288; Mass. Const, Art. XX (1780); and N.C. Const, *Declaration of Rights*, Art. V (1776).

142. *Amendments Proposed by the Virginia Convention, June 27, 1788.*

143. *See A Fragment of Facts Disclosing the Conduct of the Maryland Convention, on the Adoption of the Federal Constitution, April 21, 1788.*

144. U.S. Const, Art. I, § 8, cl. 16.

145. *Ibid.* cl. 15.

146. Blackstone, *Commentaries* at 415.

147. Matthew Hale, *Common Law of England*, 54 (1894).

148. Blackstone, *Commentaries* at 413.

149. *Ibid.*, 415.

150. Emerich de Vattel, 3 *Law of Nations* § 8 (1758).

151. *Ibid.*, § 17.

152. *Ibid.*

153. St. Thomas Aquinas, 1 *Summa Theologica*, 1043 (1920).

154. Vattel, 3 *Law of Nations* at § 18.

155. *Ibid.*

156. *Ibid.*

157. Charles, *Washington's Decision: The Story of George Washington's Decision to Reaccept Black Enlistments in the Continental Army, December 31, 1775* at 111.

158. Vattel, 3 *Law of Nations* at § 3.

159. *Ibid.*, § 18.

160. Aquinas, 2 *Summa Theologica* at 1359–60.

161. Vattel, 3 *Law of Nations* at § 231.

162. Vattel makes multiple mentions of the individual's natural right to self-defense. In Section 3 he states, "In treating the right to security, we have shown that nature gives men a right to employ force, when it is necessary for their defence, and for the preservation of their rights." *Ibid.*, § 3.

163. *Ibid.*, § 231.

164. *Ibid.*, § 24.

165. *Ibid.*, § 187.

166. *Ibid.*

167. *Ibid.*, § 4.

168. *Ibid.*, § 187.

169. Vattel, 3 *Law of Nations* at § 28.

170. *Ibid.*, § 35.

171. *Ibid.*

172. *Ibid.*, § 26.

173. *Ibid.*, § 44.

174. *Ibid.*, § 9.

175. *Ibid.*, § 8, 10.

176. *Ibid.*, § 10.

## Chapter Five

1. "That the people have a right to bear arms for the defence of themselves and the state; and as standing armies in the time of peace are dangerous to liberty, they ought not be kept up; And that the military should be kept under strict subordination to, and governed by, the civil power." Pa. Const, *Declaration of Rights*, Art. XIII (1776). "That the right of citizens to bear arms, in defence of themselves and the State, shall not be questioned." Pa. Const, Art. IX, § 21 (1790).

2. "That the people have a right to bear arms for the defence of themselves and the State, and, as standing armies, in the time of peace, are dangerous to liberty, they ought not to be kept up; and the military should be kept under strict subordination to, and governed by, the civil power." Vt. Const, *Declaration of Rights*, Art. XV (1777). "That the people have a right to bear arms, for defence of themselves and the State: and as standing armies, in time of peace, are dangerous to liberty...." Vt. Const, *Declaration of Rights*, Art. XVIII (1786). "That the people have a right to bear arms, for defence of themselves and the State; and, as standing armies in time of peace are dangerous to liberty...." Vt. Const, *Declaration of Rights*, Art. XVI (1793).

3. Kentucky Constitution of 1792 did not provide a bill of rights. Ky. Const (1792). "That the rights of the citizens to bear arms in defence of themselves and the State shall not be questioned." Ky. Const, Art. X, § 23 (1799). A statutory and textual analysis of Ohio, Vermont, Pennsylvania, and Kentucky's "right to bear

arms" provisions only protect just that, "the right to bear arms." In none of these state's provisions was the word "keep," or any word which may be interpreted by individual right theorists as a right to gun ownership, incorporated. Even if "keep" had been incorporated, as has already been shown, such a word would have only meant "to service" or "to maintain." Moreover, the use of the phrase "bear arms" in the eighteenth-century laws was limited to military service, thus the only protection these state provisions afforded was the right to bear arms "in defence of themselves and the state" in a military capacity.

4. "That the people have a right to bear arms for the defense of themselves and the state: and as standing armies in time of peace, are dangerous to liberty, they shall not be kept up; and that the military shall be kept under strict subordination to the civil power." Ohio Const, Art. VIII, § 20 (1802).

5. "Every citizen has a right to bear arms, in defence of himself and the State...." Miss. Const, Art. I, § 23 (1817).

6. "Every citizen has a right to bear arms, in defence of himself and the state...." Conn. Const, Art. I, § 17 (1818).

7. "Every citizen has a right to bear arms in defence of himself and the State...." Ala. Const, Art. I § 23 (1819).

8. "That the freemen of this State have a right to keep and bear arms for their common defence." Tenn. Const, Art. XI, § 26 (1796).

9. "That the people have a right to bear arms, for the defence of the State; and as standing armies, in time of peace, are dangerous to liberty, they ought not to be kept up; and that the military should be kept under strict subordination to, and governed by the civil power." N.C. Const. *Declaration of Rights* § 17 (1776). It was not until 1868 that the word "keep" was incorporated. It read, "A well-regulated militia being necessary to the security of a free State, the right of the people to keep and bear arms shall not be infringed; and as standing armies in time of peace are dangerous to liberty, they ought not to be kept up, and the military should be kept under strict subordination to and governed by the civil power." N.C. Const. *Declaration of Rights*, Sec. 24 (1868).

10. "The people have a right to keep and bear arms for the common defence. And as, in time of peace, armies are dangerous to liberty, they ought not to be maintained without the consent of the legislature; and the military shall be always held in an exact subordination to the civil authority and be governed by it." Mass. Const, *Declaration of Rights*, Art. XVII (1780).

11. Neither the Georgia Constitutions of 1777, 1789, nor 1798 included a "right to bear arms" provision. See Ga. Const (1777); Ga. Const (1789); Ga. Const (1798). It was not until the Georgia Constitution of 1861, following its secession in the midst of the American Civil War, that such a provision was incorporated. It reads, "The right of the people to keep and bear arms shall not be infringed." Ga. Const, Art. I, § 6.

12. There is no bill of rights in the 1777 New York Constitution. N.Y. Const (1777). It was not until 1821 that New York provided a bill of rights in its constitution, but even in this instance there was no article put in place protecting the "right to bear arms." The only section of it that mentions arming the militia reads, "The militia of this State shall at all time hereafter be armed and disciplined and in readiness for service; but all such inhabitants of this State, of any religious denomination whatever, as form scruples of conscience may be averse to bearing arms, shall be excused therefrom by paying to the State an equivalent in money; and the legislature shall provide by law for the collection of such equivalent, to be estimated according to the expense, in time and money, of an ordinary able-bodied militia-man." N.Y. Const, Art. VII, § 5 (1821).

13. The New Jersey Constitution of 1776 only afforded that the "common law of England, as well as so much of the statute law, as have been heretofore practices in this Colony, shall still remain in force, until they shall be altered by a future law of the Legislature." N.J. Const, Art. XXII (1776). Even the New Jersey Constitution of 1844 did not afford a "right to bear arms" provision. N.J. Const (1844).

14. The Declaration of Rights and Fundamental Principles of 1776 did not incorporate a "right to bear arms" provision. Del. *Declaration of Rights and Fundamental Principles*, Art. 18, 19 (1776). The Delaware Constitution of 1792 does have a bill of rights but did not incorporate a "right to bear arms" provision. Del. Const (1792). Neither did the Delaware Constitutions of 1831 nor 1897. Del. Const (1831); Del. Const (1897).

15. The New Hampshire Constitution of 1776 did not have a bill of rights. N.H. Const (1776). Article I of the New Hampshire Constitution of 1784 only provided, "No person who is conscientiously scrupulous about the lawfulness of bearing arms, shall be compelled thereto, provided he will pay on equivalent" (Section XIII); "A well regulated militia is the proper, natural, and sure defence of a state" (Section XXIV); "Standing armies are dangerous to liberty, and ought not to be raised or kept up without the consent of the legislature" (Article XXV); and "In all cases, and at all times the military ought to be under strict subordination to,

and governed by the civil power (Section XXVI). N.H. Const, Art. XIII, XXIV, XXV, XXVI (1784). It was not until New Hampshire's Constitution of 1982 that the "right to bear arms" was incorporated. It reads, "All persons have the right to keep and bear arms in defense of themselves, their families, their property and the state." N.H. Const, *Bill of Rights*, Art. II (1982).

16. The Maryland Constitution of 1776 only provided, "That a well-regulated militia is the proper and natural defence of a free government" (chapter XXV); "That standing armies are dangerous to liberty, and out not to be raised or kept up, without the consent of the Legislature" (chapter XXVI); and "That in all cases, and at all times, the military ought to be under strict subordination to and control of the civic power" (chapter XXVII). Md. Const, *Declaration of Rights*, Chap. XXV, XXVI, XXVII (1776). The same wording was incorporated in the Maryland Constitutions of 1851 and 1864. Md. Const (1851); Md. Const (1864).

17. The South Carolina Constitution of 1776 reads, "The colonists were therefore driven to the necessity of taking up arms, to repel force by force, and to defend themselves and their properties against lawless invasions and depredations." S.C. Const (1776). This phrase does not say the colonists taking up of arms was their constitutional or natural right and does not address the right to own firearms. In 1778 the South Carolina Constitution incorporated, "The military be subordinate to the civil power of the State" (article XLII), but made no mention of the "right to bear arms." S.C. Const, Art. XLII (1778). It was not after the Civil War that South Carolina addressed the "right to bear arms" in its 1868 constitution. Article I, Section 28 reads, "The people have a right to keep and bear arms for the common defence. As, in times of peace, armies are dangerous to liberty, they ought not to be maintained without the consent of the general assembly. The military power ought always be held in an exact subordination to the civil authority, and be governed by it." S.C. Const, Art. I, § 28 (1868).

18. The Virginia Constitution of 1776 reads, "That a well regulated militia, composed of the body of the people trained to arms, is the proper, natural, and safe defence of a free State; that standing armies, in times of peace, should be avoided, as dangerous to liberty; and that in all cases the military should be under strict subordination to, and governed by, the civil power." Va. Const, *Declaration of Rights* § 13 (1776). Article I in the 1829 Virginia Constitution affirmed the same right. Va. Const, Art. I (1829).

19. Connecticut did not adopt its constitution until 1818, more than thirty years after the ratification of the U.S. Constitution. Section 17 of the *Declaration of Rights* states, "Every citizen has a right to bear arms in defence of himself and the state." Conn. Const, Art. I, § 17 (1818). Its "right to bear arms" provision has been often cited by individual right supporters to show the intent of the Framers in drafting the Second Amendment. The Connecticut provision guarantees "[e]very citizen has the right to bear arms in defence of himself and the state." Since the provision grants the right to "every citizen" it has been argued that the prefatory clause of the Second Amendment, which reads "a well organized militia being necessary to the security of a free state," serves no purpose other than to explain why the Second Amendment was established. Thus, it is argued the true meaning behind the Second Amendment resembles the language in the Connecticut "right to bear arms" provision, and should be interpreted as such. This argument is flawed though. Although the Connecticut provision extends the right to bear arms to "every citizen," it only grants the right to "bear arms." This means if we interpret Connecticut's provision through the statutory language used in eighteenth-century militia laws, Connecticut's citizens are only guaranteed the right to use arms in a military capacity to defend themselves and the state, not own them.

20. The next five states to be incorporated into the Union following Ohio were Louisiana (18th), Indiana (19th), Mississippi (20th), Illinois (21st), and Alabama (22nd). Out of these five states, four adopted a provision protecting the right to bear arms — Louisiana, Indiana, Mississippi, and Alabama adopted provisions protecting the right to bear arms. Indiana's read, "That the people have a right to bear arms for the defence of themselves, and the state; and that the military shall be kept in strict subordination to the civil power." Ind. Const, Art. I, § 20 (1816). Louisiana's read, "The free white men of this State, shall be armed and disciplined for its defence; but those who belong to religious societies, whose tenets forbid them to carry arms, shall not be compelled so to do, but shall pay an equivalent for personal service." La. Const, Art. III, § 22 (1812). Alabama's read, "Every citizen has a right to bear arms in defence of himself and the State." Ala. Const, Art. I, § 23 (1819). Mississippi's read, "The right of every citizen to keep and bear arms in defense of his home, person, or property, or in the aid of the civil power when thereto legally summoned, shall not be called into question, but the legislature may regulate or forbid the carrying of concealed weapons." Miss. Const, Art. I, § 23 (1817).

21. Citing *United States v. Sprague*, 282 U.S. at 731.

22. Before Ohio was incorporated into the United States it was regulated by the provisions of the Northwest Ordinance of 1787. Even then, Ohio's vast territory was governed by a legislative assembly. In cooperation with the governor appointed by Congress, the legislature passed laws for Ohio's governance.

23. *A law respecting crimes and punishments*, Sec. 8 (Ohio 1788). Another example exists in Section 6 regarding "burglary." It states, "if the person or persons so breaking and entering any dwelling house ... shall commit, or attempt to commit any personal abuse, force, or violence, or shall be so armed with any dangerous weapon or weapons as clearly to indicate a violent intention, he, she or they so offending ... shall forfeit all his, her or their estate...." *Ibid.*, Sec. 6.

24. *Ibid.*, Sec. 3.

25. *Ibid.*, Sec. 1.

26. See *An act respecting crimes and punishments* (Ohio 1805); *An act respecting crimes and punishments* (Ohio 1809); *An act for the punishment of crimes* (Ohio 1815); *An act for the punishment of certain offences therein mentioned* (Ohio 1815); *An act for the punishment of crimes* (Ohio 1821); *An act for the punishments of crimes* (Ohio 1824); *An act for the punishments of crimes* (Ohio 1831); *A supplement to an act for the punishment of crimes* (Ohio 1831); and *An act providing for the punishment of Crimes* (Ohio 1835).

27. *An act respecting crimes and punishments*, Sec. 5 (Ohio 1805).

28. The first law against dueling actually appeared in 1799. It stipulated that "if any person within this territory, shall challenge, by word or in writing, the person of another to fight at sword, rapier, pistol, or other deadly weapon, the person so challenging" shall be found guilty. *An act for the prevention of vice and immorality*, Sec. 10 (Ohio 1799). The wording in this law is important because if "bearing arms" equated to the use of arms, would not the legislature have worded the act to state something to the effect "if any person shall bear arms against another" or "if any person shall bear a sword, rapier, pistol ... the person so challenging..."? The lack of use of "bear" in this in other contexts affirms "bear" was meant to be limited to military or militia service.

29. *Ibid.*, Sec. 26.

30. *An act for the punishment of crimes*, Sec. 25 (Ohio 1815).

31. *An act for the prevention of vice and immortality*, Sec. 1 (Ohio 1799).

32. *Ibid.*

33. *An act for the prevention of certain immoral practices* (Ohio 1805); *An act to amend that act, An act for the prevention of certain immoral practices* (Ohio 1815); *An act for the prevention of certain immoral practices* (Ohio 1816); and *An act for the prevention of certain immoral practices* (Ohio 1824).

34. *An act for suppressing and prohibiting ever species of gaming for money or other property, and for making void all contracts and payments made in consequence thereof, and also for restraining the disorderly practice of discharging fire arms at certain hours and places*, Sec. 3 (Ohio 1790).

35. *Ibid.*, Sec. 4.

36. *Ibid.*

37. *A law for regulating and establishing the militia*, Sec. 3 (Ohio 1788).

38. *A law in addition to a law entitled 'A law for regulating and establishing the militia,'* Sec. 2 (Ohio 1788).

39. *Ibid.*, Sec. 3.

40. *A law for regulating and establishing the militia*, Sec. 4 (Ohio 1788).

41. 1 *American State Military Papers* at 163.

42. *Ibid.*

43. *Ibid.*

44. *Ibid.*, 189.

45. *Ibid.*

46. *Ibid.* In 1810 the debate over a select militia would arise again. It was communicated to Congress: "The song which has been incessantly sung, ever since the constitution was adopted, that the militia are the sure bulwark of our nation, the safe-guardians of our liberties, is not in the mouth of every one, and he who doubts the truth of it is deemed a political infidel; yet, with all the odium attached, I acknowledge myself no convert of such doctrine. Let the Government proceed to regulate the militia to the utmost length their masters, the sovereign people, will bear — it will be just so far as to make them food for powder in the day of battle; and death, or what is worse, loss of honor, must be expected by every officer of spirit connected with them. General Knox's system is the only system I have seen, that can be considered as possessing any efficiency." *Ibid.*, 263. Another proposal resurfaced in 1812. It was stated: "[M]en who might be useful at home, but who would have neither arms, accoutrements, or discipline, would be thus designated? Whose rout and slaughter would only serve to mark our calamity, and spread dismay among our friends." *Ibid.*, 318.

47. *Ibid.*, 256.

48. *Ibid.*, 604.

49. *Ibid.*, 323.

50. *Ibid.*, 324.

51. *Ibid.*

52. *Ibid.*, 605–7.

53. *Ibid.*, 605.

54. *Ibid.*

55. The federal government may call upon

the militia to "execute the Laws of the Union, Suppress insurrections and repel Invasions." U.S. Const, Art. I, § 8, cl. 15.

56. 1 *American State Papers Military Affairs* at 605.

57. *Ibid.*, 606.

58. *Ibid.*, 605.

59. *Ibid.*, 607.

60. 2 *Circular Letters of Congressmen to Their Constituents 1789–1829* at 959.

61. U.S. Const, Art. I, § 8, ¶ 15.

62. *An act to alter and amend the militia laws,* Sec. 2 (Ohio 1791). A similar provision existed in Ohio's first militia law of 1788. *A law for regulating and establishing a militia,* Sec. 4 (Ohio 1788).

63. *An Act to oblige the Male white Persons in the Province of Georgia to carry Fire-arms to all Places of publick Worship* (Ga. 1757). Before Georgia's act, South Carolina was the only other state to ever enact such a law. *An Act for the better Security of this Province against the Insurrections and other wicked Attempts of Negroes, and other Slaves; and for reviving and continuing, and act of the General Assembly of this Province, entitled an Act for the better Ordering and Governing Negroes and other Slaves in this Province* (S.C. 1743).

64. *An act for suppressing and prohibiting ever species of gaming for money or other property, and for making void all contracts and payments made in consequence thereof, and also for restraining the disorderly practice of discharging fire arms at certain hours and places,* Sec. 4 (Ohio 1790).

65. 2 *The St. Clair Papers,* 309 (William Henry Smith ed., 1882).

66. *Ibid.*, 567.

67. *Ibid.*, 569.

68. 2 *The Republic of Letters: The Correspondence Between Jefferson and Madison 1776–1826,* 1224 (James Morton Smith ed., 1995).

69. Randolph Chandler Downes, "Thomas Jefferson and the Removal of Governor St. Clair in 1802," 36 *Ohio Archeological and Historical Society Publications,* 62, 69 (1927).

70. 2 *The Republic of Letters: The Correspondence Between Jefferson and Madison 1776–1826* at 1230.

71. 2 *The St. Clair Papers* at 582–3.

72. *Ibid.*, 583.

73. *An act establishing and regulating the militia* (Ohio 1799).

74. *Ibid.*, Sec. 1.

75. *Ibid.*

76. *Ibid.*, Sec. 24.

77. *Ibid.*, Sec. 25.

78. *Ibid.*, Sec. 35–7.

79. *Ibid.*, Sec. 42.

80. *Ibid.*, Sec. 30.

81. *An act to amend the act, entitled, 'An act establishing and regulating the militia,'* Sec. 1 (Ohio 1802)

82. See *An act to provide for organizing and disciplining the militia* (Ohio 1803); *An act for disciplining the militia* (Ohio 1807); and *An act to amend the act entitled, 'An act disciplining the militia'* (Ohio 1808).

83. *An act for disciplining the militia,* Sec. 35 (Ohio 1809).

84. *Ibid.*, Sec. 36.

85. *An act for disciplining the militia,* Sec. 70 (Ohio 1813).

86. The returns only included the states of New Hampshire, Massachusetts, Connecticut, New York, North Carolina, Georgia, and Kentucky. 1 *American State Papers Military Affairs* at 163.

87. *Ibid.*, 168.

88. *Ibid.*, 171–2.

89. *Ibid.*

90. *Ibid.*, 190.

91. *Ibid.*, 202–3.

92. *Ibid.*

93. *Ibid.*, 198.

94. *Ibid.*, 233–4.

95. *Ibid.*

96. *Ibid.*

97. Jefferson had written to Congress: "The dangers of our country, arising from the contests of other nations, and the urgency of making preparation for whatever events might affect our relations with them, have been intimated in preceding messages to Congress. To secure ourselves by due precautions, an augmentation of our military force, as well regular as of volunteer militia, seems to be expedient. The precise extent of that augmentation cannot as yet be satisfactorily suggested; but that no time may be lost, and especially as a season deemed favorable to the object, I submit to the wisdom of the Legislature whether they will authorize a commencement of this precautionary work, by a present provision for raising and organizing some additional force, reserving to themselves to decide its ultimate extent on such views of our situation as I may be enabled to present at a future day of the session. If an increase of force now be approved, I submit to their consideration the outlines of a plan proposed in the enclosed letter from the Secretary of War. I recommend, also, to the attention of Congress, term at which the act of April 18, 1806, concerning the militia, will expire, and the effect of that expiration." 17 *Annals of Congress* 151 (1808).

98. *An Act procuring an additional number of arms, and for the purchase of saltpetre and sulphur* authorized "a sum of money, not exceeding three hundred thousand dollars, be, and the same is hereby, appropriated, out of any moneys in the Treasury not otherwise appropriated,

for the purpose of procuring by purchase, or causing to be manufactured within the United States, and under the direction of the President of the United States, an additional number of stands of arms, to be deposited in safe and suitable places." 18 *Annals of Congress, 2839* (1808). See also 2 *U.S. Stat* at 473.

99. 18 *Annals of Congress* at 1581. Burwell further commented "[l]et us have arms and I fear not any mischief from combinations of any kind against the country." *Ibid.*

100. *Ibid.,* 1582.

101. 1 *U.S. Stat* at 576.

102. 18 *Annals of Congress* at 1581.

103. 2 *U.S. Stat* at 481. Although this act was officially passed into law before the Arming the Whole Militia Act, the latter was actually approved by Congress first. There was some reluctance to pass the Sale of Public Arms Act because of this. A contingent of Congressmen believed the resolution was pointless given they had already authorized the arming of the entire militia through federal arms. In the end, the Sale of Public Arms Act passed because states such as Georgia and South Carolina were in dire need of arms not only to protect their borders from external threats, but from internal slave uprisings. As long as the states wished to "pay for their arms, and not receive them as a donation from the General Government," Congress did not see why they should not allow such a bill to pass. 18 *Annals of Congress* at 1697–8.

104. Mr. Macon described the bill as "the most important question which the House had had before them this session." *Ibid.,* 2179.

105. 2 *U.S. Stat* at 490–1.

106. It was originally proposed that the annual sum should be one million dollars. 18 *Annals of Congress* at 2175. After much debate his amount was reduced to two hundred thousand dollars. *Ibid.,* 2191; 2 *U.S. Stat* at 490.

107. *Ibid.,* 490.

108. *Ibid.,* 491. Even after passing an act providing arms for the entire militia, there were still members in Congress that wanted a select militia. Mr. Smith delivered a report stating, "The aw of 1792 already provides for organizing and disciplining the militia; and the subsequent act [1808 act arming the militia] makes provision for arming them.... All, therefore, within the power of Congress, seems to have been already done, unless it should be deemed expedient to make a new organization, by a classification which shall constitute a select and reserve militia." 1 *American State Papers Military Affairs* at 256.

109. 2 *Circular Letters of Congressmen to Their Constituents 1789–1829* at 545.

110. 18 *Annals of Congress* at 2175.

111. *Ibid.,* 2176.

112. *Ibid.,* 2177.

113. *Ibid.*

114. *Ibid.,* 2177–8.

115. *Ibid.,* 2180.

116. *Ibid.,* 2180–1.

117. *Ibid.,* 2182.

118. *Ibid.,* 2184.

119. *Ibid.,* 2178.

120. *Ibid.,* 2189.

121. *Ibid.,* 2180.

122. *Ibid.,* 2193.

123. *Ibid.,* 2194–5.

124. *Ibid.,* 2197.

125. *Ibid.,* 1463.

126. 2 *U.S. Stat* at 473.

127. 18 *Annals of Congress* at 1582.

128. 1 *American State Papers Military Affairs* at 329.

129. 2 *The Worthington Papers,* 59 (Richard C. Knopf ed., 1956).

130. *Ibid.*

131. *Ibid.*

132. At time Worthington wrote this the *Act for disciplining the militia* of 1808 was in effect. It allowed any person to find a substitute to march in their stead, but would be liable "to all the penalties, incurred by persons refusing to serve, when called on tours of duty." *Act for disciplining the militia,* Sec. 34 (Ohio 1808). The first substitute law in Ohio appeared in 1799. See *An act establishing and regulating the militia,* Sec. 38 (Ohio 1799).

133. War was not officially declared by Congress until June 18, 1812. 2 *U.S. Stat* at 755.

134. 3 *The Worthington Papers* 12 (Richard C. Knopf ed., 1956).

135. *Ibid.,* 187.

136. 1 *American State Papers Military Affairs* at 331–4.

137. 3 *The Worthington Papers* at 17.

138. *Ibid.,* 43.

139. *Ibid.,* 170–1.

140. 4 *The Worthington Papers,* 22 (Richard C. Knopf ed., 1956).

141. *Ibid.,* 57.

142. See *An act for organizing and disciplining the militia* (Ohio 1815). The next major act regarding the militia would not be passed until 1831. *An act for organizing and disciplining the militia* (Ohio 1831).

143. *An act directing the collection and repairs of public arms and accoutrements* (Ohio 1815). An example of a certificate showing an individual returning the public arms and accoutrements can be found in 1 *The Samuel Huntington Papers,* 3 (1976).

144. *An act to provide for the distribution and safe-keeping of the public arms; and for other purposes,* Sec. 7 (Ohio 1823).

145. *An act amendatory to 'An act to provide*

for the safe keeping of the public arms, and for other purposes (Ohio 1827).

146. *An act to provide for drawing from the United States, and distributing the public arms apportioned to the militia of this state* (Ohio, 1828).

147. *An Act to regulate the Militia* (Ohio 1844).

148. *An act for organizing and disciplining the militia*, Sec. 28 (Ohio 1831).

149. *Ibid.*

150. *Ibid.*, Sec. 33.

151. *An act to provide for organizing and disciplining the militia*, Sec. 24 (Ohio 1799).

152. *An act for organizing and disciplining the militia*, Sec. 35 (Ohio 1831).

153. *An Act to regulate the Militia*, Sec. 1 (Ohio 1844).

154. *Ibid.*, Sec. 2

155. 1 *Official Opinions of the Attorney Generals of the State of Ohio* 43, 43–46 (Wade H. Ellis ed., 1905).

156. *An Act to regulate the Militia*, Sec. 5 (Ohio 1844).

157. *Ibid.*, Sec. 20.

158. *Ibid.*, Sec. 22.

159. *Ibid.*, Sec. 19.

160. 1 *American State Papers Military Affairs* at 664.

161. *An act for organizing and disciplining the militia*, Sec. 50 (Ohio 1831).

162. *An Act to amend the act entitled "An Act to organize and discipline the Militia*, Sec. 6 (Ohio 1843).

163. 2 *Circular Letters of Congressmen to Their Constituents 1789–1829* at 959.

164. 1 *American State Papers Military Affairs* at 256.

165. For instances see *An act to amend the act, entitled, 'An act establishing and regulating the militia*, Sec. 1 (Ohio 1802) ("that he is conscientiously scrupulous of bearing arms"); *An act to provide for organizing and disciplining the militia*, Sec. 28 (Ohio 1803) ("whenever any person ... who may be conscientiously scrupulous of bearing arms"); *An act for disciplining the militia*, Sec. 10 (Ohio 1807) ("That when any person may be desirous of being excused from attending and bearing arms at any must of the militia"); and Congressman William Henry Harrison's speech to Congress on January 17, 1817, 1 *American State Papers* at 663–5.

166. 18 *Annals of Congress* at 2193.

167. 1 *Papers of Thomas Jefferson* at 363. The first draft read, "No freeman shall ever be debarred the use of arms," *Ibid.*, 344, while the second draft read the same as the third, *Ibid.*, 353.

168. The Second Amendment conditions that right on "A well-regulated militia being necessary to the security of a free State." U.S. Const, Amend. II.

169. Ohio Const, Art. VIII, § 20 (1802). This argument is further supported by the fact that the next two sections of the Ohio Constitution refer to the militia, standing armies, and the military. The first reads, "That no person in this state, except such as are employed in the army or navy of the United State, or militia in actual service, shall be subject to corporal punishment under the military law." Ohio Const, Art. VIII, § 21 (1802). Section 22 reads, "that no soldier, in time of peace, be quartered in any house without consent of the owner; nor in time of war, but in the manner prescribed by law." Ohio Const, Art. VIII, § 22.

170. Ohio Const, Art. VIII, § 1 (1802).

171. *A law respecting crimes and punishments*, Sec. 1, 9 (Ohio 1788). For an example of an act after the passing of the 1802 constitution, see *An act to prevent certain acts hostile to the peace and tranquility of the United States, within the jurisdiction of this state* (Ohio 1807).

172. Ohio Const, Art. VIII, § 1 (1802).

173. *Ibid.*

## Chapter Six

1. Ohio Const, Art. I, Sec. 4 (1851).

2. *Arnold v. City of Cleveland*, 67 Ohio St. 3d 35, 53 (Ohio 1993).

3. 8 W.L.J. 145 (1850).

4. *Ibid.*, 145–6.

5. *Ibid.*, 148.

6. *Ibid.*

7. *Ibid.*, 149.

8. The Ohio legislature would pass an act against the carrying of concealed weapons in 1859.

9. Indiana passed its first concealed weapon law in 1820 very similar to the Kentucky law. Clayton E. Cramer, *Concealed Weapon Laws of the Early Republic: Dueling, Southern Violence, and Moral Reform* 80 (1999).

10. Kentucky's first concealed weapon law was passed on February 3, 1813. It read: "That any person in this commonwealth, who shall hereafter wear a pocket pistol, dirk, large knife, or sword in a cane, concealed as a weapon, unless when traveling on a journey, shall be fined in any sum, not less than one hundred dollars; which may be recovered in any court having jurisdiction of the sums, by action of debt, or on the presentment of a grand jury — and a prosecutor in such presentment shall not be necessary. One half of such fine shall be to the use of the informer, and the other to the use of this commonwealth." *An Act to prevent persons in this Commonwealth from wearing concealed Arms,*

*except in certain cases* (Ky. 1813). The act immediately following this concealed weapon law was an amendment to the Kentucky militia law. It too differentiated between the use of "carry arms" and "bear arms" because it had a provision exempting any "who may conscientiously [be] scruple to bear arms." *An Act to amend the Militia Law*, Sec. 4 (Ky. 1813).

11. In January 1838, Tennessee passed its first concealed weapon law. Section 2 stipulated, "That if any person shall wear any Bowie knife, Arkansas tooth pick, or other knife or weapon that shall in form, shape or size resemble a Bowie knife or Arkansas tooth pick under his clothes, or keep the same concealed about his person, such person shall be guilty of a misdemeanor, and upon conviction shall be fined in a sum not less than two hundred dollars, and shall be imprisoned in the county jail not less than three months and not more than six months." Section 3 stipulated, "That if any person shall maliciously draw or attempt to draw any Bowie knife, Arkansas tooth pick, or any knife of weapons that shall in form, shape or size resemble a Bowie knife or Arkansas tooth pick, from under his clothes or form any place of concealment about his person, for the purpose of sticking, cutting, awing, or intimidating other person, such person so drawing or attempting to draw, shall be guilty of a felony, and upon conviction thereof shall be confined in the jail and penitentiary house of this State for a period of time not less than three years, nor more than five years." Section 4 made the use of such a weapon to max this penalty up to fifteen years. See *An Act to suppress the sale and use of Bowie Knives and Arkansas Tooth Picks in this State*, Sec. 2–4 (Tenn. 1838).

12. West Virginia did not become a state until 1863. Therefore, Virginia was Ohio's neighbor up to that year. Just like Tennessee, in 1838 Virginia passed its first concealed weapon law. It stipulated, "That if any person shall hereafter habitually or generally keep or carry about his person any pistol, dirk, bowie knife, or any other weapon of the like kind, from the use of which the death of any person might probably ensue, and the same be hidden or concealed from common observation, and he be thereof convicted, he shall for every such offence forfeit and pay the sum of not less than fifty dollars nor more than five hundred dollars, or be imprisoned in the common jail for a term not less than one month nor more than six months." Furthermore, the act set a provision in place if such a weapon was used to kill another person. Even if the jury acquitted the accused of murder, they could still find him guilty of carrying a concealed weapon if evidence suggested it. This shows that the Virginia legislature did not feel the carrying of concealed weapons was even allowable in events such as self-defense. See *An Act to prevent the carrying of concealed weapons* (Va. 1838).

13. Ohio Const., Art. VIII, § 20 (1802).

14. Ohio Const, Art. I, § 4 (1851).

15. 1 *Report of the Debates and Proceedings of the Convention for the Revision of the Constitution of the State of Ohio*, 47 (1851).

16. *Ibid.*, 23.

17. *Ibid.*, 51.

18. *Ibid.*, 64.

19. *Ibid.*, 69.

20. *Ibid.*, 70.

21. *Ibid.*

22. *Ibid.*

23. 2 *Report of the Debates and Proceedings of the Convention for the Revision of the Constitution of the State of Ohio*, 231 (1851).

24. *Ibid.*

25. *Ibid.*, 326, 462.

26. *Ibid.*, 326.

27. 1 *Ohio Bench and Bar*, 84–87 (1897).

28. Henry Stanbery, *Manual of the Constitutions of All the United States, in Which the Various Provisions and Departments of Power Are Arranged Under Distinct Heads* (1850).

29. 12 *Official Opinions of the Attorneys General of the United States* (1944).

30. 1 *Official Opinions of the Attorneys General of the State of Ohio* at 180–3.

31. 1 *Ohio Bench and Bar* at 262–3. See also Elizabeth Baer, "Groesbeck of Ohio, Lawyer of the Nineteenth Century," 37 (1958).

32. William Groesbeck, *An Address on the True Scope of Human Governments* (1855).

33. *Ibid.*, 10.

34. *Ibid.*

35. *Ibid.*

36. *Ibid.*

37. *Ibid.*, 12.

38. *Ibid.*

39. *Ibid.*, 17.

40. *Ibid.*

41. William Groesbeck, *Speech of Hon. Wm. Groesbeck at Steubenville, Ohio, September 13, 1871* 9 (1892).

42. *Ibid.*, 3.

43. *Ibid.*

44. Simeon Nash, *Morality and the State* (1859).

45. Simeon Nash, *Crime and the Family* (1876). This was originally written in 1861, but he chose not to publish it until 1876. *Ibid.*, iv.

46. Nash, *Morality and the State* at 288.

47. *Ibid.*

48. *Ibid.*

49. *Ibid.*, 294.

50. *Ibid.*, 295–303.

51. "Walker," 8 *W.L.J.* at 148.

52. Nash, *Morality and the State* at 281.
53. *Ibid.*
54. *Ibid.*
55. *Ibid.*, 252.
56. *Ibid.*
57. *Ibid.*, 312–3.
58. *Ibid.*, 391.
59. 1 *Report of the Debates and Proceedings of the Convention for the Revision of the Constitution of the State of Ohio* at 450.
60. *Ibid.*
61. *Ibid.*, 451.
62. *Ibid.*, 462.
63. *Ibid.*, 463.
64. *Ibid.*, 451.
65. *Ibid.*
66. *Ibid.*, 452–3.
67. *Ibid.*, 453.
68. *Ibid.*
69. *Ibid.*, 454.
70. *Ibid.*
71. *Ibid.*, 456.
72. *Ibid.*
73. *Official Report of the Proceedings and Debates of the Third Constitutional Convention of Ohio 1873–74*, 142, 144, 1119 (J.G. Adel ed., 1874).
74. *An Act to prohibit the carrying or wearing of Concealed Weapons*, Sec. 1 (Ohio 1859).
75. *Ibid.*, Sec. 2.
76. *Cleveland Plain Dealer*, May 17, 1855.
77. *Annals of Cleveland*, 529 (1856).
78. *Ibid.*
79. *Cleveland Plain Dealer*, April 11, 1859.
80. 55 *Journal of the House of Representatives of the State of Ohio* (1859).
81. 55 *Journal of the Senate of the State of Ohio* (1859).
82. 795 N.E.2d 633 (Ohio 2003).
83. 9 *W.L.J.* 290 (1852).
84. *Ibid.*, 298.
85. *Ibid.*
86. 58 N.E. 572 (Ohio 1900).

87. *Ibid.*, 572.
88. *Ibid.*, 575.
89. *Ibid.*
90. *Ibid.*
91. 101 Ohio St. 409 (Ohio 1920).
92. *Ibid.*, 410.
93. *Ibid.*, 413.
94. *Ibid.*, 415.
95. *Ibid.*, 414 (citing *Hogan*, 58 N.E. at 575).
96. *Photos v. City of Toledo*, 19 Ohio Misc., 147, 161. (Ohio Misc., 1969).
97. *City of Akron v. Dixon*, 36 Ohio Misc., 133, 134 (Ohio Misc., 1972).
98. *Ibid.*
99. 8 *W.L.J.* at 146.
100. 2 *Report of the Debates and Proceedings of the Convention for the Revision of the Constitution of the State of Ohio* at 27.
101. *Ibid.*
102. *Ibid.*
103. *Ibid.*, 31.
104. *Ibid.*, 32.
105. *Ibid.*
106. 67 Ohio St.3d 35 (Ohio 1993).
107. *State v. Winkelman*, 2 Ohio App.3d 465, 466 (Ohio Ct. App. 1981); see also *State v. Fant*, 53 Ohio App. 2d, 87, 90 (Ohio Ct. App. 1977) (citing *Miller*, 307 U.S. 174).
108. 67 Ohio St.3d at 53.
109. *Ibid.*, 47.
110. *Ibid.*, 48.
111. *Ibid.*, 43.
112. *Ibid.*
113. 58 N.E. at 219.
114. *Arnold*, 67 Ohio St. 3d at 43.
115. Patrick Charles, *Irreconcilable Grievances: The Events That Shaped the Declaration of Independence* (2008).
116. 67 Ohio St. 3d at 43.
117. 99 Ohio St. 3d, 537 (2003).
118. *Nieto*, 101 Ohio St. 409.

# Bibliography

The following list only comprises cases, sources, and laws cited in the manuscript. The list is not a cumulative list of all sources that were reviewed; an exhaustive review of every state's laws was made up to 1800, and in some circumstances past this. Moreover, the book also examines countless state constitutional provisions, and the debates and proceedings of the United States Constitution — all of which are not included.

## CASES CITED

### Supreme Court

*District of Columbia v. Heller,* 128 S.Ct. 2783 (2008)
*United States v. Miller,* 307 U.S. 174 (1939)
*Presser v. Illinois,* 116 U.S. 252 (1886)
*United States v. Cruikshank,* 92 U.S. 542 (1875)
*Miller v. Texas,* 153 U.S. 535 (1894)
*Holmes v. Jennison,* 39 U.S. 540 (1840)
*Houston v. Moore,* 18 U.S. 1 (1820)
*Printz v. United States,* 521 U.S. 898 (1997)
*United States v. Sprague,* 282 U.S. 716 (1931)
*Federal District and Appellate Courts-*
*Parker v. District of Columbia,* 478 F.3d 370 (2007)
*Parker v. District of Columbia,* 311 F.Supp.2d 103 (D.C. Cir. 2004)
*Love v. Pepersack,* 47 F.3d 120 (4th Cir. 1995)
*United States v. Warin,* 530 F.2d 103 (6th Cir. 1976)
*Gillespie v. City of Indianapolis,* 185 F.3d 693 (7th Cir. 1999)
*Hickman v. Block,* 81 F.3d 98 (9th Cir. 1996)
*Cases v. United States,* 131 F.2d 916 (1st Cir. 1942)
*United States v. Rybar,* 103 F.3d 273 (3d Cir. 1996)
*United States v. Hale,* 978 F.2d 1016 (8th Cir. 1992)
*United States v. Oakes,* 564 F.2d 384 (10th Cir. 1977)
*United States v. Wright,* 117 F.3d 1265 (11th Cir. 1997)

### State Courts

*Hilberg v. F.W. Woolworth Co.,* 761 P.2d 236 (Colo. Ct. App. 1988)
*Brewer v. Commonwealth,* 206 S.W.3d 343 (Ky. 2006)

*State v. Blanchard*, 776 So. 2d 1165 (La. 2001)
*State v. Nickerson*, 247 P.2d 188 (Mont. 1952)
*Stillwell v. Stillwell*, 2001 WL 862620 (Tenn. Ct. App. 2001)
*State v. Anderson*, 2000 WL 122218 (Tenn. Crim. App. 2000)
*State v. Williams*, 158 Wash. 2d 904 (Wash. 2006)
*Rohrbaugh v. State*, 216 W. Va. 298 (W. Va. 2004)
*Sandidge v. United States*, 520 A.2d 1057 (D.C. 1987)
*Commonwealth v. Davis*, 369 Mass. 886 (Mass. 1976)
*In re Atkinson*, 291 N.W.2d 396 (Minn. 1980)
*Burton v. Sills*, 53 N.J. 86 (N.J. 1968)
*In re Cassidy*, 268 A.D. 282 (N.Y. App. Div. 1944)
*State v. Fennell*, 95 N.C. App. 140 (N.C. Ct. App. 1989)
*Mosher v. City of Dayton*, 48 Ohio St. 2d 243 (Ohio 1976)
*Masters v. State*, 653 S.W.2d 944 (Tex. App. 1983)
*State v. Vlacil*, 645 P.2d 677 (Utah 1982)
*Kalodimos v. Village of Morton Grove*, 103 Ill. 2d 483 (Ill. 1984)
*Aldridge v. Commonwealth*, 2 Va.Cas. 447 (1824)
*Waters v. State*, 1 Gill 302 (1843)
*United States v. Sheldon*, 5 Blume Sup.Ct.Trans. 337 (1829)
*Nunn v. State*, 1 Ga. 243 (1846)
*Hill v. State*, 53 Ga. 472 (1874)
*Commonwealth v. Blanding*, 20 Mass. 304 (1825)
*Arnold v. City of Cleveland*, 67 Ohio St.3d 35 (Ohio 1993)
*Ohio v. Walker*, 8 W.L.J. 145 (1850)
*State v. Hogan*, 58 N.E. 572 (Ohio 1900)
*State v. Nieto*, 101 Ohio St. 409 (Ohio 1920)
*Photos v. City of Toledo*, 19 Ohio Misc. 147, (Ohio Misc. 1969)
*City of Akron v. Dixon*, 36 Ohio Misc. 133 (Ohio Misc. 1972)
*State v. Fant*, 53 Ohio App.2d 87 (Ohio Ct. App. 1977)

# SOURCES

Adams, John. *A Defence of the Constitution of Government of the United States of America*. Vol. 2. London: John Stockdale, 1794.

*Annals of Cleveland* 39. Cleveland: 1856.

Aquinas, St. Thomas. *Summa Theologica*. 22 vols. London: Burns, Oates & Washburne, 1920

*American Archives: Documents of the American Revolution, 1774–76*. Edited by Peter Force. 4th ed. 6 vols. 1837–53.

*American Archives: Documents of the American Revolution, 1774–76*. Edited by Peter Force. 5th ed. 3 vols. 1837–53.

Attorney General. *Whether the Second Amendment Secures an Individual Right: Memorandum Opinion for the Attorney General*. 2004.

Baer, Elizabeth. "Groesbeck of Ohio, Lawyer of the Nineteenth Century." Thesis, Miami University, 1958.

Bailyn, Bernard. *The Ordeal of Thomas Hutchinson*. Cambridge: Belknap Press, 1974.

*Baron Von Steuben and His Regulations*. Edited by Joseph R. Riling. Philadelphia: R. Riling Arms Books, 1966.

*Bench and Bar of Ohio: History and Biography*, Edited by George Irving Reed. Vol. 1. Chicago: Century Publishing and Engraving, 1897.

Blackstone, William. *Commentaries on the Laws of England: With Notes and Reference to the Constitution and Laws of the United States, and the Commonwealth of Virginia.* Edited by St. George Tucker. 5 vols. South Hackensack: Rothman Reprints, 1969.

Boynton, Lindsay. "Martial Law and the Petition of Right," *English Historical Review* 79 (1964): 255.

Brand, C.E. *Roman Military Law.* Austin: University of Texas Press, 1968.

Chandler, Peleg W. *American Criminal Trials.* Vol. 1. Freeport: Books for Library Press, 1970.

Charles, Patrick. *Washington's Decision: The Story of George Washington's Decision to Reaccept Black Enlistments in the Continental Army, December 31, 1775.* Charleston: Booksurge, 2006.

_____. *Irreconcilable Grievances: The Events that Shaped the Declaration of Independence.* Westminster: Heritage Books, 2008.

Christianson, Paul. "Arguments on Billeting and Martial Law in the Parliament of 1628." *History Journal* 37 (1994): 539.

*Circular Letters of Congressmen to Their Constituents 1789–1829.* Edited by Noble E. Cunningham. Vol. 1. Chapel Hill: University of North Carolina Press, 1978.

*The Correspondence of Thomas Gage.* Edited by Clarence Edwin Carter. 2 vols. Hamden: Archon Books, 1962.

Cox, Caroline. *A Proper Sense of Honor: Service and Self Sacrifice in George Washington's Army.* Chapel Hill: University of North Carolina Press, 2004.

Cramer, Clayton E. *For Defence of Themselves and the State: The Original Intent and Judicial Interpretation of the Right to Keep and Bear Arms.* Westport: Praeger, 1994.

_____. *Concealed Weapon Laws of the Early Republic: Dueling, Southern Violence, and Moral Reform.* Westport: Praeger, 1999.

Cramer, Clayton E., and Olson, Joseph Edward. "What Did Bear Arms Mean in the Second Amendment?" *Georgetown Journal of Law and Public Policy* 2 (2008).

Cress, Lawrence Delbert. "Radical Whigery on the Role of the Military: Ideological Roots of the American Revolutionary Militia," *Journal of the History of Ideas* 40 (1979): 47.

*Dictionary of the English Language.* Edited by Timothy Cunningham. Vol. 1. 1773.

*Documents of the American Revolution.* Edited by K.G. Davies. 10 vols. Shannon: Irish University Press, 1972–81.

Downes, Randolph Chandler. "Thomas Jefferson and the Removal of Governor St. Clair in 1802." *Ohio Archeological and Historical Society Publications* 36 (1927): 62.

Fields, William S., and Hardy, David T. "The Third Amendment and the Issue of the Maintenance of Standing Armies." *American Journal of Legal History* 35 (1991): 395.

Frey, Sylvia. *Water from the Rock: Black Resistance in a Revolutionary Age.* Princeton: Princeton University Press, 1991.

Groesbeck, William. *An Address on the True Scope of Human Governments.* Cincinnati: C.F. Bradley, 1855.

_____. *Speech of Hon. William Groesbeck at Steubensville, Ohio, September 13, 1871.* Cincinnati: 1892.

Hale, Matthew. *Common Law of England.* Birmingham: Legal Classics Library, 1987.

Horton, James Oliver. *Slavery and the Making of America.* New York: Oxford University Press, 2005.

Hume, David. *Essays: Moral, Political, and Literary.* Edited by Eugene R. Miller. Indianapolis, Literary Classics, 1985.

Hutchinson, Peter Orlando. *The Diary and Letters of Thomas Hutchinson.* 2 vols. New York: AMS Press, 1973.

*Ideal Commonwealths: More's Utopia, Bacon's New Atlantis, Campanella's City of the sun, and Harrington's Oceana.* Edited by Henry Morley. New York: P.F. Collier, 1901.

*Journal of the House of Representatives of the State of Ohio* 55 (1859).

*Journal of the Senate of the State of Ohio* 55 (1859).

Kates, Don B. "Handgun Prohibition and the Original Meaning of the Second Amendment." *Michigan Law Review* 82 (1983): 204.

*Landmark Briefs and Arguments of the Supreme Court of the United States Constitutional Law.* Edited by Philip B. Kurland. Arlington: University Publications, 1975.

Machiavelli, Niccolo. *The Prince and Discourses.* Edited by Max Lerner. New York: Random House, 1950.

Maier, Pauline. *American Scripture: Making the Declaration of Independence.* New York: Random House, 1998.

Martyn, Charles. *The Life of Artemas Ward: The First Commander-in-Chief of the American Revolution.* New York: A. Ward, 1921.

Nash, Simeon. *Morality and the State.* Columbus: Follett, Foster, 1859.

_____. *Crime and the Family.* Cincinnati: Robert Clarke, 1876.

*Official Opinions of the Attorney Generals of the State of Ohio.* Edited by Wade H. Ellis. Vol. 1. Springfield: Springfield Publication, 1905.

*Official Opinions of the Attorney Generals of the State of Ohio.* Vol. 12. Springfield: Springfield Publication, 1944.

*Official Report of the Proceedings and Debates of the Third Constitutional Convention of Ohio 1873–74.* Edited by J.G. Adel. 1874.

Oliver, Benjamin. *The Rights of an American Citizen.* Boston: Marsh, Capen & Lyon, 1832.

*The Origin of the Second Amendment: A Documentary History of the Bill of Rights.* Edited by David F. Young. Ontonagon: Golden Oak Books, 1995.

*The Papers of Benjamin Franklin.* Edited by W.B. Wilcox. Vol. 22. New Haven: Yale University Press, 1982.

*The Papers of George Mason.* Edited by Robert Rutland. Vol. 1. Chapel Hill: North Carolina University Press, 1970.

*The Papers of George Washington.* Edited by W.W. Abbot. Revolutionary Series. 15 Vols. Charlottesville: University of Virginia Press, 1985.

*The Papers of George Washington.* Edited by W.W. Abbot. Confederation Series. Vol. 4. Charlottesville: University of Virginia Press, 1992–97.

*The Papers of James Madison.* Edited by Robert Rutland. Vol. 9. Washington, DC: Langtree & O'Sullivan, 1840.

*The Papers of John Adams.* Edited by Robert Taylor. Vols. 3–5. Boston: Little, Brown, 1979.

*The Papers of John Marshall.* Edited by Herbert A. Johnson. Vol. 1 Raleigh: University of North Carolina Press, 1974.

*The Papers of Nathanael Greene.* Edited by Richard K. Showman. Chapel Hill: University of North Carolina Press, 1976.

*The Papers of Thomas Jefferson.* Edited by J.P. Boyd. Vol. 1. Princeton: Princeton University Press, 1950.

*The Political Writings of John Adams.* Edited by George W. Carey. Washington, DC: Regnery Publications, 2000.

*Portrait of a Patriot: The Major Political and Legal Papers of Josiah Quincy Junior.* Edited by Daniel R. Coquillette. Charlottesville: University of Virginia Press, 2005.

Potter, Janice. *The Liberty We Seek: Loyalist Ideology in Colonial New York and Massachusetts.* Cambridge: Harvard University Press, 1983.

Rawle, William. *A View of the Constitution of the United States of America.* New York: Da Capo Press, 1970.

*Report of the Debates and Proceedings of the Convention for the Revision of the Constitution of the State of Ohio.* 2 vols. 1851.

*The Republic of Letters: The Correspondence Between Jefferson and Madison 1776–1826.* Edited by James Morton Smith. 3 vols. New York: Norton, 1995.

*Revolutionary Virginia: The Road to Independence.* Edited by W.J. Vanschreevan. 7 vols. Charlottesville: University of Virginia Press, 1973–83.

Sabine, Lorenzo. *Biographical Sketches of Loyalists of the American Revolution.* 2 vols. Boston: Little, Brown, 1864.

*The St. Clair Papers: The Life and Services of Arthur St. Clair, Soldier of the Revolutionary War, President of the Continental Congress, and Governor of the North-Western Territory, with his Correspondence and Other Papers.* Edited by William Henry Smith. 2 vols. New York: Da Capo Press, 1971.

*The Samuel Huntington Papers.* (Columbus: Ohio Historical Society, 1976), reels 1–3.

Schwartz, Bernard. *The Bill of Rights: A Documentary History.* 2 vols. New York: Chelsea House Publishers, 1971.

Schwoerer, Lois G. *The Declaration of Rights, 1689.* Baltimore: John Hopkins University Press, 1981.

Selby, John E. *The Revolution in Virginia, 1775–1783.* Williamsburg: Colonial Williamsburg Foundation, 1988.

Sidney, Algernon. *Discourses Concerning Government.* Edited by Thomas G. West. Indianapolis: Liberty Classics, 1990.

Smith, James M. "The Constitutional Right to Keep and Bear Arms." J.D. thesis. Cambridge: Harvard Univesrity, 1959.

Stanbery, Henry. *Manual of the Constitutions of All the United States, In Which the Various Provisions and Departments of Power are Arranged Under District Heads.* Columbus: J.H. Ripley, 1850.

Stark, James H. *The Loyalists of Massachusetts and the Other Side of the American Revolution.* Salem: Salem Press, 1910.

Story, Joseph. *Commentaries on the Constitution of the United States.* 3 vols. New York: Da Capo Press, 1970.

*The Thomas Worthington Papers 1731, 1779–1907.* Edited by Richard c. Knopf. 4 vols. Columbus: Ohio Historical Society, 1956.

Trenchard, John. *A Short Historie of Standing Armies in England.* London: 1698.

Tucker, St. George. *View of the Constitution of the United States: With Select Writings.* Indianapolis: Liberty Fund, 1999.

United States. *American State Papers: Military Affairs.* Vol. 1. Washington, DC: 1832.

United States. *Annals of Congress: The Debates and Proceedings of the Congress of the United States.* Washington, DC: 1789–1824.

United States. *Journals of the Continental Congress, 1774–89.* Edited by Kenneth Harris, 34 vols. Washington: National Archives and Records, 1905.

United States. *Naval Documents of the American Revolution.* Edited by William Bell Clark. 19 vols. Washington, DC: 1964.

Vattel, Emerich de. *Law of Nations.* Vol. 3. Indianapolis: Liberty Fund, 2008.

*Vegetius: Epitome of Military Science.* Trans. By N.P. Milner. Liverpool: Liverpool University Press, 1993.

Wiener, Frederick Bernays. *Civilians Under Military Justice: The British Practice since 1689 Especially in North America.* Chicago: University of Chicago Press, 1967.

Winthrop, William. *Military Law and Precedents.* Washington, DC: Government Print Office, 1920.

*The Writings of George Washington.* Edited by J.C. Fitzpatrick. Vol. 29. Washington, DC: 1931–44.

# Laws Cited

## Delaware

An Act for the Trial of Negroes (Del. 1797).
An Act for establishing a Militia within this State (Del. 1782).
An Act for establishing the Militia in this state (Del. 1793).
An Act for establishing a Militia within this state (Del. 1778).
A Supplement to an act, intitled, An Act for establishing the Militia in this state (Del. 1796).

## Georgia

An Act to oblige the Male white Persons in the Province of Georgia to carry Fire-arms to all Places of publick Worship (Ga. 1757).
Act for the better ordering the Militia of this Province (Ga. 1765).
An Act for Establishing and regulating Patrols (Ga. 1757).
An Act to amend and continue an Act, intitled "An Act for establishing and regulating Patrols" (Ga. 1760).
An Act to alter and amend the Militia Law of this State, and to provide for arming the militia thereof (Ga. 1799).

## Kentucky

An Act for regulating the Militia of this Commonwealth (Ky. 1792).
An Act to prevent persons in this Commonwealth from wearing concealed Arms, except in certain cases (Ky. 1813).
An Act to amend the Militia Law (Ky. 1813).

## Maryland

An Act for the speedy trial of criminals, and ascertaining their punishment in the county courts when prosecuted there, and for payment of fees due from criminal persons (Md. 1715).
An Act for the Preservation of the Breed of Wild Deer (Md. 1729).
An Act for the more effectual preservation of the breed of deer (Md. 1773); An Act for the preservation of the breed of wild deer, and for other purposes therein (Md. 1789).
A Supplement to the act entitled, An act to regulate and discipline the militia of this state (Md. 1799).
An Act to regulate and discipline the militia of this state (Md. 1793).
A Supplementary Act, to the Act for the Ordering and Regulating the Militia of this Province for the better Defense and Security thereof (Md. 1732).
An Act his Majesty's Service, and further Defence and Security of this Province (Md. 1756).
An Act relating to Free Negroes and Slaves (Md. 1831).
An Act to Enroll, Equip, and Regulate the Militia of this State (Md. 1834).
A Supplement to the act entitled, An act to regulate and discipline the militia of this state (Md. 1799).

## Massachusetts

An Act to prevent Routs, Riots, and tumultuous Assemblies, and the evil Consequences thereof (Mass. 1786).
An Act for regulating and governing the Militia of the Commonwealth of Massachusetts, and for repealing all Laws heretofore made for that Purpose; excepting and Act, intitled "An Act for establishing Rules and Articles for governing the Troops stationed in Forts and Garrisons, within this Commonwealth, and also the Militia, when called into actual Service" (Mass. 1793).

*An Act for forming and regulating the Militia within the Commonwealth of Massachusetts, and for repealing all the Laws heretofore made for that Purpose* (Mass. 1781).

*An Act, describing the Disqualifications to which Persons shall be subjected, who have been, or may be guilty of Treason, or giving Aid or Support to the present Rebellion, and to whom a Pardon may be extended* (Mass. 1787).

*An Act for regulating and governing the Militia of the Commonwealth of Massachusetts, and for repealing all Laws heretofore made for that Purpose; excepting and Act, intitled "An Act for establishing Rules and Articles for governing the Troops stationed in Forts and Garrisons, within this Commonwealth, and also the Militia, when called into actual Service* (Mass. 1793).

*An Act in Addition to the several Acts already made to the prudent Storage of Gun Powder within the Town of Boston* (Mass. 1783).

*An Act, describing the Disqualifications to which Persons shall be subjected, who have been, or may be guilty of Treason, or giving Aid or Support to the present Rebellion, and to whom a Pardon may be extended* (Mass. 1787).

*An Act for the more speedy and effectual suppression of tumults and insurrections in the commonwealth* (Mass. 1787).

## New Hampshire

*An Act to Prevent the Killing of Wild Deer, at Unreasonable Times* (N.H. 1758).

*An Act for the Regulating the Militia*, Sec. 1 (N.H. 1718).

*An Act for the Regulating the Militia* (N.H. 1759).

*An Act for forming and regulating the Militia within this State, and for repealing all the Laws heretofore made for that Purpose* (N.H. 1780).

*An Act for forming and regulating the Militia within this State, and for repealing the laws heretofore made for that purpose* (N.H. 1786).

*An Act for forming and regulating the Militia within the State of New Hampshire, in New England, and for repealing all the Laws heretofore made for that Purpose* (N.H. 1776).

*An Act for forming and regulating the militia within this State, and for repealing all the laws heretofore made for that purpose* (N.H. 1792).

*An Act for the Commission of Joseph Dudley as Governor of New Hampshire, Dated April 1, 1702* (N.H. 1702).

## New Jersey

*An Act to prevent Routs, Riots and tumultuous Assemblies* (N.J. 1797).

*An Act to restrain Tavern-keepers and others from selling strong Liquors to Servants, Negroes and Mulatto Slaves, and to prevent Negroes and Mulatto Slaves, from meeting in large Companies, from running about at Nights, and from hunting or carrying a Gun on the Lord's Day* (N.J. 1751).

*An Act to prevent Killing of Deer out of Season and against Carrying Guns and Hunting by Persons not Qualified* (N.J. 1722).

*A Supplementary Act to the act entitled, An Act to prevent the killing of Deer out of Season and against carrying of Guns, and hunting by persons not qualified* (N.J. 1751).

*An Act for the better regulating the Militia* (N.J. 1777).

*An Act for better settling and regulating the Militia of this Colony of New-Jersey, for the Repelling of Invasions and Suppressing Insurrections and Rebellions* (N.J. 1746).

*A Supplementary Act to the Act, entitled, An Act for better settling and regulating the Militia of this Colony of New-Jersey, for the repelling Invasions, and suppressing Insurrections and Rebellions; as also for continuing such Parts and Clauses of the said Law as are not altered and amended by this Act* (N.J. 1757).

*A Supplement to the Act, intitled, "An Act for organizing and training the Militia of this State"* (N.J. 1793).
*An Act for organizing and training the Militia of this State* (N.J. 1792).
*An Act for making current Thirty Thousand Pounds, in Bills of Credit, for his Majesty's Service in the Present War* (N.J. 1757).
*An Act for the Preservation of Deer and other Game, and to prevent trespassing with Guns,* Sec. 3 (N.J. 1771).

## New York
*An Act to prevent the firing of Guns and other Fire-Arms within this Colony* (N.Y. 1773).
*An Act to prevent hunting with Fire-Arms in the City of New-York, and the Liberties thereof* (N.Y. 1763).
*An Act for regulating the Militia of the Colony of New York* (N.Y. 1772).
*An Act for regulating the Militia of the State of New York* (N.Y. 1778).
*An Act to regulate the Militia* (N.Y. 1786).
*An Act to organize the Militia of this State* (N.Y. 1793).

## North Carolina
*An additional act to an act, entitled, An act to prevent killing deer at unreasonable times and for putting a stop to many abuses committed by white persons, under pretence of hunting* (N.C. 1745); *An act to amend an act entitled "An additional act to an act, entitled, an act to prevent killing deer at unreasonable times and for putting a stop to many abuses committed by white persons under pretence of hunting"* (N.C. 1768).
*An Act to revise and amend the Militia Laws* (N.C. 1800).
*An Act for raising troops for the protection of the inhabitants of Davidson county* (N.C. 1786).

## Ohio
*A law respecting crimes and punishments* (Ohio 1788).
*An act respecting crimes and punishments* (Ohio 1805).
*An act respecting crimes and punishments* (Ohio 1809).
*An act for the punishment of crimes* (Ohio 1815).
*An act for the punishment of certain offences therein mentioned* (Ohio 1815).
*An act for the punishment of crimes* (Ohio 1821).
*An act for the punishments of crimes* (Ohio 1824).
*An act for the punishments of crimes* (Ohio 1831).
*A supplement to an act for the punishment of crimes* (Ohio 1831).
*An act providing for the punishment of Crimes* (Ohio 1835).
*An act for the prevention of vice and immorality* (Ohio 1799).
*An act for the punishment of crimes* (Ohio 1815).
*An act for the prevention of certain immoral practices* (Ohio 1805).
*An act to amend that act, "An act for the prevention of certain immoral practices"* (Ohio 1815).
*An act for the prevention of certain immoral practices* (Ohio 1816).
*An act for the prevention of certain immoral practices* (Ohio 1824).
*An act for suppressing and prohibiting ever species of gaming for money or other property, and for making void all contracts and payments made in consequence thereof, and also for restraining the disorderly practice of discharging fire arms at certain hours and places* (Ohio 1790).
*A law for regulating and establishing the militia* (Ohio 1788).
*A law in addition to a law entitled "A law for regulating and establishing the militia"* (Ohio 1788).

*An act to alter and amend the militia laws* (Ohio 1791).

*An act establishing and regulating the militia* (Ohio 1799).

*An act to amend the act, entitled, "An act establishing and regulating the militia"* (Ohio 1802).

*An act to provide for organizing and disciplining the militia* (Ohio 1803).

*An act for disciplining the militia* (Ohio 1807).

*An act to amend the act entitled, "An act disciplining the militia"* (Ohio 1808).

*An act for disciplining the militia* (Ohio 1809).

*An act for disciplining the militia* (Ohio 1813).

*An act for organizing and disciplining the militia* (Ohio 1815).

*An act for organizing and disciplining the militia* (Ohio 1831).

*An act directing the collection and repairs of public arms and accoutrements* (Ohio 1815).

*An act to provide for the distribution and safe-keeping of the public arms; and for other purposes* (Ohio 1823).

*An act amendatory to "An act to provide for the safe keeping of the public arms, and for other purposes"* (Ohio 1827).

*An act to provide for drawing from the United States, and distributing the public arms apportioned to the militia of this state* (Ohio, 1828).

*An Act to regulate the Militia* (Ohio 1844).

*An Act to amend the act entitled "An Act to organize and discipline the Militia"* (Ohio 1843).

*An Act to prohibit the carrying or wearing of Concealed Weapons* (Ohio 1859).

### Pennsylvania

*An Act to suppress the disorderly practice of firing guns, & c. on the times therein mentioned* (Pa. 1774).

*An Act against riots and rioters* (Pa. 1705).

*An Act to prevent the hunting of deer, and other wild beasts, beyond the limits of the lands purchased of the Indians by the Proprieties of this province, and against killing deer out of season* (Pa. 1760).

*An Act to prevent the killing of Deer out of Season, and against carrying of Guns or Hunting, by Persons not qualified* (Pa. 1721).

*An Act to regulate the Militia of the Common-Wealth of Pennsylvania* (Pa. 1777).

*An Act for the regulation of the Militia of the commonwealth of Pennsylvania* (1793).

*An Act for the regulation of the Militia of the Commonwealth of Pennsylvania* (Pa. 1802).

*An Act to repeal part of the additional supplement to the Acts for the regulation of the Militia of this Commonwealth* (Pa. 1790).

*An Act to provide for the suppressing an insurrection in the Western Counties of this commonwealth* (Pa. 1794).

*An Act to provide arms for the use of the commonwealth* (Pa. 1797).

*An Act to suppress the disorderly practice of firing guns, & c. on the times therein* (Pa. 1774).

### Rhode Island

*An Act for embodying and brining into the field Twelve Hundred able-bodied effective Men, of the Militia, to serve within this State for One Month, from the Time of their Rendezvous, and no longer Term, and not to be marched out of the same* (R.I. 1781).

### South Carolina

*An Act for the better Security of this Province against the Insurrections and other wicked Attempts of Negroes, and other Slaves; and for reviving and continuing, and act of the General Assembly of this Province, entitled an Act for the better Ordering and Governing Negroes and other Slaves in this Province* (S.C. 1743).

*An Act for the better establishing and regulating of Patrols in this Province* (S.C. 1746).

*An Act for the better Ordering and Governing of Negroes and other Slaves in this Province* (S.C. 1740).

*An Act for the Preservation of Deer, and to prevent the Mischiefs arising from Hunting at unreasonable Times* (S.C. 1769).

*An Ordinance for the Preservation of Deer, and to prevent the Mischiefs arising from Fire-Hunting* (S.C. 1785).

*An Act for the Regulation of the Militia of this State* (S.C. 1782).

*An Act to Organize the Militia throughout the State of South Carolina, in conformity with the act of Congress* (S.C. 1794).

## Tennessee

*An Act for the better establishment and regulation of the militia in this state* (Tenn. 1798).

*An Act for the better establishment and regulation of the militia of this state* (Tenn. 1798).

*An Act to suppress the sale and use of Bowie Knives and Arkansas Tooth Picks in this State* (Tenn. 1838).

## United States

United States, *Statutes at Large*. Vols. 1–2. Washington, DC: 1799.

## Vermont

*An Act for regulating and governing the Militia of the State of Vermont, and for repealing all Laws heretofore passed for that purpose* (Vt. 1793).

*An Act for forming and regulating the militia, and for encouragement of military skill, for the better defence of state* (Vt. 1779).

*An Act regulating the Militia of this State* (Vt. 1786).

*An act regulating the Militia of the State of Vermont* (Vt. 1787).

## Virginia

*Statutes at Large of Virginia*. Edited by William H. Hening. 13 vols. New York: R. & W. & G. Bartow, 1823.

*An act, to amend an Act, entitled an Act for regulating the Navigation of James River, above the Falls of the said River* (Va. 1811).

*An act farther to amend the penal laws of this commonwealth* (Va. 1823).

*An Act to prevent the carrying of concealed weapons* (Va. 1838).

# Index